# Establishing & Sustaining Learning-Centered Community Colleges

Edited by Christine Johnson McPhail

Foreword by George R. Boggs

Community College Press®
a division of the American Association of Community Colleges
Washington, DC

The American Association of Community Colleges (AACC) is the primary advocacy organization for the nation's community colleges. The association represents more than 1,100 two-year, associate degree-granting institutions and more than 11 million students. AACC promotes community colleges through six strategic action areas: national and international recognition and advocacy, learning and accountability, leadership development, economic and workforce development, connectedness across AACC membership, and international and intercultural education. Information about AACC and community colleges may be found at www.aacc.nche.edu.

Design: McGaughy Design
Editor: Deanna D'Errico
Printer: Kirby Lithographics, Inc.

Community College Press
American Association of Community Colleges
One Dupont Circle, NW
Suite 410
Washington, DC 20036

Printed in the United States of America.

ISBN 0-87117-366-2

# Contents

# Foreword

Establishing and Sustaining Learning-Centered Community Colleges is a book about substantive change in higher education. The chapter authors include today's most prominent thinkers on what has come to be known as the learning college movement, the learning revolution, or the learning paradigm. The learning paradigm was born and evolved in the community colleges in America in an environment of decreasing resources and increased calls for accountability and attention to institutional effectiveness. The ideas behind the learning paradigm were first articulated in the early 1990s, perhaps noted first in 1991 in the vision statement for Palomar College, a community college in southern California.

> Readers of these statements will note that they reflect perhaps a subtle but nonetheless profound shift in how we think of the college and what we do. We have shifted from an identification with process to an identification with results. We are no longer content with merely providing quality instruction. We will judge ourselves henceforth on the quality of student learning we produce...

Thanks to the early work of scholars including Bob Barr, John Tagg, and Terry O'Banion, the concepts of the learning paradigm were refined and spread throughout higher education to the point that learning and learning outcomes have become the themes of countless conferences and the focus of dissertations, articles, and books. Higher education accreditation standards in the United States today give more prominence to evidence of learning outcomes while placing much less emphasis on resources and processes. The authors of this book bring even greater clarity to this movement.

For those college leaders, faculty members, trustees, and staff members who want to move their institutions toward a greater focus on student learning and student success, this book is a wonderful resource, exploring issues such as developing an environment that is receptive to change, engaging internal and external constituencies, the role of student development, changing institutional language and structure, strategic planning, establishing learning outcomes, assessment of learning outcomes, changes in budgeting and resource allocation, changes in governance, the effective use of technology, creating a culturally responsive climate, and measuring institutional progress.

The need for change in how colleges and universities operate is becoming apparent. Projections done by the Bureau of Labor Statistics show a growing disparity between job requirements and employee skills. Higher education institutions, including community colleges, need to accept more responsibility for what our students learn. Even at the macro level, there is an obvious need for improvement. Although 42% of community college students in the United States indicate that they intend to earn a baccalaureate, only 26% of them actually transfer to an upper-division institution. Thirty-three percent of community college students are ethnic minorities, but they receive only 27% of the degrees and certificates.

The learning paradigm is an often misunderstood concept. The most common reaction when someone first hears it described is, "isn't that what we are already doing?" Although it is probably true that most faculty and staff in higher education today chose their careers because they want to make a difference in people's lives and they themselves love teaching and learning, unfortunately our institutions are probably not structured in ways to facilitate student learning and success. We even describe the purpose of our institutions as providing instruction in a variety of subjects, indicating an identification with methods rather than the expected outcome of student learning. Of course, when we identify with methods, we are less likely to see other methods or structures that could improve the desired outcomes.

It is always easier not to rock the boat or to make changes incrementally. If one were to keep a log of the time spent in committee discussions or trustee meetings, I doubt that a significant amount of it would be spent on the topic of students' learning and success. I wonder how common it is that Terry O'Banion's two questions, (1) How will this decision affect student learning? and (2) How will we know how this decision affects student learning? are used in planning and decision making. Even if plans are made to become more learning-centered, Irving McPhail makes the point that positive rhetoric makes little difference unless planning is linked to resource allocation.

The shift to a focus on learning rather than instruction can also be threatening to the constituencies of a college. In its broadest terms, the learning paradigm calls for institutional change and institutional responsibility for learning outcomes and improving them. That puts the responsibility for improved outcomes on all of the college's people: trustees, presidents, instructional faculty, student service professionals, and staff, as well as students themselves. Institutional leaders will have to develop structures and processes that allow for more flexibility and creativity. Decisions will have to become more data-driven as the institution moves toward a culture of improvement and documentation. Barriers to student success will have to be identified and removed. In spite of the hard work ahead for those who embrace the changes described in this book, the rewards for changes that result in greater student success and improved institutional climate are worth the effort.

In my first speech to the faculty at Palomar College in 1985, I talked about the importance of students and referred to our mission as student learning. However, it took several more years for the faculty and staff at Palomar to articulate the vision that would lead to the learning paradigm. The work at Palomar continues, as it does at the other

Vanguard Colleges that were part of the League for Innovation's Learning College Initiative and, now, at many other colleges and universities. For those who truly want to make a difference for their institutions and for their students, *Establishing and Sustaining Learning-Centered Community Colleges* is a book that will be of significant value. I appreciate the groundbreaking wok of Christine Johnson McPhail and her fellow authors. And I appreciate all of those college leaders who have dedicated themselves to improving student learning.

George R. Boggs
*President and CEO*
*American Association of Community Colleges*

# Preface

Community colleges continue to identify new and different ways to address the learning needs of their students. In recent years, the learning revolution has challenged community colleges to shift their focus (paradigm) from teaching to learning, and the number of community colleges transitioning from teaching to learning is growing dramatically larger. Almost daily community colleges are making changes in their instructional programs and services, recruitment, hiring, training of faculty, and service delivery. Although some colleges may have shown signs of moving beyond the paradigm shift, the impact of the learning revolution on community colleges—how colleges have been transformed—lacks a cohesive explanation.

Almost two decades have passed since the advocates of the learning-centered college spoke about the malaise caused by the teaching focus of the community college. Some viewed the shift from teaching to learning as a means to recapture the drive that founded the community college movement, reinforced its multiple missions, and now finds expression in the success of the learner. The learning-centered college movement offered many community colleges a renewed context to reaffirm their commitment to educate large populations of students underserved by other segments of higher education and make substantial changes in their delivery of programs and services. The velocity of the learning-centered community college was fueled by intense and sometimes conflicting scenarios: major strides in the use of technology, declining fiscal resources, increasingly diverse student populations, and impending retirements of faculty and leaders. These scenarios created the capacity for community colleges to move beyond the paradigm shift to participate in a new evolution of learning.

Education research reveals that new knowledge grows out of the process of relating new ideas to what we already know and exploring the interrelationships among ideas. *Establishing and Sustaining Learning-Centered Community Colleges* is about people and colleges who translated the paradigm shift into results—people and colleges who have been actively involved in the evolution of the learning-centered community college. Throughout the book, practitioners and scholars—people who are integrating learning-centered principles into programs and services at their colleges on a daily basis— share what they did and how they did it. Some of these practitioners and scholars are creating a new norm for community colleges.

Any effort to assess institutional effectiveness begins with the mission of the institution. From that mission we can identify the more specific goals of programs and other activities of the institution. From the program and activity goals we can develop processes by which we determine whether and how well the programs and activities of the institution lead to the achievement of the institution's mission. What skills and strategies can we learn from our observations of the learning revolution? How does a college make the transition from teaching to learning, and how do colleges maintain the momentum?

The first of its kind since the publication of the classic works of Robert Barr, John Tagg, and Terry O'Banion, this book has the potential to become the flagship book on the learning college. First, the book brings together a group of authoritative voices to go beyond the learning paradigm shift to examine the progress of the learning college over the past 15 years. Second, the authors' perspectives are based on real-life experiences of implementing learning principles at their respective institutions. Third, the book offers new and different perspectives on how it might be necessary to add elements to or expand the paradigm to effectively deal with the learners in 21st-century community colleges. The book also identifies emerging organizational changes as a result of implementing learning college principles.

### Overview of Contents

*Establishing and Sustaining Learning-Centered Community Colleges* provides rich field-based insight for practitioners and institutions interested in creating and sustaining a learning college. In Part 1, The Context of the Learning College, William Flynn, Robert Barr, Frank Fear, and David Shupe offer a comprehensive range of ideas for defining and understanding the context of the learning college. In Part 2, Toward a Deeper Understanding of the Learning College, Shirlene Snowden, Mark Battersby, Henry Linck, Rosalie Mince, and Tara Ebersole provide practical advice on how to define and recognize quality learning and how to assess and analyze learning outcomes. In Part 3, Implications for Expanding the Learning Paradigm, Evelyn Clements, Alicia Harvey-Smith, Ted James, Mark Milliron, and Mary Prentice offer timely information and authoritative advice about major issues and administrative problems that expands the focus of the learning paradigm. Part 4, Emerging Organizational Changes, allows William Flynn, Irving Pressley McPhail, and I an opportunity to analyze and critique organizational culture, suggesting ways to implement strategic changes to improve and expand learning in community colleges. In Part 5, Surviving and Sustaining the Paradigm Shift, Renate Krakauer and Cynthia Wilson provide well-researched information about the learning college that is grounded in the real world that will help community colleges evaluate, survive, and sustain the learning college momentum. In the Epilogue, I explore some of the challenges and opportunities associated with understanding the complexities of an organization's culture, focusing on changes conducive to implementing learning-centered principles at the community college. Finally, the Appendix presents a comprehensive bibliography of learning college literature, updated from Terry O'Banion's original by O'Banion and Kelley Costner.

The wealth of knowledge contributed by some of America's most noted scholars and practitioners in the learning college movement makes this book an asset for professionals interested in learning-centered education. I believe that this book will challenge community college professionals to develop bases of understanding and ideas upon which they can become involved in or strengthen their involvement in the learning college movement.

Christine Johnson McPhail
*Coordinator, Community College Leadership Doctoral Program*
*Morgan State University*

# PART 1

# The Context of the Learning College

CHAPTER 1

# The Search for the
# Learning-Centered College

WILLIAM J. FLYNN

The American community college has gone through evolutionary and generational changes, much like a family. Known in the past as junior colleges, technical colleges, or vocational colleges, this singular institution carved out a special niche in the life of the community it served. Often neglected by other higher education constituencies or undervalued by funding sources, it continues to be a uniquely American institution, quietly serving all citizens through degree and certificate programs, easy transfer opportunities to four-year institutions, continuing professional education offerings, community services programming, cultural events, and community and economic development.

This multi-pronged mission has some historical precedent. *Building Communities*, a project developed by the American Association of Community Colleges in 1988, identified dual influences on educational institutions. The first, the colonial influence, focused on the student, general education, and loyalty to the college. The second, the German model, emphasized the teacher, specialization, and loyalty to the discipline. This duality—some might call it an internal tension-has not abated since American higher education was born at Harvard University, and community colleges are not immune to its spell. Although many sectors of American society have changed and adjusted to new influences and trends, higher education has been resistant to any meaningful change, and community colleges are no exception.

Then came the 1990s, when the United States went through a significant economic restructuring. Technology vastly increased the amount of information available. The nature of work, jobs, and careers drastically changed and may never be the same again. The Internet made knowledge available in a way never imagined a few years ago. Corporations began to move into the training and education sector. And never before had the nation seen so much public policy debate about accountability in education.

These multiple challenges—pervasive technology, increased calls for accountability, and unprecedented competition—continually force educators to rethink the usual mode of operation, the mandate to provide cost-effective, accessible, undergraduate education and preparation for the world of work. Given the enormous size of the educational system, the sheer scope of change required, and the entrenched forces opposing such change, significant innovations are scattered. What is needed is not only incremental or even institutional change but grand-scale transformation. Unless community college instructors can transform their institutions to be relevant, competitive, accessible, and accountable, these schools may lose their sanction. Yet of all the challenges community colleges face, one born in the 1990s is perhaps the most demanding and, potentially, the most rewarding. And it came from within the community college community.

## Finding a Metaphor for Institutional Transformation

Over the years, many external observers and critics have called for change and improvement in American education. The current discussion on the need for change in undergraduate education comes largely from an article that appeared in the November/December 1995 issue of *Change*. The authors, Barr and Tagg, both worked in the Palomar Community College District in Southern California. Although their backgrounds were in community colleges, the impact of their analysis and vision was felt throughout higher education. The Barr and Tagg article was the most cited in the magazine's recent history.

Barr and Tagg tapped into a deeply ingrained sense that something had to change. By applying to the current educational scene the theories of scientist Thomas Kuhn and futurist Joel Barker, they developed a simple, penetrating analysis of the current status of colleges, called the "instruction paradigm." Stated simply, in their present configuration, colleges provide instruction to students.

## What Institutions Are

In the instruction paradigm, the focus is on the teacher, who often employs lecture as the primary method of delivering instruction. Learning is clearly the responsibility of the student, and its measurement is not a high priority. This centuries-old model of the scholar possessing knowledge and transferring it to eager students has changed little since before the invention of the printing press.

This emphasis on instruction rather than learning is ingrained in the culture, structure, and missions of community colleges. One example is revealing: In the mid-1990s, Barr investigated the mission statements of virtually every community college in California, more than 100 institutions that enrolled some 1.5 million students. He concluded that the institutions' mission statements "failed to use the word learning as a statement of purpose."

A central component of the instruction paradigm is that college offerings and organizations are atomistic and compartmentalized. In this metaphor, the atom is the 50-minute lecture period and the molecule is the three-credit course offered in a 15-week semester or a 10-week quarter. In this environment, time is constant and learning varies. Meaningful assessment tends to occur at the conclusion of a course. The entire college shifts gears as it enters exam week—instruction is no longer provided and what has been transferred to the student is, effectively, requested back in test format. The degree or certificate awarded recognizes accumulation of credit hours, not a demonstration of interrelated knowledge, competencies, or skills.

Other characteristics of the instruction paradigm are readily recognizable. Independent, discipline-centered departments are repositories of specialized and somewhat isolated knowledge, rarely interacting with colleague departments. Significant resources and planning efforts are committed to maintaining traditional values and keeping teachers current in their disciplines through professional development programs. A subtle but perceptible caste system exists on many campuses in which the instructors are the upper class and all other employees are support staff. To ensure that a teacher has the requisite preparation to convey knowledge, minimum academic qualifications are required in the instructor-hiring process. Simply put, any expert can teach.

Despite the significant body of literature on the value of collaborative or self-paced learning environments, the learning-community movement, and assessment as a pedagogical tool, colleges did little to infuse these approaches into curriculum except on the fringe. Everyone agreed that students bring to the classroom multiple learning styles and that critical thinking should be incorporated into every course. Yet little concrete evidence points to instructors implementing these beliefs. Colleges were, and remain, teaching institutions, and within that context, it was the student's responsibility to learn. It has always been so.

## What Institutions Must Become

Barr and Tagg argued that the very mission, vision, culture, and structure of a college must undergo a shift from being an institution that provides instruction to students to an institution that produces learning in students. Once that shift is made, everything has the potential for change. This deceptively simple semantic change has profound implications for what colleges can become and redefines how participants design and shape the complex relationship between the teacher and the student that will exist in the future.

As Barr and Tagg saw it, this paradigm shift results in several benefits for the college: All instructors have the potential to become the designers of powerful learning environments. Curriculum design would be based on an analysis of what a student needs to know to function in a complex world rather than on what the teacher knows how to teach. The college would be judged not on the quality of the entering class but on the quality of the aggregate learning growth possessed by its graduates. Compartmentalized departments would be replaced by cross-disciplinary cooperatives. And every employee, not just the teacher, would have a role to play and a contribution to make in maintaining a student-centered environment.

The implications for change and transformation are considerable. Committing to the learning paradigm, would allow colleges to reconfigure their interaction with students, particularly with the emergence of learning technology options. They can shift from delivering instruction in traditional methods to discovering the many ways in which learning can be stimulated in every student. Although lecturing would continue to be a valid method of delivering information, encouraging discussion and promoting interaction using other collaborative ways to enhance learning would be more fully explored and adopted. Commitment of professional development resources to train instructors in stimulating and assessing student learning would be highly desirable. Planners and curriculum designers, given their diverse access to information today, would begin to question the notion that all subjects fit easily into three- or four-credit-hour modules.

Moving to the learning paradigm could be empowering. Instructors, liberated from the tyranny of the Carnegie unit, could design powerful learning environments that address multiple learning styles and needs. Colleges could redefine the term full-time teaching load to include mentoring, proactive academic advisement, creating and monitoring of learning environments, and strategic community involvement. To support this movement on a macro level, state systems, accreditation bodies, and other regulatory agencies should initiate serious discussion on the continuing validity and practicality of the semester or quarter system as the most effective way to produce student learning, particularly as more colleges move toward asynchronous learning options.

## Barriers to Change

Given the nature of American community colleges—their history and traditions, their commitment to shared governance and consensus building, and a substantial institutional culture that seems to resist change—the impediments to organizational transformation in these colleges are formidable. The search for the learning-centered college is not without obstacles.

The concept of shared governance implies that all campus constituencies have an active role to play in determining the goals, direction, and operation of the college. No other entity in society embraces this collectivist approach to managing its affairs. But truly shared governance is honored more often in the breach than in the observance. Although instructors zealously guard the curriculum as their exclusive property, they often determine their role in institutional management decisions case-by-case, effectively holding veto power over meaningful change. Within the campus political climate, significant intellectual energy and precious time go to positioning and posturing.. Reaching consensus requires long deliberation and consultation. With every hand on the tiller, the collegiate ship of state does not change course easily or often.

Too often, competitive instincts tend to be focused inward on rivalries between or among departments, divisions, instructors, and administration. Scant attention is paid to the environment outside the academic community or to potential threats to higher education as a whole. Compartmentalization hinders a process-oriented perspective. Quality is defined as adherence to self-defined standards (i.e., accreditation), and few meaningful reward systems recognize initiative, innovation, or efficiency. There are few college-wide discussions on refining and improving the educational process or on how each employee can contribute to creating a powerful learning environment.

Unfortunately, colleges and instructors are prisoners of a system, structure, and history that prevent meaningful collaboration between and among campus stakeholders. Creative, innovative teachers are still held hostage by the Carnegie unit and by the recurring rhythms of the academic year with its long holiday breaks and light summer schedule, implying that learning can occur only in familiar patterns and at set times of the year. Archaic and discriminatory grading practices continue, in some cases predefining how instructors will distribute letter grades in a class without concern for students' prior preparation, abilities, or academic potential.

All of the college community—instructors, administrators, support staff—are ultimately caught up in defending a system not of their creation. It is the system in which they were educated. It is the system that annoys or infuriates them when, as parents, they see their children endure some of its inanities. Yet because they are inside it, because they work in it or teach in it, they become the system, and amazingly, they resist changing it.

If instructors were allowed to redesign colleges today, by changing their organizational structures, functions, processes, governance, mission, and values, as well as the way in which teachers and students interact, how many would simply duplicate the status quo? Or would instructors work together to design the most efficient, effective, and productive organization they could collectively imagine to ensure the future?

This precisely is the challenge American community colleges face in the new millennium: the need to transform themselves into colleges that place learning first in every decision and action-learning-centered institutions. Colleges must use their internal communication mechanisms to fully inform instructors and staff of the current external climate and competitive forces and to actively encourage collaborative leadership among all employees in defining how they will reconfigure and position their college in the new century.

## Other Perspectives on Change

Another significant contributor to the discussion on becoming learning-centered was Terry O'Banion, founder and first CEO of the League for Innovation in the Community College. His extensive writing on the learning-centered college identified the traditional limits on higher education: time-bound, place-bound, bureaucracy-bound, and role-bound. All four limitations place significant restrictions on the ability to design a student-centered environment. Indeed, Prometheus was most likely to less bound than colleges appear to be today, with restrictions embedded in education codes, procedures manuals, state master plans, legislatively driven budgets, and organizational cultures. A more detailed examination of some of these long-standing limitations reveals each to be a significant barrier to quality teaching and effective student learning.

O'Banion's definition of a learning college had several key precepts: It placed learning first in all actions and decisions; it provided as many options as possible for learning; it enabled students to take responsibility for their own choices; and it based its staffing on student needs. Success was achieved only when the college could document that its students had acquired "improved and expanded learning" (O'Banion, 1997). It also defined the role of the learning facilitator by the needs of the student and encouraged the student to participate in collaborative learning activities.

Indeed, the concepts of Barr, Tagg, and O'Banion had precedent. K. Patricia Cross, a longtime astute observer of education, noted in 1976 that excessive reliance on time- and place-bound instruction defined much of the virtual architecture of academic institutions (for more about institutional architecture, see chapter 9). Studies have clearly shown that reliance on the time spent on a task is an invalid measure of learning. Instead, the emphasis should be on measuring mastery. Given the tremendous growth of asynchronous learning opportunities (online courses, virtual colleges and universities, computer-based training, and mediated courses), educators have to question the validity of continuing to schedule learning activities exclusively in the semester or quarter format. Equally worthy of debate is the notion that all subjects fit easily into a three- or four-credit-hour module.

Another focus on learning came from outside the educational arena. Senge's (1990) landmark book, *The Fifth Discipline*, gave the corporate sector plenty of food for thought and action. Senge's vision of a corporation where people continually expanded their capability to create results, where collective aspirations were set free to nurture and grow, where new and expansive patterns of thinking were nurtured, and where people were encouraged to see the organization in its totality, struck a responsive chord in the business world; he became a highly sought-after speaker and writer.

## Restructuring the Old Order

Another paradigm that needs to be reexamined is the notion that learning takes place in a specially designed place called a college. In fact, most standard classrooms are anything but specially designed and are not the most conducive locations for meaningful learning to occur. Today's student has a choice of accessing information and learning electronically in his or her home at any time by means of the Internet or televised courses. The provider of this educational experience can be the local community college or a college thousands of miles away. What competitive advantages do local colleges have when they require students to battle gridlocked freeways and confront crammed parking lots in order to sit in crowded lecture halls to acquire the same knowledge? Which of these two options available to the student-learning delivered to any location via technology or a lengthy commute to a crowded campus-can be more accurately described as distance learning?

Granted, class discussion and interaction are important and valuable. But challenging the classroom means challenging not only a location, but also its residents. For many instructors, the classroom is a familiar and comforting environment. As Plater (1995) observed in looking to the future: "The metaphor of the classroom is a powerful one. The most basic and fundamental unit of academic life—the sanctity of the classroom and the authority of the teacher in it—is about to be turned inside out."

One formidable challenge is to plan and implement, in a sensitive but comprehensive way, the evolving role of instructors in an age where technology has made information accessible in efficient and cost-effective ways, thereby challenging the unique franchise undergraduate education has enjoyed for so long. In addition to their subject expertise, instructors need to be trained in identifying learning styles, modular curriculum development, and instructional technology and methodology to become effective assessors of a student's abilities and potential, as well as designers of learning environments and trainers in accessing information and data. Readily available access to information anywhere means that the classroom has lost its place of primacy as the central location where knowledge is acquired. This, in turn, forces the redefinition of the teacher-student relationship and the traditional geography that houses it.

This trend is not necessarily something to be feared. Technology allows the expansion of instructional design principles and practices; these in turn allow instructors to employ a variety of presentational styles to match multiple learning styles. Professional development resources must be committed to train instructors in how to understand and use the new technology to design and implement powerful learning environments. The end result could be the liberation of instructors from the tyranny of the traditional academic calendar and a dramatic increase in meaningful student learning.

Another area where the traditional model impedes colleges from becoming learning-centered is the way legislation institutionalizes educational bureaucracy. New education initiatives are signed into law annually, many of them the product of intense lobbying by special interest education groups, including various unions and organizations, which define progress as creating new jobs or granting salary increases. An instructive example emerges in current trends outside the traditional K-12 education bureaucracy. The popularity of the charter school movement, home schooling, franchised for-profit local learning and tutoring centers, and the rapid growth of online educational alternatives are all clear indications that both the public and its elected officials are looking for ways to avoid the educational bureaucracy that is choking traditional institutions.

Publicly funded institutions are increasingly subjected to calls for accountability and must obtain the results a particular constituency desires. If they do not, they are deemed to be unaccountable and their funding is jeopardized. Legislators are in the forefront of those calling for increased accountability, yet they regularly attempt to micromanage education, oblivious to the fact that their tampering with the system directly impacts its effectiveness and accountability. Colleges must be careful not to fall into the trap of responding to calls for accountability with hastily developed changes that have no positive systemic impact. The best response is to infuse institutional assessment into the very culture of the college, enabling instructors to accurately and regularly gauge the educational progress of their students—to demonstrate that deep learning is taking place. Such a commitment to assessment also provides administrators with solid data on which to make decisions to improve student learning and institutional effectiveness. However, assessment should not be linked to the negative implications of externally mandated accountability; it should be an internal quest for continuous quality improvement of the learning process conducted by all college employees.

## The New Curriculum

Whereas *Building Communities* urged a strong core curriculum, community colleges must also address the growing needs of a workforce constantly seeking skills upgrade, retraining, and lifelong learning—in many cases, adults who have already been through the core curriculum in earlier years and now need training or retraining. To effectively serve these constituencies, community colleges will need to commit resources to prior learning assessment to ensure efficient and effective assistance to these older students. Adult students who need to develop new skills or seek retraining to ensure employability find that their needs are not fully met by the traditional core curriculum—what they all seek when they return to college campuses is learning.

In *The End of Work*, Rifkin (1995) convincingly argued that rethinking the very nature of work would be the most pressing concern facing society in the coming years. If this is true, and if community colleges are being asked to provide training, education, and certification to citizens of all ages in a society struggling with this monumental issue, it is time to ask some fundamental questions about how colleges position themselves to meet this challenge. Perhaps it is time to question what a contemporary work-related curriculum should be, and why it takes so long to conceive, design, seek approval for, and implement it. Perhaps colleges should question why student support programs are structured to serve recent high school graduates when the average age of the national community college student body creeps toward 30 and above. Perhaps colleges should reexamine institutional priorities that marginalize lifelong learning and continuing education programs despite the evidence of growing popularity nationwide.

*Building Communities* cited a U.S. Department of Labor study indicating that an individual would experience three career changes and seven job changes in his or her lifetime. Since the original study was published, the number of job changes in a person's lifetime has no doubt increased, and some of those changes will likely be to careers that currently do not exist. The challenge to community colleges, therefore, is to anticipate the job market and develop curricula to meet workforce training and retraining needs.

Colleges must be able to develop and offer courses and programs in a rapid-response mode, an operating behavior in short supply on today's campuses. Instructors must become leaders in streamlining the process of developing, approving, and offering courses and programs that are relevant and responsive to the needs of their communities.

Curriculum is most important to instructors. They have a heavy intellectual and emotional investment in the current curriculum. As Knefelkamp (1990) observed, it is their "collective autobiography." Because their primary allegiance is to their department or discipline, there is little or no sense of the collective whole, no meaningful comprehension of the overall process of a student's education. Taken collectively, the curriculum is enormous and compartmentalized, tied to its contributing departments. To the student, the curriculum is incoherent and unwieldy, and stands as an impediment to intellectual achievement or academic progress. In a learning-centered environment, instructors can make great strides in developing a new curriculum that is flexible, contemporary, and easily adapted to new opportunities, markets, and services.

Even what is currently called the core curriculum (or distribution requirements) also needs transformation. This prescribed set of required courses from an array of departments, assembled in the hope that a well-rounded general education will miraculously occur from what is basically a cafeteria menu, is without design or merit. Coherence, if there is any, is to be supplied by the student. The core curriculum is not learning-centered or outcomes-based. A further complication is that community colleges cannot be innovative in developing a truly effective curriculum that contains core knowledge and skills, despite the efforts of future-thinking instructors, because upper-level institutions often dictate the shape and content of general education requirements to meet their own internal political needs. The student is trapped in the academic crossfire.

Competence in life requires the appropriate use of knowledge; academic success demands the ability to recognize and recall knowledge. Students leave college knowing things, but they are unable to understand concepts or apply knowledge across particular contexts, because the curriculum has often failed to focus on competency. The rapid increase in popularity for learning on demand will affect the existing curriculum, causing increasing modularization and new methods of delivery. To design a true core curriculum, instructors should define collectively what graduates should know and be able to do and create learning experiences to achieve those ends. Curriculum should be designed around the critical learning outcomes necessary for success in a field, building the sequence of courses around students' active involvement in real-life case studies. A curriculum based on outcomes gives students the knowledge, skills, and attitudes that are valued by employers.

Community colleges must anticipate what the future job market will be and what curricula must be developed to meet the training and retraining needs of the workforce. They must find ways to streamline and shorten the cycle of curriculum development, approval, and implementation to be responsive partners in workforce development. While the traditional curriculum will remain a core offering of community colleges, the development of competency certification, often in partnership with the private sector, should be a strong and viable alternative to degree or certificate programs. Instructors must define collectively what graduates should know and be able to do and design learning experiences and outcomes necessary for success in work and in life.

## Looking to the Future

The concepts contained in Barr and Tagg's learning paradigm, as well as O'Banion's learning-centered college, provide an overarching metaphor for organizational transformation and not merely change. They are not concepts that can be applied to only one portion of a college. They must permeate all aspects of its structure, fabric, and culture to effectively complete and go beyond the paradigm shift. Planning, resource allocation, facilities design, curriculum development, policy governance, the infusion of technology into pedagogy, and the nature and quality of all supportive services must be aligned with the vision of a college unified in causing, enhancing, and producing student learning. Various management tools and organizational development practices can be effectively applied to hasten the transformation, but the concepts alone, without vision and commitment, are ultimately insufficient.

When new facilities are constructed or existing facilities are renovated, colleges must abandon the familiar aspects of the conventional classroom. Connectivity is essential and the ability to connect to the incredible information network of the Internet with the click of a mouse must be available in every facility. Classrooms must be easily reconfigured to permit small group discussion, collaborative learning exercises, and maximum individualized interactions between teacher and student. Instructors should be given appropriate presentational technology to enhance their efforts.

Placing learning at the core of every decision and action means rethinking how instructors organize themselves, how colleges are structured, and most importantly, how employees interact with each other and with students. Job roles and descriptions must be rethought and modified. Technology must be thoughtfully applied to relieve staff of busy work and meaningless repetitive tasks, freeing them to assume new roles in support of the central learning mission. Above all, a new spirit of mutual trust and cooperation must evolve, so that the energies of everyone are focused on student learning rather than the preservation of old allegiances, privileges, and mindsets.

As instructors, staff, and administrators plan for the colleges of the future, they must anticipate the tremendous societal changes and technological challenges that all will face. They need not eliminate the place-bound campuses and locations in which so much is invested, but they cannot allow the physical institutions to continue to function on a part-time or selective basis. Colleges must move from the old agrarian-based calendar to a 365-

day-a-year operation. Colleges must develop a virtual presence to match their community presence to meet the incredible increased need for learning for all ages. In the process of creating a responsive learning institution, both virtually and in reality, they will have to re-examine employee contracts, labor agreements, full- and part-time employment, and the definition of the responsibilities and privileges of tenure. In an age where information can flow freely across state and national lines, state master plans quickly will be rendered obsolete, district boundaries will be meaningless, and educational sector politics will become moot. Available will be a new pool of potential colleagues.

## Maximizing Resources in the Transformative Process

Colleges need to invest in supporting the crucial and evolving role of instructors as subject experts, learning mentors, and role models, while adding the new responsibilities of learning environment designer and holistic curriculum leader. Freed from the time- and place-bound curriculum and classroom, the 21st-century instructor can have more freedom to experiment with new methods, techniques, and approaches to ensure that all students learn in whatever manner is most appropriate.

Another resource to maximize is the tremendous potential of every college employee. Rather than continuing a hierarchical structure in which there are teachers and those who support teaching, college communities must engage in a dialogue that examines the potential of all people to be used in the most cost-effective and sensible way so they may become active contributors to the learning process. Indeed, all academic, student services, and administrative personnel need to become involved in the transformation process. Leadership must come from those who have dealt with both the internal obstacles and external challenges that will affect higher education's future. The ultimate goal is to become a college where everyone is focused on learning. With learning at the center of the organizational culture, this approach becomes an analytical matrix against which current problems may be evaluated, a target toward which institutional energies and resources may be directed, and a unifying goal that will bring campus constituencies together in common purpose.

Those who develop and manage budgets must have the political courage to allocate resources in a way that supports student learning. Academic planners must think outside the instruction box to complement instructors who commit to becoming the designers of learning environments rather than simply maintaining the comfort zone of traditional lecturing. Strategic planning efforts must be free of the restrictive elements of paradigmatic thinking that filter out new information that does not agree with the current direction.

## The Search Without an Ending

Today, the United States is a nation of lifelong students. Students come to college campuses for community services workshops and seminars that enhance their maturation. Older adults seek enrichment through noncredit programs and activities. Workforce members of all ages come back to colleges for refresher courses, skills upgrades, and retraining. Two-year colleges are evolving as institutions, no longer simply technical colleges, no longer merely junior colleges. As technology impacts lives, jobs, and the society, and as the very definition of community changes, these institutions will become more than just community colleges. They will become the learning centers of their communities.

This is the agenda for the journey to the learning-centered college in the 21st century: to move from the comfort of the instruction paradigm to the challenge of the learning paradigm, and to retain and enhance colleges' strengths and resources while courageously daring to transform and thereby advance student learning. It will not be easy. In the words of Proust, we need not find new lands, but to see with new eyes. By seeing each institution with new eyes, the search for the learning-centered college can truly begin.

## References

AACC Commission on the Future of Community College. (1988). *Building communities: A vision for a new century.* Washington, DC: American Association of Community Colleges.

Barr, R., & Tagg, J. (1995, November/December). From teaching to learning: A new paradigm for undergraduate education. *Change, 27*(6), 13–25.

Knefelkamp, L. (1990, May/June). Seasons of academic life: Honoring our collective autobiography. *Change, 76,* 4–23.

O'Banion, T. (1997). *A learning college for the 21st century.* San Francisco: AACC and ACE/Oryx Press.

Plater, W. (1995, May/June). Future work: Faculty time in the 21st century. *Change, 27,* 23–33.

Rifkin, J. (1995). *The end of work: The decline of the global labor force and the dawn of the post-market era.* New York: Putnam.

Senge, P. M. (1990). *The fifth discipline: The art and practice of the learning organization.* New York: Currency.

# CHAPTER 2

# The Learning Paradigm as Bold Change: Improving Understanding and Practice

ROBERT B. BARR AND FRANK A. FEAR

In this chapter, we reexamine the nature of the learning paradigm, including the requirements and challenges in making the shift from the instruction paradigm to the learning paradigm. Our thesis is that making this shift is bold, transformative change. Bold change requires answering fundamental questions about the purpose of higher education, the nature of learning, the nature of organizations, organizational change, and the approaches change agents take. To do this, we will extend the observations made in earlier commentaries by Barr (1998); Fear, Adamek, and Imig (2002); and Fear, Doberneck, and colleagues (2003) and consider what the learning paradigm is; how it came to be; how we interpret its meaning; and how institutional leaders and instructors attempt to shift colleges and universities from teaching to learning.

Successfully shifting from teaching to learning requires answering fundamental questions thoughtfully, deliberately, and systematically. That will challenge campus change agents. Although the learning paradigm provokes response, it offers no blueprint that change agents can adopt routinely or implement mechanistically. Authentic expressions of the learning paradigm are products of ingenuity; bold efforts that seek to change the fundamental nature of how colleges operate in the classroom and throughout the entire institution.

Perhaps more than anything else, becoming a learning college requires liberating organizational members from historical processes, approaches, and systems. For many colleges, that requires organizational transformation. What often happens is that change in the name of becoming a learning college takes place within the constraints of the existing instructional culture, which does not change the fundamental essence of teaching and learning. Such changes preserve the status quo, breathing life into the bromide the more things change, the more things stay the same.

Because shifting from teaching to learning is a paradigmatic change, change agents' actions must go beyond the realm of conventional change practices in higher education. They must go beyond fixing what is not working—reformation—and beyond introducing new ideas or practices—innovation. Shifting from teaching to learning involves core change and represents a radically different vision of higher education. How radical is the learning paradigm? To articulate the essential dimensions of the learning paradigm for the 1995 article published in *Change,* Barr and Tagg identified a series of counter-positions to the instruction paradigm. In other words, the learning paradigm and instruction paradigm are opposites. Shifting from teaching to learning means replacing the dominant paradigm's set of fundamental operating principles with an opposing and alternative set. It means replacing what instructors know how to do and have been doing successfully with a new vision and practice in higher education.

This shift demands that campus change agents think beyond the realm of how change is typically conceived and enacted on college campuses—as a process. To be sure, process is important. But whereas process acumen is necessary, it is insufficient for paradigmatic change (Fear, Adamek, & Imig, 2002). At its core, paradigmatic change is about an idea, a startling idea, which contrasts sharply with the core ideas of conventional thinking. Shifting from teaching to learning requires, first and foremost, a deep understanding of this startling idea, which, in turn, requires a deep understanding of theories of learning.

The instruction paradigm-governed college has a theory of learning that is never really discussed. It exists in structures and actions as a theory-in-use, not as an espoused theory. This is a distinction discussed by organizational theorists Argyris and Schön (1974). It refers to the fact that people and organizations can say one thing and do another. An espoused theory is a set of principles governing the behavior of a person or organized entity. A theory-in-use, on the other hand, is the set of principles that disinterested observers infer governs that behavior. Thus, a manager might profess belief in participatory management, while observers agree that her behavior is authoritarian.

The theory of learning in place in an instruction paradigm-governed college might be called the particle theory of learning. Professors, as source of light, bombard students with knowledge particles in the hope that some of those particles will be absorbed and stored. Although this theory is too outrageous to be explicitly supported, it lives in what instruction paradigm-governed colleges actually do. On the other hand, the learning paradigm-governed college develops an explicit, institutional theory of learning. This is both an advantage and a problem from an operational standpoint. It is an advantage because an institution can be conscious, deliberate, and systematic in how it seeks to accomplish learning. It is a problem because it challenges instructors and administrators to agree on a core set of learning assumptions, concepts, and perspectives.

Making the shift to learning requires answering fundamental questions, including: What is to be learned? Where? When? By whom? For what purpose? With what outcomes? And, most importantly, according to what theory of learning? Answers to these questions will drive an aligned plan for enabling robust and meaningful learning environments and experiences. Enabling the learning theory and plan will require revamping funding and resource allocation, support systems, and instructors roles and rewards, as well as adjusting the metrics used to monitor efficiency, evaluate effectiveness, and gauge overall success. All of this must be done in a way that meshes with the campus context in which transformative change is sought. That means fitting change to the historical, economic, political, mission-related, and other realities that make any campus environment distinctive, if not unique.

## Origins of the Learning Paradigm

### Historical Background

To understand the essence of the learning paradigm as bold change, it may help to know, first, its historical origins and, second, the genesis of the concept. The instruction paradigm, we submit, is part of a larger encompassing paradigm, the grand narrative of the modern world, usually called moderism. In one form or another, this larger paradigm has been a dominant force for approximately 400 years. Moderism began with the scientific revolution of the 17th century, continued with the Enlightenment of the 18th century, evolved during the Industrial Revolution of the 19th century, and reached ascendancy with the rise of transnational corporatism in the 20th century. This shift moved society from traditional authority, humanism, and smaller-scale modes of operations to rational administration, technical procedures, and systematic management of large-scale operations with economies-of-scale. The outcomes are manifest in a variety of expressions including the positivist scientific method, behavioral psychology, and the factory model of production, which includes bureaucratic organizational systems, higher education among them. As an outgrowth of this historically dominant paradigm, the instruction paradigm emphasizes teachers as information givers, learning as an individual activity, and students as passive recipients.

Many analysts, including Capra (1982) and Drucker (1992), believe that current times represent a period of epochal change, a time when society literally rearranges itself, organizing around new and different philosophies, values, forms, and goals. Called postmodernism by some, the new society includes a variety of counter-positions to the historically dominant paradigm. Among the core ideas are multiplicity of meaning and interpretation; diversity of expression and form; centrality of interpersonal relationships and connectedness; and recognition of and appreciation for non-linearity, complexity, and emergence. For Capra (1996) and others, one of the essential ways the new alternative paradigm differs from the old is in how power is exercised and structured-with less emphasis on authority exercised through hierarchies and more emphasis on discovery mediated through interaction. This new way of thinking and practicing is embodied in such contemporary expressions as shared leadership, participatory management, and collaborative learning. As an outgrowth of this new larger social narrative, the learning paradigm emphasizes learning, instructors as co-learners and learning environment designers, and students (often working together) as active constructors of meaning (Gibbs, 1995).

### *The Learning Paradigm Concept*

Whereas other thinkers and writers have applied this general understanding to higher education, including the Wingspread Group in *An American Imperative* (1993), the learning paradigm concept was created independently by Barr during 1991 while serving as director of institutional research and planning at Palomar College, a San Diego-area community college. Barr first shared his essential insight and conception of a paradigm shift with John Tagg, a friend and English professor at Palomar. A more expanded and developed set of materials were later shared with George Boggs, president of the college.

As a kindred spirit, Tagg recognized instantly the significance of Barr's insight. After authoring several initial articles on the learning paradigm published in California newsletters and in *Leadership Abstracts* (Barr, 1993, 1994, 1995), Barr invited Tagg to join him in writing an article for *Change* (Barr & Tagg, 1995). Boggs recognized the learning paradigm's significance but wondered whether others, especially leaders in higher education, would respond to an idea that had such radical and subversive implications for the normal view of how colleges were to function. Boggs first used Barr's materials in a speech to an administrators' conference held in May 1992. Those attending thought that Boggs, now president of the American Association of Community Colleges, was saying something that needed to be heard across higher education. Consequently, the National Institute for Staff and Organizational Development (NISOD), the sponsor of the conference, published the speech (Boggs, 1993). Still later, Barr and Boggs shared the learning paradigm ideas with Terry O'Banion, president and CEO of the League for Innovation in the Community College. O'Banion took up the cause and published a book, *A Learning College for the 21st Century* (1997), which became a best-seller.

What lead Barr to his insight? Twenty years earlier, Barr was taking a graduate course in the sociology of innovation at the University of Michigan. Barr focused his course attention on innovation in higher education. Through this study, he was introduced to an innovation at a Midwestern liberal arts college. Thinking that there was a more powerful and effective way to educate undergraduates, an innovator at this college championed the creation of a college-within-a-college at his institution. Wanting to know if his program was in fact more effective than the traditional methods used there, the program founder developed multiple pre- and post-measures of student learning and success. The results showed that on every measure students in the program outperformed by a large margin those in the traditional program. The fact that the program did not cost any more than the traditional program made it even more impressive.

Clearly, Barr thought, this innovation was a great success. But the rest of the story was distressing. Not only was this innovation not replicated or adapted anywhere else in higher education, so far as Barr could find, it disappeared from the very institution where it was created, once its founder and champion retired. Most troubling about this story, however, was that it seemed to Barr that this case paralleled the story of virtually every innovation for improving student learning he studied. So, for the next 20 years, he persistently searched for answers to these questions: Why is there a lack of innovation in the core educational practices of institutions of higher education? Why do educational practices not evolve and lead to improved outcomes over time? Why are colleges not getting better and smarter at their work? Up to the spring of 1991, he found every proposed explanation to be wanting.

As it happened, in the fall of 1989 and not long after his arrival at Palomar, Barr became the leader of a major planning effort that included the president, Boggs, and colleague Tagg. The Vision Task Force, officially chaired by Boggs with de facto leadership by Barr, was charged with creating a compelling vision of Palomar to be achieved during the next 15 years. In the course of the work of the task force, Barr sought a powerful and concise way to express Palomar's core mission. He was inspired in this by the mission statement of FedEx, "To deliver every package, overnight, every time." This contrasted sharply to the mission and vision statements that Barr had collected and studied from other colleges as background research for the task force. The vision expressed in virtually all of these documents was a variation on the theme: We will be number one. In contrast to the colleges' self-aggrandizing statements, FedEx aspired to make a significant contribution to customers—to deliver their packages, on time, every time. In addition, Barr found that most college mission statements emphasized activities and throughputs (not outcomes or results), such as offering a rigorous curriculum. Barr did not find these statements very satisfactory and searched for an impassioned and inspiring expression, something that might proclaim "We have a dream!" rather than assert "We have a strategic plan."

In the spring of 1991, shortly after the task force's mission and vision proposals were approved by the board of trustees, Barr was still grappling with his twin concerns about the lack of innovation in core educational practices and his desire to find a powerful and concise mission statement for Palomar. Then, in a reflective moment, it hit him. The focus—the mission—of his college, and of all other colleges as far as he knew, was not on learning. It was on instructing. No wonder, he thought, there is so little, lasting innovation in educational practice. The educational practices currently in use, dominated by 50-minute lectures from experts to passive students, were themselves the end—not (as he had assumed) a means to an end. Both in their explicit statements of mission and in their everyday practices, colleges and universities sought to teach, that is, to instruct and profess. Universities expressed their essential functions as "teaching, research, and public service," and community colleges touted themselves as "America's premier teaching institutions." Despite his awareness of these statements, it was a huge surprise to him that they were to be taken literally. He had simply assumed, perhaps like most others, that the purpose of a college was to educate, that is, to empower students to learn as much and as profoundly as possible. What Barr realized was that the theory-in-use of institutions of higher education was to provide instruction rather than to produce learning.

## Essence of the Learning Paradigm

With this insight, Barr recognized that the shift of colleges from teaching to learning constituted change at the paradigmatic level. Barr knew from his studies of Thomas Kuhn's *Structure of Scientific Revolutions* (1970) that paradigms do not live in what is said about practice, but rather in what is done in practice. In fact, the point of calling a framework of assumptions a paradigm is to emphasize that assumptions are not only being taken for granted but may also operate unconsciously, some so deeply that they are not even known to exist. Paradigms are compelling forces because they govern the nature of behavior. Joel Arthur Barker (1992b) elaborates: "A paradigm is a set of rules and regulations (written or unwritten) that does two things: (1) It establishes or defines boundaries; and (2) It tells you how to behave inside the boundaries in order to be successful" (p. 32) .

Barr began charting the differences between the dominant paradigm, which he later named the instruction paradigm, and his proposed alternative paradigm, the learning paradigm. The instruction paradigm, as the theory-in-use of colleges and universities as organizations, revealed itself in their structure and practice. The learning paradigm arose literally and simply from reversing just about every principle and feature of current practice.

Thus, shifting to the learning paradigm represents a subversive act—a breaking of conventional rules and regulations, establishing new boundaries, and requiring fresh behaviors. What, then, are the rules, regulations, boundaries, and roles associated with the learning paradigm? In their 1995 article, Barr and Tagg defined a college governed by the learning paradigm as one which conducts an organized and systematic effort to "create environments and experiences that bring students to discover and construct knowledge for themselves, to make students members of communities of students that make discoveries and solve problems . . . and . . . to create a series of ever more powerful learning environments" (p. 15).

In a comparison chart published in the article, Barr and Tagg contrasted the learning paradigm-governed college with the instruction paradigm-governed college on a number of dimensions:

- mission and purposes—from providing instruction to producing learning
- success criteria—from producing student credit hours to achieving student learning outcomes
- teaching-learning structures—from organizing classes in 50-minute lecture blocks to having flexibly structured learning arrangements, in other words, whatever works best for learning
- learning theory—from viewing students as passive recipients to seeing them as active knowledge constructors
- productivity and funding—from being defined in terms of inputs and resources, such as enrollments, to being defined in terms of outcomes, especially student learning outcomes

- nature of instructor and student roles—from regarding instructors as knowers and students as knowledge recipients to reframing all (including non-instructional staff) as learners and designers of learning environments

Although this contrast has proven to be an excellent tool by which to grasp the radical implications of the learning paradigm, it can be misleading in four ways.

First, the contrast might be interpreted to mean that everything associated with the instruction paradigm is wrong. But rather than thinking of the two paradigms in terms of good and bad, a broader perspective would understand the learning paradigm as an inevitable development due to changing socio-contextual conditions. Because paradigms are nested in socio-contextual conditions and other more fundamental paradigms, when such conditions and paradigms change, it affects paradigms nested within them. Consequently, contemporary challenges and circumstances have combined to make the instruction paradigm lag behind current thinking. The instruction paradigm made sense during an earlier era when learning theory was dominated by the notion of transferring knowledge from experts to novices and scientific management theory influenced the creation of machine-like organizational systems. Today, we recognize the value of constructivist learning theory; understand the limitations associated with knowledge transfer; and affirm the value of learning organizations aiming to improve over time.

Second, the from-to presentation might give readers the impression that each dimension represents a continuum. In this way of thinking, a particular college could be seen as operating midway between focusing on inputs and focusing on outcomes. Suggesting that the difference between the instruction and learning paradigms is a matter of degree—rather than seeing the contrast as a difference of kind—impoverishes the underlying principles of the respective paradigms and veils the radical implications of the learning paradigm as a governing system in higher education. The learning paradigm is not an amalgamation of the instruction and learning paradigms.

Third, in any rendition of from-to, readers typically focus on the to because they are interested in learning about the new idea but may fail to truly appreciate the robust influence of the from. Paradigms are meaning structures, and people use meaning structures to filter what they experience and learn. If the instruction paradigm is higher education's dominant meaning structure, then it stands to reason that instructors might expect to find situations where new ideas, such as the learning paradigm, are filtered through the instruction paradigm meaning structure. What happens, for example, if instructors interpret students discovering and constructing knowledge for themselves through an instruction paradigm lens?

That happened to co-author Fear and his associates as they were involved in the final planning phase for launching a learning paradigm program. They realized that they were preparing to launch a learning paradigm program using an instruction paradigm design. Shocked and dismayed at this realization, they struggled with what to do. In the end, they decided that the way forward—just as Barr and Tagg (1995) had learned when creating the learning paradigm itself—was to "literally and simply reverse just about every principle or feature of current practice." This traumatic and disorienting realization represented the pathway to profound discovery and enlightenment: Individually and collectively, Fear and his associates entered the learning paradigm.

Fourth, identifying and describing specific features of the learning paradigm may be interpreted as saying that learning colleges have a specific and fixed form. To the contrary, expressions of the learning paradigm are not determined. They can be multiple, varied, fluid, and evolving over time. As a means to illustrate core features of the learning paradigm, Barr and Tagg considered drawing examples from what colleges were doing (chief among them, Alverno College) as they were writing their 1995 article. They decided not to use such examples because they did not want to suggest that only particular forms or practices embody the learning paradigm. What the authors really hoped to accomplish was that readers would apprehend the gestalt of the learning paradigm. Barr and Tagg conceive the learning paradigm as a whole, greater than the sum of its parts. Paradigms are not the sum of their parts, they reasoned; rather, the parts receive meaning from the paradigm. Too much focusing on parts, as critics and even supporters of the learning paradigm sometimes do, interferes with understanding and internalizing the gestalt.

We believe paradigm shifts are ultimately internalized holistically and, eventually, all at once. Just as in learning to ride a bicycle, plenty of trial and error is required; a rider peddling for the first time without assistance experiences the event holistically and tacitly. When asked what that first ride was like, the rider is unlikely to talk about the ride mechanics. That is because no amount of analysis of any specific feature comes close to capturing the essence of this deep experience. In fact, the rider is likely to talk about it as a deep experience, that is, what it means in personal terms to ride a bike unfettered. We believe this is what happens with experience in the learning paradigm. Over time, participants shift their understanding to a gestalt and resonate with its essence rather than with the identified parts.

This was co-author Fear's experience, as well as the experience of executive administrators responsible for his learning paradigm program. In both cases, with increasing practice, experience, and deeper understanding, the gestalt of the program came into clearer view. As a program founder, Fear has described it as "engaged learning" (Fear, Bawden, et al., 2002), a learning approach defined by collaborative and participatory inquiry that he uses not only in his teaching work, but also in his research and public service endeavors. As administrators observed the evolution of Fear's work, they also developed ways of expressing their understanding of the program as a gestalt. For example, one administrator described it as "Students taking control of their own learning."

Fear and Barr worked together with colleagues (Fear, Doberneck, et al., 2003) experimenting with using imagery and metaphor to help supporters and students of the learning paradigm mine and deepen their understanding, express what they were learning, and share their struggles as they implemented it. For example, participants in a conference session were able to talk easily about their work that way and significant insights emerged about the essence of the learning paradigm. Among other things, this strategy enabled conversants to capture and express the emotional aspects associated with making a paradigm shift, especially what it feels like during stressful times. Some found it useful to express their feelings pictorially and then talk about what they had drawn.

## Deepening Our Understanding of the Learning Paradigm

Because making the shift from teaching to learning involves adopting new roles and establishing new boundaries, having opportunities to engage in dialogue about the experience helps sharpen understanding, including quickening the pace of comprehending the gestalt. That is why we believe every campus initiative should include abundant opportunities for authentic dialogue about what is happening and why and how. Also important is encouraging dialogue among diverse parties, people representing different institutions, who can learn from what others are doing; make available to others what they are doing; and possibly even develop—together—a common understanding of significant matters associated with the learning paradigm.

This is exactly what happened with Barr and Fear. Fear was involved in making the learning shift as the founder of the Liberty Hyde Bailey Scholars Program, an undergraduate program at Michigan State University (MSU). That work provoked Barr to think about how he might use this example to better articulate the essence of the learning paradigm. As Fear and his colleagues moved forward with the Bailey program, Barr and Fear developed a working relationship beginning in the spring of 1999 at a National Conference on the Learning Paradigm held in San Diego, where Fear and his students presented. The conversations continued when Fear hosted Barr during his visit to MSU, and as Fear and his colleagues continued participating in annual learning paradigm conferences.

As the relationship evolved, Barr and Fear engaged in a dialogue about the learning paradigm and how it was being interpreted in practice. A fascinating dynamic emerged early on in this dialogue. Barr pointed out passages from the *Change* article that Fear and associates had either overlooked or underemphasized in their change work. With time, Fear and others realized that they had read what they had already believed, in effect, using the article to confirm thinking and validate the direction of their work. By the same token, when re-reading the Barr and Tagg article with fresh eyes, Fear and his associates found themselves reacting negatively to some of its language, such as the words "producing learning" (conjuring up a factory image). In addition, Fear and his colleagues would often complain to Barr about how they felt others in the movement to shift from teaching to learning, now catching fire, were misinterpreting what they felt was its essence.

Through these discussions, Barr and Fear began to see how preferred learning and change theories affect what people believe and how they practice. Emerging from this unexpected conflict was a deeper understanding of the learning paradigm and how it is interpreted. After significant discussion with Fear, Barr proposed this gestalt of the learning paradigm: A learning paradigm-governed institution is one whose purpose is to enable deep learning and to continually get better at it over time. When stated this way, the essence of the learning paradigm is like an abstract principle that can take many different, even conflicting, forms in practice. Deep learning can mean different things to different people in different circumstances. Likewise, getting better at enabling learning over time can mean a variety of achievements and ways of measuring those achievements. Nevertheless, as abstract and simple as this may be, it is not without content.

For colleges as organizations, the shift from teaching to learning involves two related but distinct shifts. First, colleges must shift their espoused theory and theory-in-use from providing instruction to enabling deep learning. Although an obvious assertion, it is a statement with far-reaching implications. It means that colleges must decide what it means to enable learning, in the first place and, more so, what it means to enable learning deeply. Engaging in this effort begins with an assessment of current conditions. Are we enabling deep learning? When? Where? How?

Second, colleges must shift from operating as problem-solving organizations to operating as learning organizations. This is a distinction well developed by Senge in *The Fifth Discipline* (1990). A problem-solving organization engages in single-loop learning; it establishes and uses a fixed set of methods to define and solve problems. A learning organization, on the other hand, engages in double-loop learning, learning new problem definitions and methods and constantly changing how it envisions the future and addresses challenges. A learning college recognizes that it is on a never-ending quest to develop ever more powerful environments for deep learning.

## Making the Shift From Teaching to Learning: Common Responses

### *Paradigmatic Straddle*
Attempting bold change is complex, difficult, and stressful. It stands to reason that individuals and institutions might engage in behaviors that diminish the prospects for transformative change. There are two common obstructive practices in the shift from teaching to learning-paradigmatic straddle and creating alternative settings.

Paradigmatic straddle occurs when ideas and practices from multiple paradigms are mixed. Paradigmatic straddle can take several forms. Shifting from one paradigm to another requires unlearning as much as it does learning anew; habits are difficult to shed, even with intentionality. Consequently, in one form change agents can talk new and practice old. This happened to co-author Fear during the early years of his personal experience in shifting from teaching to learning in the context of a department's graduate program. His classroom practices continued to reflect the instruction paradigm and lagged behind colleagues' efforts, even though he (as unit chairperson) articulated the need for making the shift, impelled colleagues to see the wisdom and benefits of shifting, crafted the intellectual foundation for the change, and co-designed two core courses.

Only after experiencing another learning paradigm experiment at the undergraduate level was Fear able to align intention with practice. It took him years to let go of teaching-centered education and to replace it—competently and confidently—with learning-centered practice. When he finally made the shift, the contrast was so compelling that he wrote about it as "turning things upside down" (Fear, McCarthy, et al., 2003). As this personal example suggests, transacting a paradigmatic shift is made neither automatically nor easily. Even when a person is eager to make the shift, one finds that time, practice, and dialogue are necessary, as is administrative support and patience.

A second form of paradigmatic straddle has potentially insidious consequences for people and colleges. This happens when the new paradigm is adopted partially, such that ideas are incorporated selectively into the current paradigm and the current paradigm is retained as the primary interpretive frame of reference. Often experienced in the early stages of a paradigm shift, this is a type of paradigmatic cheating, especially if it endures or is enacted intentionally. The antidote for this form of straddle is open and honest conversation about whether change intentions are becoming change reality. This is often more easily said than done, however. Individuals and institutions are often unaware that they are straddling this way. Worse yet, the politics of change sometimes means that shifts are undertaken for symbolic purposes only, that is, to give the impression that transformation is underway.

Even when there is a sincere attempt to change, an underemphasized element in the politics of change is the nature of the leadership required. In our consulting work we have seen numerous examples of instructors and institutional leaders who do not seem to be as adept in learning-centered environments as they are in teaching-centered programs. No matter how successful one has been in the old reality, the new reality requires acquiring and demonstrating new and different competencies. Making the shift can be an excruciatingly difficult, if not a painful, process. Barker (1992a) described this phenomenon as "the Back to Zero principle."

There is a third straddle form: seeking alternative paradigm ends while, at the same time, employing means associated with the historically dominant paradigm. The antidote for this form of paradigmatic straddle is straightforward: philosophically and procedurally, aligning change means with change goals. How does this apply to the learning paradigm?

Recall from our earlier discussion how Barr and Tagg (1995) defined a college governed by the learning paradigm:

> as one which conducts an organized and systematic effort to create environments and experiences that bring students to discover and construct knowledge for themselves, to make students members of communities of learners that make discoveries and solve problems . . . and . . . to create a series of ever more powerful learning environments. (p. 15)

Just as instructors seek to create environments and experiences that bring students · to discover and construct knowledge for themselves so, too, should instructors create environments and experiences that enable all on campus to understanding the value of the learning paradigm and how it might influence their lives. And, just as instructors seek to gather students in learning communities to make discoveries and solve problems so, too, should instructors seek to engage members of the campus community in learning communities to make discoveries and solve problems related to the learning paradigm.

Aligning means and ends is not unlike what happens when a business department teaches its students about collaborative management and also conducts department business that way. This radical way of proceeding includes, but goes well beyond, process; it fundamentally changes the way that instructors think about innovations, organizations, and change. It does that by opening the door to a variety of counter-positions to conventional practice.

### Creating Alternative Settings

A second form of diminishing the prospects for making a paradigm shift is introducing change in one or more specific locations in an institution rather than introducing change across the institution. This is another way in which institutions hold core practices sacred—maintaining the general system and, at the same time, experimenting with change, often in fringe locations. With strategic intent, institutional leaders can observe these experimental efforts and decide what (if anything) can be diffused to the broader environment or be replicated in other smaller-scale locations.

Called *alternative settings* in the literature (Cherniss & Deegan, 2000) they are created by those who embrace countercultural (to the mainstream) ideas. Co-author Fear has experience with designing and directing a learning paradigm program that was created as an alternative setting in a university context (see Fear, Latinen, Woodward, & Gerulski, 2001). Concerned about the narrowness of student training in a technically focused curriculum, a dean asked Fear and his associates to create a learning environment that would broaden undergraduates' perspectives and, at the same time, stimulate students' leadership capabilities and contribute to their character development. What emerged was the Bailey Scholars Program mentioned earlier in this chapter. Fear and his associates soon discovered that surviving required nimble boundary crossing: remaining true to the ethos of the learning paradigm and, at the same time, abiding by university norms and regulations. A key to program viability has been demonstrating the valued-added aspects of the program to outsiders. It is not enough for the program to succeed on terms it has established; politically, the program has had to succeed on terms others value. For example, when the program won a campus-wide award given for excellence in interdisciplinary scholarship (almost always given for research achievements) that signaled to outsiders that the program functioned well in the mainstream.

In their experience, Fear and his associates found what research findings have revealed: Alternative settings are dicey operations that often succumb to the varied challenges they face. Always created with compelling vision and conviction, and launched with considerable sweat and passion, it is challenging to sustain these characteristics over time. Creep can set in-often below the radar-such that as time passes the alternative setting looks more and more like the conventional setting. That almost always signals the death knell because an alternative setting's market value lies in being different from mainstream expressions, not the same. Alternative settings also face scaling up challenges. It is often difficult to take ideas that work in smaller settings and transfer them effectively in macro operations.

Nevertheless, alternative settings can serve a useful purpose because they represent a spawning ground of bold ideas. Conventionally organized institutions, including higher education, would lead outsiders to believe that radical ideas emerge as a matter of course as these institutions do their business and evolve. Without question, new ideas and programs are created on a regular basis. Yet, programs that embrace an alternative paradigm threaten the status quo and are often rejected (or at least marginalized) by them. Consequently, radical ideas are often expressed and take root as social movements, outside the mainstream of institutional life.

When an institution adopts an idea from a social movement, it is often because the idea has been around for a period of time and feels less threatening. Even then, institutions rarely absorb the radical concept holistically or completely. Rather, the idea is modified to fit an institution's culture and systems architecture. In other words, unless an institution seeks to become an alternative setting itself (with respect to the wider sociocultural context), the process of adopting a radical idea diminishes the radical edge of the original concept. This leads to a paradox of transformational change. One would think that a radical idea has the power to potentially change an institutional core, that is, to change the way business is done. What typically happens, though, is just the opposite: A bold idea is changed to fit the way business is already done. When that happens, transformational change is impeded in favor of institutional reform.

What are the implications of the accommodations we have discussed—paradigmatic straddle and the creation of alternative settings—for the learning paradigm? More than anything else they demonstrate the enormity of the challenge associated with affecting the paradigmatic shift from teaching to learning. The instruction paradigm is engrained in higher education's psyche, structure, and operational systems. Affirming the shift from teaching to learning is one thing; making the shift intellectually is another thing; becoming a learning college is the most difficult task of all.

## Embarking on the Journey to a Learning College

With individual and organizational obstacles standing in transformation's way, how does bold change net a chance? Although there is no recipe for success, observation and experience inspire these five interrelated guidelines:

1. Identify intended learning outcomes.
2. Use the outcomes as a starting point for designing curriculum.
3. Develop a system for measuring the achievement of learning outcomes.
4. Create a wide range of powerful options for achieving the required learning outcomes.
5. Continually explore new and alternative methods for empowering learning.

We consider these five guidelines as we treat three broad topics: creating an intellectual foundation for learning, operationalizing the intellectual foundation, and using transformative means to achieve transformative ends.

### *Creating an Intellectual Foundation for Learning*

We view learning- and student-centered education as a scholarly endeavor—that is, informed by theory and practiced thoughtfully. Learning is a complex subject. In designing a learning program, choices need to be made, and these choices are affiliated with distinctly different philosophical and scholarly traditions. Consequently, it is prudent to make informed decisions grounded in an understanding of the literature of learning.

We recommend launching the planning process by reading extensively, analyzing alternative learning theories (including robust consideration of campus experiences), and engaging in dialogue about ideas, perspectives, and possibilities about learning. This is exactly what Fear and his associates did at Michigan State. Launching the Bailey program involved a semester-long seminar for instructors and administrators co-lead by Fear and a colleague who had led a learning-centered college at another university. Seminar participants engaged in vigorous discussion about core issues. Overall, the seminar influenced the design of the program and helped establish a culture of scholarly engagement.

This example illustrates one of our fundamental beliefs: becoming a learning college requires, first and foremost, becoming a student of learning. There are many rich and provocative readings that help to inform the process. In addition to O'Banion's *A Learning College for the 21st Century* (1997), consider Tagg's *The Learning Paradigm College* (2003) and Abbott and Ryan's *The Unfinished Revolution* (2001). Various theories of learning are described, including the historical debate and evolution of ideas about how students learn best. At the same time, these authors speak specifically as to why the learning shift is difficult for organizations and what can be done to facilitate it. Readings like this set the stage for reading more deeply about various theories of learning and how to enable deep learning in collegiate contexts. Examples are Fink's *Creating Significant Learning Experiences* (2003); *Theoretical Foundations of Learning Environments* (2000) edited by Jonassen and Land; and *The Theory and Practice of Learning* (2003), by Jarvis, Holford, and Griffen. Instructors can also benefit from reading and discussing colleagues' attempts at designing, implementing, and evaluating theoretically grounded, student-centered undergraduate programs. *Learning-in-Community: Reflections on Practice* (2003) by Venkatesh, Small, and Marsden is a recent example.

Reading and engaging in dialogue will help create an intellectual foundation that fits instructors needs and campus sociocultural realities. Following the semester-long seminar at Michigan State, Fear (1997) drew on seminar readings and dialogue to write and disseminate an essay on the learning model that became the foundation for his program. Doing that had great value: It provided an intellectual frame of reference for the program and offered a point of departure for discussing the program's implementation strategy.

### *Operationalizing the Intellectual Foundation*

It is far from a straightforward process to operationalize the intellectual foundation. Fear and his associates found how difficult it was—and how long it took—to translate their model into reality. Only with time and reflection was the reason forthcoming: The model they created stretched them beyond their current capabilities. The transition to the new reality was painfully slow. When Fear and his colleagues articulated the program's desired learning outcomes, the nature of the problem became obvious: The vision and outcomes did not align. In making this discovery, this group experienced a common plight in making the shift from teaching to learning. The group learned that it was trying to use ordinary means (approaches and techniques with which they were familiar) to achieve extraordinary (transformative) ends. Although shifting from teaching to learning does not require having an entirely new tool kit, transformative change will not happen if instructors rely exclusively on known and familiar tools.

With learning outcomes and skills identified, the exhilarating part of becoming a learning college begins—the curriculum design process. We suggest designing the curriculum backwards, starting with learning outcomes. Approaching it this way will enable instructors to constantly keep the goals of a learning college in focus. This is especially important as instructors experiment with various tools, approaches, and forms. Learning-community members will need to determine what is and is not working so that instructors can make in-course adjustments. To accomplish that end, we suggest developing a set of indicators for learning outcomes, indicators that can be used to measure progress as planning and implementation process evolves. This measurement system should be used less at the beginning to evaluate success and more to inform the planning process.

Shifting from teaching to learning requires patience and dedication to aspects of non-linear planning. That means being open to discovering things that participants could not have possibly imagined at the outset and, then, being able to act on new discoveries. Although this will sometimes involve departures from pre-determined routines, these are often valuable destinations on the twisting road from teaching to learning. Indeed, a journey metaphor applies well. From conversations with learning paradigm practitioners we have discovered that, at its extreme, the journey can feel "like moving into the unknown, propelling you out of your comfort zone. It can prompt visceral responses such as joy, fear, or dissonance, and the feeling that you are 'on and at the edge'" (Fear, Doberneck, et al., 2003, p. 163).

For thoughtful, non-linear planning to happen, gather data and plenty of opportunities to consider the findings in contextual and theoretical terms. That means considering what the transformation requires as a research project. Think of the work as an empirical expression of, and also as a contribution to, the scholarship of learning and organizational transformation. What follows automatically is the ability to share with colleagues at conferences and in publications an elevated view (in scholarly terms) of what the college is doing. Otherwise, professional sharing can be limiting, overly attentive to instrumental matters with little or no reference to theory, empirical evidence, or critique. For the learning paradigm movement to remain vital and for instructors to be included as credible partners in that movement, campus experiences must contribute to scholarly understanding about learning and change.

### Using Transformative Means to Achieve Transformative Ends

These scholarly contributions may yield the great benefit of refreshing the way that transformational change is introduced in higher educational settings. There is a conventional view of the change process that conforms quite well to the Newtonian view of organizations as machines, executive leaders strategically pulling levers of change to introduce, diffuse, and sustain change. We find this mechanistic view similar in genre to the instruction paradigm's theory of learning-teachers transferring knowledge to students.

In contrast to a mechanistic way of proceeding, consider the implications of the fourth guideline we suggest for becoming a learning college: create a wide range of powerful options for achieving the required learning outcomes. It asserts that there are many and divergent ways—not just one standard approach—for learning best. That means we refuse to invest in discovering and transferring across campuses one best approach. We intentionally walk a different path by encouraging multiplicity of approaches and outcomes. It also demands that we dedicate ourselves to identifying options with impact.

Now, consider the implications of our fifth guideline: continually explore new and alternative methods for empowering learning. Key words here are continually, new, and alternative. These are important words: Continually means never-ending; new means dedication to discovery; and alternative means diverse, that one size cannot possibly fit all. A key operating rule of this guideline is that effective learning models, once discovered, represent only points of departure for ongoing explorations. This journey is about a learning quest and not about a learning destination.

Adopting the way of shared thinking involves another shift-requiring an essential change in the historic way we envision executive leadership. Among other things, the historically dominant paradigm has executive leaders articulating a vision, translating the vision in programming terms, marketing the program, securing support, and then transferring the program to users. In the alternative paradigm, executive leaders recognize they do not have it all figured out. Shifting to the alternative paradigm requires high levels of collegial interaction, participation, and—perhaps most important of all—engagement. Executive leaders in the alternative paradigm know they cannot force people to be engaged. What they can do, though, is help create an environment where people want to engage. For that to happen, executive leaders enable and empower others—just as teachers in the learning paradigm do—to participate in an exciting and meaningful journey of discovery. When executive leaders believe and act this way, they are more likely to launch change platforms that are "more *embracing* (of different ideas and approaches) than declarative; more *inviting* (to people) than directive; and more *connecting* (across campus divides) than restrictive" (Fear, Adamek, & Imig, 2002, p. 50).

## Imagine With Us

Consider this image of a campus where the alternative paradigm is animate. Learning about learning has become a campus focus. Learning is more than something to be acquired, codified, and applied. This campus is a dynamic, yeasty environment where multiple experiments are taking place. Not everyone shares the same opinions or theories about what it means to learn powerfully or what learning model is best. Rather than becoming points of conflict, however, these differences are points of departure for discourse about learning. Participants explore learning alternatives and share what they are learning with each other. This is a vibrant, energetic place dedicated to constantly discovering new and innovative ways for advancing learning and achieving critical learning outcomes. It is a learning organization, dedicated to constantly improving the way its core business is conducted. The learning paradigm beckons.

## References

Abbot, J., & Ryan, T. (2001). *The unfinished revolution: Learning, human behavior, community and political paradox.* Alexandria, VA: Association for Supervision and Curriculum Development.

Argyris, C., & Schön, D. (1974). *Theory in practice: Increasing professional effectiveness.* San Francisco: Jossey-Bass.

Barker, J. (1992a). *Future edge: Discovering the new paradigms of success.* New York: Morrow.

Barker, J. (1992b). *Paradigms: The business of discovering the future.* New York: HarperBusiness.

Barr, R. (1993, October). A new paradigm for community colleges: Focus on learning instead of teaching. *Adcom,*

Barr, R. (1994, February). A new paradigm for community college. *The News.*

Barr, R. (1995, March). From teaching to learning: A new reality for community colleges. *Leadership Abstracts, 8*(3).

Barr, R. (1998, September/October). Obstacles to implementing the learning paradigm. *About Campus,* 18–25.

Barr, R., & Tagg, J. (1995, November/December). From teaching to learning: A new paradigm for undergraduate education. *Change, 27*(6), 13–25.

Boggs, G. R. (1993). Community colleges and the new paradigm. *Celebrations.* Austin, TX: National Institute for Staff and Organizational Development.

Capra, F. (1982). *The turning point: Science, society, and the rising culture.* New York: Bantam Books.

Capra, F. (1996). *The web of life.* New York: Anchor Books.

Cherniss, C., & Deegan, G. (2000). The creation of alternative settings. In J. Rappaport & E. Seidman (Eds.), *Handbook of community psychology.* New York: Plenum Press.

Drucker, P. (1992). *Managing for the future.* New York: Penguin Books.

Fear, F. (1997). *The road to Bailey: A vision for The Liberty Hyde Bailey Scholars Program.* East Lansing, MI: College of Agriculture and Natural Resources, Michigan State University. Available from http://www.bsp.msu.edu/background/baileyrd.cfm

Fear, F., Adamek, M., & Imig, G. (2002). Connecting philosophic and scholarly traditions with change in higher education. *Journal of Leadership Studies, 8,* 42–51.

Fear, F., Bawden, R., Rosaen, C., & Foster-Fishman, P. (2002). A model of engaged learning: Frames of reference and scholarly underpinnings. *The Journal of Higher Education Outreach and Engagement, 7*(3), 55–68.

Fear, F., Doberneck, D., Robinson, C., Fear, K., & Barr, R. (with Van Den Berg, H., Smith, J., & Petrulis, R.). (2003). Meaning making and the learning paradigm: A provocative idea in practice. *Innovative Higher Education, 27,* 151–168.

Fear, F., Latinen, L., Woodward, D., & Gerulski, K. (2001). Fusing competence and character: Celebrating postmodern expressions in higher education. *The Journal of College and Character*. Available from http://collegevalues.org/articles.cfmevalues.org/articles.cfm?id=373&a=1

Fear, F., McCarthy, C., Diebel, A., Berkowitz, S., Harvey, L., & Carra, C. (2003). Turning the all around upside down: The graduate classroom as an alternative, self-organizing system. *Encounter, 16*(2), 34–39.

Fink, L. D. (2003). *Creating significant learning experiences.* San Francisco: Jossey-Bass.

Gibbs, J. (1995). *Tribes: A new way of learning and being together.* Sausalito, CA: Source Center Systems.

Jarvis, P., Holford, J., & Griffin, C. (2003). *The theory and practice of learning.* Sterling, VA: Kogan Page.

Jonassen, D., & Land, S. (2000). *Theortical foundations of learning environments.* Mahwah, NJ: Erlbaum.

Kuhn, T. (1970). *The structure of scientific revolutions.* Chicago: The University of Chicago Press.

O'Banion, T. (1997). *A learning college for the 21st century.* San Francisco: AACC and ACE/Oryx Press.

Senge, P. (1990). *The fifth discipline: The art and practice of the learning organization.* New York: Currency.

Tagg, J. (2003). *The learning paradigm college.* Boston: Anker Publications.

Venkatesh, M., Small, R., & Marsden, J. (2003.) *Learning-in-community: Reflections on practice.* Boston: Kluwer Academic.

Wingspread Group on Higher Education. (1993). *An American imperative: Higher expectations for higher education.* Racine, WI: The Johnson Foundation.

CHAPTER 3

# Engaging Constituencies on Behalf of a Learning College

DAVID A. SHUPE

The success of any college that engages in a sustained, systematic focus on student learning will depend largely on how different constituencies perceive and respond to that effort. Internal constituent groups include students, instructors, student advisors, institutional researchers, and college staff. External constituencies include accreditors, employers, community leaders, parents, the system office, and political officials. The response of any one of these constituents can range from active support to neutral indifference to active opposition; the last two are equally effective in preventing organizational change.

For each of these groups, a college should look clearly at its intended solution and make a critical self-examination: In what ways does the college's intended solution acknowledge the interests and concerns of this constituent group? Does it offer something positive to that group? If it does, are supporters of the change prepared to make a case that this constituency will understand and appreciate? Finally, college administrators deserve special consideration. Arbiters of all of the other constituencies, their support for a learning-centered college can never be assumed, because this transformation requires changing the rules from those that administrators have already mastered to new and unfamiliar ones whose political effect is unknown and, from their point of view, unpredictable.

A learning college can follow different models, some that are probably yet to be developed (Tagg, 2003). Additionally, this task of transforming a college to systematically focus on student learning will require a sustained effort. For any given college, the appropriate model can draw on goals and strengths that are distinctive to that institution. This process will be a linear series of changes that will take time to accomplish, easily (perhaps even optimistically) 5 to 10 years. Both the model of transformation a college uses and the significant time investment required for transformation underlies the need to thoughtfully engage a college's many constituencies in support of that transformation. It is the college's particular constituencies that will collectively define the model and care about and protect its distinctiveness. A college's ability to introduce a change in an academic year that becomes firm enough to move on to a subsequent change in the next academic year will depend on both the active support of key constituencies and the absence of significant opposition from others.

The ability to sustain momentum over 5 to 10 years requires attention to this very practical consideration of attending to constituencies. In any given year of the transformation, not everyone will like the new steps required. The members of a specific constituency may well feel that their interests are not being attended to or, even worse, may feel that that they are losing something. The next year, however, they may have their turn, in that the changes for that year provide something valuable from their perspective. Opposition is certain to arise when a constituent group comes to feel disregarded time and again, year after year. To move forward, colleges need to ensure that each group has its own reason (or several reasons) for buying into the eventual goal of establishing a learning college.

Those who support the learning-college idea at a specific college have a careful route to steer. On one side, they must avoid making decisions about changes without attending to the interests of the various constituencies; on the other side, they must be wary of eliciting and acting on suggestions from the constituencies that do not yet have a clear sense of the overall goal. Neither approach will succeed. The first will fail because the concept cannot become a reality without the support of these constituencies. The second will fail because the many disparate suggestions that will be elicited will be much too colored with self-interest to consider what, overall, would be best for the college. Few respondents will be operating from a vision of transforming a college to a learning college.

There may, however, be a safe path through the middle. Some sense of a shared positive vision of a learning college seems a prerequisite. If the leaders of the endeavor lack such a vision, how can it be explained to differing constituencies in a way that makes sense to them? There will be alternative ways to get there, and those alternatives need to be carefully examined internally with this question: How will different constituencies be likely to view these alternatives? The leaders are advised to look clearly at their intended approach and to engage in a critical self-examination. For each of these constituencies, these are the key generic questions:

- In what ways does this set of changes acknowledge the interests and concerns of this constituent group?
- Do the changes offer something positive to the group?
- If so, are supporters of this set of changes prepared to make a case that this constituency will understand and appreciate?

Engaging constituencies does not assume that any of these constituencies speak with a single voice. There will always be a range of opinions, and decisions may come down to who actually represents this constituency in the local setting. Given that, any college making global changes will want to include the local characteristics of each of its constituencies in its evaluation. Nevertheless, if only as a starting point, it is helpful to step inside what is often a consistent point of view for each constituency. There will certainly come a time to present this proposed change to representatives of these constituencies for feedback. Those who want to make that transformation should—before presenting it to others as a proposal—first carefully evaluate how constituent groups are likely to receive any given change. Such evaluation, for each proposed change, needs to consider each of the constituencies, because their support or lack of support could make a difference for the college.

## Engaging Constituent Groups

### Students

A learning college is constructed first for the students. However, it is not easy to start with the student constituency, because such a concept is itself rarely an idea in students' minds. Words will have to be carefully chosen. Students are so accustomed to the present paradigm, that if they hear that the college is to be a learning college, their first response is likely to be, "Isn't this already a learning college?" Their second response may be, "How can it be any different than what it is?" To work successfully with students, colleges should choose less conceptual and more practical terminology. Appropriate questions for engaging the students include: How will students come to know about the proposed changes? How will they come to understand that these changes will make a positive difference for them? Why do they have a reason to care about this?

Colleges should view the proposed changes through the students' perspective. As well conditioned by the present paradigm, many students will evaluate any proposed changes through criteria grounded in that paradigm. If students hear the changes as not making any real changes in the system of rewards, they will be uninterested. However, if they hear them as authentic changes in the rewards system, students may be inclined to oppose them as unilateral changing of the rules for them to achieve success, which in turn may make it (from their perspective) more difficult to get through school.

Fairness will also be a primary consideration: Whatever applies to one applies to others as well. I recall being told about the results of a student survey: Students who enrolled in course sections that featured special grant-funded active-learning activities thought they had learned more because of this approach but also expressed a high level of dissatisfaction. The students felt they had had to work harder to get the same result (earned credits) than their peers in the regular sections. Finally, nearly all students will want to see some positive change during the time they themselves are in college. They will be quick to ask: Will this actually make a positive difference to me?

Those working for a new paradigm will need to respond to these common student concerns. Although these will not be the students' only concerns, they are the ones almost certain to emerge. Until they are addressed, students are unlikely to pay attention to any other logic. The first concern (fear of change) suggests that students will need to be offered something positive beyond the transcript. The second concern (need for fairness) suggests that the minimum size of a change may be the boundary of a credential-giving program. (Thus learning-college features may best be addressed program by program.) The third (need for relevance) suggests that several steps along the way will need to provide something concrete for students.

Why should students support changes leading to a learning college? Intrinsic reasons for students to support proposed changes—they will learn more and enjoy their experience more—will work with some students but not the majority. Others need a more extrinsic reason. This could be an eventual college record through which students can demonstrate to employers what they know and what they can do. This record, rather than comparing a student to other students, would best compare a given student to a defined set of educational achievements and goals. Better still if this record were to acknowledge a student's individual strengths. If students were to begin college with the understanding that their task is to create the best possible record of learning achievements for themselves, it would begin to address what Tagg (2003) calls "one of the fundamental challenges that colleges face today: to change the way incoming students think about the school setting, about academic work, and about their own relationship to academic institutions" (p. 47).

This is a good example of the value of attending to the students' point of view. It also shows that listening to a constituency can affect what a college decides to incorporate into its own model. Colleges may create or select different possible changes but with the same aim in mind, both to provide something of value to a constituency and to constitute a building block for developing a learning college.

Nevertheless, students are not an easy constituency to take into account. Students are an external constituency: Each academic term they choose to enroll and pay tuition or not. If they are at all uncertain about changing conditions at the college, the decision to go elsewhere is not difficult. They are also an internal constituency in that it is the results of their work—student-learning outcomes—that constitutes the reason-for-being for a community college and increasingly constitutes the primary measure of its effectiveness (Shupe, 1999).

Putting a learning-college concept into place will change the nature of classroom activities. But even conventional institutional planning processes are honed in an environment that does not easily attend to students. Given that, in the process of thinking through a learning college, a college can be tempted to avoid engaging the student constituency. It should be immediately apparent how ironic such an omission would be.

### Instructors

A college's prospects for becoming a learning college rest largely on the kind of support instructors give it. No constituency will be more affected than instructors are. Add to this a working environment that encourages and protects individualism, and it is not surprising that there is a wide range of opinion about most educational topics. Some of the strongest supporters of the learning-college concept are instructors. So are some of the strongest skeptics and most vocal critics. This range of views is to be expected, even valued. Colleges will vary somewhat in the degree to which instructors are expected to follow the directions given them by administrators. Instructors must have their own reasons for supporting moves toward a learning college.

Instructors will be concerned about workload. Will this add or subtract work to the teaching hours, office hours, even academic term? There are two workload factors to consider. The first is the transitional work it will take to get from here to there, that is, to take the steps that lead to becoming a learning college. The second is the amount of work that can be regularly and continuously expected once the college has more or less arrived at its goal. An example of transitional work is the committee work that will be needed to hammer out a new proposal on student advising. An example of regular work is the time it would take in any given week to advise students. The question colleges need to address directly is the amount of work (in either sense) that becoming a learning college will require of instructors.

Instructors will also be concerned about academic standards. Some instructors believe there is a zero sum game between paying attention to student learning and maintaining academic standards—the more there is of the one, the less there is of the other. This is not an unreasonable stance. Because the current instruction paradigm does not (and arguably cannot) really attend to student learning itself, the phrase is understood as attention to students' interests. Students who understand that their task is to accumulate course credits as quickly and easily as possible view academic standards (or what they sense instructors mean by academic standards) as an impediment. Why should this be any different as a learning-college concept? For instructors, this question needs to be answered early on.

Another clear concern for instructors is academic freedom, a phrase that has come to be used for protecting an instructor's individuality. This is as much about teaching style as it is about course content. Here are the underlying questions: Is there a real change intended here? Will it affect the way an instructor teaches, or will it affect the way that teaching is perceived? Will it acknowledge instructional strengths or devalue them? What will instructors need to do differently? How comfortable will they be making these changes? Those who are promoting the change to a learning college need to address these questions directly.

Maintaining student data privacy is likely to be another concern of instructors. A learning college will maintain new organizational information about student achievement, both in a specific instructor's course and prior to a student enrolling in that course. In terms of student data in a specific course, an instructor may care deeply about who sees that information and how it will be read and used. Concerning students' prior performance data, instructors themselves may not wish to see that information. Some instructors consider the absence of information a virtue; it allows them to avoid prejudging students based on their earlier performance. If, in becoming a learning college, one of the goals is to increase the learning of students by better meeting each student at the point where he or she is most ready to learn, then knowledge of what each student has accomplished prior to the course-not relative to other students but relative to defined expectations-becomes the kind of new and valuable information that could make a positive difference in student learning.

The criteria for evaluating the set of changes required to become a learning college is best drawn from the new paradigm toward which a college is moving, not from the status quo-not an easy task. The old criteria are so thoroughly ingrained in educational thought and practice that they are second nature. It will take time to change, but from the instructional perspective (unlike the student perspective), time is available. As long as progress along the way is discernable, most instructors will readily accept that it may take 10 years to make such a shift in a college's focus.

### Student Advisors

The active support of student advisors is critical; they interpret the official college experience for most students in sessions with students, in orientation sessions, and in other settings designed to encourage students' success. When students begin to notice changes in their courses and need to realize that these changes are not simply per course but part of a larger direction, student advisors become a potent force in reinforcing and interpreting the change process. If this internal constituency chooses not to be actively supportive, the entire process of organizational development can stall. They need not oppose learning-college ideas to have this negative effect. They could simply not engage the students positively at the time that students are beginning to wonder what they are confronting.

Remember the question: Are supporters of this set of changes prepared to make a case that students will understand and appreciate? On a daily basis, student advisors need to make the case. They may choose not to do so, however, if the college culture instills a strong dividing line between academic affairs and student affairs or if they consider that the learning-college concept is solely an interest of instructors.

What does the learning college have to offer student advisors? For a while in the college's progress, the change process may all seem simply like more work for them, in that they will be simultaneously interpreting for students both the old and new paradigm. To engage and offer student advisors something positive, the college should offer ways of making their job easier. The advisors themselves would know best how this could be accomplished, with a further goal of choosing ways to reinforce student responsibility for their own learning. For example, each student could have Web access to his or her own developing college record of achievements, and the occasions when they choose to see an advisor personally may be focused on specific questions.

### *Institutional Researchers*

Colleges are expected to maintain good data on their students, and increasingly this responsibility falls to a person whose job function, in whole or in part, is called institutional research. The learning-college concept emphasizes the need to understand the student-learning experience, and the researcher's task is to make aspects of this learning experience visible. A useful step is to consider the difference it would make to the college if this task were performed well or not so well, and what (from a learning-college perspective) *well* would mean.

Perhaps it would mean that institutional research generate information that demonstrates that the changes being introduced are making a positive difference. At the beginning, the difference may not be at all evident, but when the changes start, even in small ways, to make a difference, this progress needs to be captured in data form. If preliminary data are missed or overlooked by institutional research, for whatever reasons, making the case to external constituencies (as described later in this chapter) may be more difficult. Here, timing is everything, and the institutional researcher's commitment to thinking ahead to what kind of data would be helpful could—at some point in the progress that may not be predictable—make all the difference in generating support for the learning college.

### *College Staff*

What difference could it make whether college staff support the idea of a learning college? It depends on what the college is choosing to become. If it consciously (or unconsciously) chooses to limit change to what students learn in courses, perhaps it does not matter. However, as Light (2001) has pointed out, students themselves report that much of what they learned in college occurs outside of courses. If the college aspiring to be a learning college chooses to think of this non-classroom learning as including much or all of the total college experience, then quite quickly, the college staff becomes an important constituency.

The clearest influence of college staff is work-study programs in which students work for college staff and demonstrate their work skills, good or bad. A student's data can reflect his or her employment experience. The supervising staff will play a role in collecting and evaluating this information. The learning-college concept thus offers college staff a chance to be included in the larger vision of a place where students learn in diverse settings.

### *Accreditors*

The accreditation process is changing; it is much more concerned than in the past with student-learning outcomes. Some real overlap may exist between this emphasis and the concept of a college focused on learning, although this connection needs to be explored further. Tagg (2003) clearly distinguishes an evaluation or summative assessment from a feedback or formative assessment. The question is whether the accreditation process is primarily concerned with summative assessment, whereas the learning college is primarily interested in formative assessment. Clearly the distinction is valuable, but it is not dichotomous. If an instructor's evaluation of a student's paper indicates that it has a weak thesis but good anecdotes that fully illustrate the points being made, is this evaluation or feedback?

In the old paradigm in which nothing but a course grade really counts, it is clearly feedback. However, if a college committee takes on the challenge of carefully defining factors or criteria for students' papers and the college keeps track of this information, then a weak thesis and anecdotes that illustrate also become evaluation, without losing their character as feedback. Accreditors, while wanting colleges to be clear about this distinction, would find this particular example most interesting, especially if it can be shown that students' writing ability does improve over the course of their time at the college.

### Employers

Employers are primarily interested in students demonstrating what they know and what they can do. This is true for the student who applies for a job after completing a program of study and for the student who already works for the employer. Thus, a college aiming to become a learning college would seemingly be able to gain crucial strong support from employers. Students are far more likely to make the effort to demonstrate professional standards if employers take these standards seriously. Community leaders and political officials are far more likely to lend support when they hear that employers are pleased.

The central question may be the extent to which the college is ready to attend to the student learning that employers desire. This goal is not difficult for most technical or professional programs; their challenge is being able to demonstrate that students are well prepared for a specific field. It has been more of a challenge for liberal arts programs, an instruction paradigm for which course title and course grade were the only demonstrable measures of learning. In his 2003 work, Tagg detailed the Liberal Studies/Professional Skills program at Inver Hills as one example of an approach wherein colleges can demonstrate the relevance of liberal studies to employers.

### Community Leaders

Community leaders, including those who often serve on a college's governing or advisory board, are a constituency that, like employers, cares that students be able to demonstrate what they know and what they can do. Those who are encouraging movement toward a learning college can and should take this into account. Colleges should promote a focus on students' learning skills of engaging in citizenship and working with diverse people. Service learning opportunities are valuable, both to students and to community leaders, if those who supervise students can clearly indicate what students have learned by participating—a central tenet of the learning-college concept.

### Parents

Some community colleges do not regard the parents of their students as a constituency. This is not surprising; the students themselves do not encourage parental involvement, and, of course, many community college students are older and are parents themselves. It requires stepping outside the institutional environment and meeting people in the community to realize that most parents care deeply about how well their children are doing, whether those children are 18 or 28 or 48. In some ways, the interest is deeper even than the self-interest of students. Often no one is prouder at graduation than a student's parents.

If parents understand that the changes toward becoming a learning college have made a positive difference for their child, they will be supportive. Their role, then, may come later in the overall process, as it becomes possible to demonstrate what difference the learning-college changes have made to students. The students themselves may be relieved to complete a program; their parents will often be very pleased with the school, especially during the year in which a student has graduated. At this point and for a short while, some parents would be happy to find ways to indicate their pleasure with the college. A college can make use of these testimonials in a variety of ways to increase community support.

### The System Office

In most states, community colleges have a relationship with an agency that serves as a system office, a central interface to the legislature and other state agencies. Although its responsibilities vary from state to state, the system office is an important constituency for the community college. College administrators know that it is useful (at the very least) to have the officials who work there look favorably on the college.

In a case where a college making changes is in competition with other colleges vying for the same students, the system office can provide a degree of mediation or political cover for the college, provided that the officials there like what is developing. Keeping them regularly informed of developments at the college is politically important; for a college working on becoming a learning college, it is indispensable.

### Political Officials

Local political officials must understand well a college's aspiration to become a learning college. Sooner or later someone is likely to complain to a local official about the college's new direction. This official needs to already be fully grounded and informed about the concept of a learning college. Careful communication will garner the support of political officials eager to celebrate the college as a jewel of their community.

### College Administrators

College administrators are no less self-interested than any other constituency member. They are likely to be mediators and arbiters of all of the other constituencies' interests. If it serves their purposes to support changes leading to a learning college, they will do so; if it does not, they will not. If they were part of the group that chose to apply this concept to their own college, they are likely to stay the course. Otherwise, their support for a learning college can never be assumed, because this transformation may require a change in the rules from those that they have already mastered to new and unfamiliar rules whose political effect is unknown and, from their point of view, unpredictable. Why should administrators commit themselves to a long-term direction that poses far more chances of failure than success?

Nevertheless, some college administrators are ready to work with all the constituencies to become a learning college. Perhaps it is the challenge that motivates them or a deep personal commitment to improving student learning. For instructors, staff, and students who share that interest, their presence in a college is a gift. Without their leadership, and the risk that goes with it, the process will not succeed.

## Final Thought

To advance changes, a college needs to carefully consider the ramifications for each constituency. Colleges need to engage each constituency by acknowledging the interests and concerns of group members. They should pinpoint the positive elements of change that will emerge as a result of the new direction and be prepared to make a direct case that the group will understand and appreciate. Successfully becoming a learning college requires identifying early the constituencies whose support or lack of support will make a difference to the process. At any given institution, the actual process of becoming a learning college will depend on year-by-year developments that require drawing on the support of all constituencies. Maintaining momentum is key.

## References

Light, R. J. (2001). *Making the most of college: Students speak their minds.* Cambridge, MA: Harvard University Press.

Shupe, D. (1999, Winter). Productivity, quality, and accountability in higher education. *Journal of Continuing Higher Education, 47*(1), 2–13.

Tagg, J. (2003). *The learning paradigm college.* Boston: Anker.

# PART 2

# Toward a Deeper Understanding of the Learning College

# CHAPTER 4

# The Vanguard Learning Colleges: Lessons in Strategic Planning

## SHIRLENE LOFTON SNOWDEN

Community colleges have reached a point of crisis: Major change is inevitable. Keller (1999–2000) called for change at community colleges that goes beyond planning to restructuring—to creating a new organization. Institutional transformation for the 21st century demands deep architectural changes in higher education delivery systems (Altbach, 1999; Hooker, 1997; Keller, 1999–2000; McClenney, 1999). For community colleges to survive, boards of trustees and college presidents must view profound architectural restructuring as a high-priority agenda item.

The call for restructuring—not reform—at the end of the 20th century continues, while accountability remains a concern of policymakers. Today's community college students will not accept a 100-year-old education system that does not meet the needs of corporate America. My research indicates that education needs have changed drastically as the economy, society, and demographics have changed. These uncontrollable factors have forced visionary education leaders to continuously provide the new skills and knowledge necessary for building a responsive workforce. Since the turn of the 19th century, community colleges have struggled to meet the challenges of a changing environment. History has shown, however, that too many community colleges have not been proactive; they have instead shifted focus only incrementally to keep pace with changes.

Twenty-first century educators must be prepared to meet the needs of a more diverse student body seeking flexible learning opportunities. Unless community colleges respond by shifting from a focus on teaching to a focus on learning, the workforce will continue to explore other training and education options. O'Banion (1997) argued that "the Learning College will break the bonds of the traditional approach which are role-bound, time-bound, and efficiency-bound, giving the student the opportunity to improve and expand learning, using many options and modalities" (p. 9). Education leaders must learn more about what students want and must respond to workplace needs.

## Strategic Planning for Transformative Change

I was intrigued by the demands for change, the more recent calls for architectural transformation, the lack of strategic planning in higher education, and the constant turnover of community college presidents. I sought to determine how committed community college presidents are to using strategic planning as a vehicle for transforming the institution. My study focused on the 12 Vanguard Learning Colleges (League for Innovation, 2001). The leaders of these colleges recognized the need for revolutionary changes. Traditional teaching modes need to become a focus on learning, requiring instructors to focus on students' learning and to be guided by a new framework for education delivery. These institutions, embracing the learning-college concepts and principles, have begun to make incremental changes by focusing on students' needs. All but a few of the 12 colleges are still wrestling with how to create major infrastructure change to create a new institution—a learning college.

The more things change, the more community colleges stay the same. During my 25 years of service in both academia and administration, I served under the leadership of five presidents and several interim presidents. Each president struggled to deal with internal politics and operational deficits and found little time to assess external needs and develop a vision that was responsive to the needs of the community. Research indicates that this situation is not unusual. Some community college presidents do not experience longevity; they frequently leave institutions besieged with board and community issues or complaints. Such presidents are unprepared to handle the lengthy, complex journey required to bring about change. How does the tumultuous tenure of the executive leader influence change? Strategic planning is intimately connected to institutional change or transformation. True transformation is connected to effective leadership. Keller (1983) argued that "planning effectiveness of the institutions depends on the planning effectiveness of the presidential leaders" (p. 156).

Strategic planning is the appropriate response to the call for a transformation process. It allows leaders in organizations to bring about change, using a systematic, inclusive process. The strategic plan requires the involvement of all stakeholders at the college. It is a complex, directional blueprint with components, processes, and systems that provide the foundation for an institution to move from point A to point B. To achieve movement, the plan requires that all parts work together in harmony. With a clear vision in mind, each day assessments measure success and evaluate progress. The process is complex in an education environment in which stakeholders and resisters may impede progress in support of the status quo.

Selecting the appropriate strategic plan to move in the right direction is more critical today given the new millennium pressures on community colleges to transform the institution. As was noted earlier, educational transformation has been high on the agendas of policymakers and community college leaders for several decades. Twenty-first century demands have increased the depth and breadth of the challenges facing community colleges still struggling to make up budget shortfalls from the late 1990s. Although researchers and writers have proposed many approaches to address the process of transformation, few community colleges have fully embarked on this difficult process.

Some colleges have initiated a change process but have not committed to effecting significant changes. Most offer an education designed to meet workforce needs, but few have responded to the fast-paced changes in the economy, demographics, and technology. "Most colleges and universities are not set up with strategic planning capacity. They are basically good at operations, that is, efficiently doing the same things day after day" (Kotler & Murphy, 1981, p. 470). Educational transformation requires leaders in higher education to abandon traditionally safe environments and explore a new way of doing business. College presidents recognize that successful planning for educational transformation is difficult and requires time and commitment; therefore, they resort to management by increments because it is easier—a standard practice at too many institutions.

## Strategic Planning at the Vanguard Learning Colleges

My experiences as a community college professor and administrator and my studies in educational transformation and strategic planning drove me to further explore the change process used by learning-college institutions. I examined the impact of the strategic planning models used by the Vanguard colleges as they began the shift from traditional education systems to learning-centered colleges. The 12 colleges responded to an education crisis by undergoing a major transformation process, and the League for Innovation named them as exemplary institutions and catalysts for other colleges. These colleges embraced strategic planning as a vehicle for change and established a learning-college vision before beginning the transformation process.

I sent a survey to each of the Vanguard colleges and followed up with a more intensive case study at three of them. The survey included questions regarding the planning process, the efforts to transform their colleges, and the extent to which the colleges had adopted learning-centered activities, as well as the level at which they had implemented key learning-college components. The voice from the top (presidents as well as members of the executive teams) indicated a strong commitment to the learning-college concept, and each college embraced strategic-planning models for transformation. The Vanguard colleges began using an inclusive planning process designed to assess institutional needs and to effect a change in their organizational structures and cultures. Committed to a documented strategic planning model, these leaders shared a learning-college vision and collaboratively established their direction.

### Extent of Strategic Planning

My investigation focused on the commonalities of the strategic plans at the Vanguard colleges and the extent to which they had implemented the principles of the learning paradigm. The questions I asked were as follows: Did the colleges have a literature-based strategic plan? Did the strategic plan facilitate the transformation to the learning college? To analyze the responses, I measured the extent to which the community colleges used a strategic planning process, the linkage of the transformation process to the learning college, and the level of implementation of the learning-college key components and principles. I used Sheridan's (1998) component planning model to assess whether the colleges had a strategic plan in place. Using Sheridan's four-stage analysis—strategic plan, strategic process, strategic planning decision influence, and strategic nature—I discovered that the data clearly demonstrated that the Vanguard colleges had implemented a literature-based strategic planning process and were in various stages of implementing the change process. The elements examined at each institution included the following:

- Strategic plan—The plan component includes the vision, mission, and values of the organization, followed by strategic goals and objectives that provide direction, and an operational plan that outlines the steps needed to reach the desired goals.
- Strategic process—The process component includes external scanning and internal assessment of the environment. This phase also includes stakeholder involvement and procedures that provide for review and revision of goals and objectives.
- Strategic planning influence—The influence element measures the extent to which programs are developed, modified, or terminated and the allocation of resources to support the desired goals and objectives. This component also includes the establishment of desired targets and the marketing and promotions that would assist in reaching targeted initiatives.
- Strategic nature—This component is measured using the following four criteria:
  1. developing a blueprint for the college
  2. reviewing and clarifying the mission
  3. defining the mission's importance for public relations
  4. establishing a reasonable, clear, articulated vision of what the college is to become

My study findings were based on a strategic planning questionnaire, in-depth interviews, and a review of appropriate institutional documents. These instruments provided basic information about planning activities and contained scorable measures of the degree of influence of planning on decision making and the strategic nature of the planning process.

### Stages of Transformation

After assessing the strategic planning process at the Vanguard colleges, my next task was to determine what progress (if any) colleges were making with their efforts to link the planning process to the adoption of the learning-centered college. The two features of the implementation process were as follows:

- Institutional transformation—examined the extent to which strategic-plan components were linked to creating a learning college.

- Learning-centered principles—determined the level of implementation of the learning-college key components as established by the League for Innovation (2001).

My investigation revealed that the Vanguard colleges' change process had elements of a strategic plan, including mission and value statements that were linked to the learning college. Furthermore, the strategic plan contained written strategic directions for the next 3 to 5 years with goals and objectives designed to create a learning college. Some colleges took the next step: They incorporated documented operational plans with implementation details focused on the transformation to the learning college.

Most of the Vanguard colleges conducted an assessment of their strengths and weaknesses, including a formal analysis of the external environment. These colleges strongly emphasized the inclusion of all internal stakeholder groups in the planning process. Leaders among the staff, instructors, students, and alumni served on committees, provided input, and received valuable information regarding the transformation process. To provide flexibility, they established a process for continually reviewing and modifying the plan. Generally, the colleges supported strategic planning as an appropriate vehicle for change, but little evidence indicates that the college community at-large accepted or understood the process of transformation to the learning college. According to stakeholders, too often decisions did not support the strategic direction established during the planning process.

The Vanguard colleges have found the transformation process to be difficult and lengthy, requiring an extensive commitment of financial and human resources. Completing the environmental scan and developing strategies to transform the organization with stakeholder involvement required an inordinate amount of time. When I started my research, several colleges had spent at least 3 years developing the strategic plan and were still in the initial stage of implementing change strategies. What stood out as the most important element to successful change was the leadership's strong commitment to transformation.

The Vanguard colleges made significant gains using a strategic planning process, had multiple conversations about learning, and developed programs and improved services in support of students. In several cases, the colleges had begun to develop flexible instructional programs based on students' needs before the national focus on the learning college. Others had embraced technology and now offer an array of courses and programs via the Internet. These activities support the colleges' efforts to make the strategic plan a living document and the center of all decisions and activities in support of the shift to a learning college.

## Obstacles to True Transformation

Despite their progress in implementing the key learning-college components and principles, several Vanguard colleges had not committed to bringing about deep architectural changes.

Many were changing systems and processes only incrementally and were unable or unwilling to modify or eliminate existing programs. These colleges met little resistance when adding programs or expanding existing programs. Most used committee structures, which included pockets of instructors and staff, that supported the learning revolution, but only to the extent of facilitating minor changes. Some instructors voluntarily implemented creative learning strategies in the classroom. Others were encouraged and in some cases received financial incentives to begin implementing programs and services in support of the learning revolution. Despite these obstacles, the college leaders did not consider using force or threats to encourage buy-in or involvement. As a result, many stakeholders continued with business as usual, conducting traditional programs and services.

True transformation will not occur at these colleges without deeper architectural and structural changes. In many cases, the college leaders reported the major impediment to true transformation to be the difficulty in changing and managing the culture of the college, especially the mindset of some of the instructors. Generally, each Vanguard college found it difficult to change institutional culture and develop college-wide strategic thinking.

### *Funding*

The Vanguard colleges also faced significant statewide funding issues as they began their transformations. At many colleges, the process was derailed by deep, pervasive budget cuts that affected federal, state, and local funding, forcing many colleges to increase tuition. During a time of economic retrenchment-resulting in cuts in instructors and staff and student services-stakeholders find it difficult to focus on new initiatives and investment in new technology. Although financial hardship could instigate change or serve as the trigger point for transformation, most of the Colleges curtailed many new initiatives and continued with outdated programs and services. Thus, they have been forced to delay implementing programs and services in support of becoming learning-centered colleges.

## Barriers to Implementing the Learning College

Based on my study, the success or failure in transforming the institutions to learning colleges goes beyond the tenure of the college presidents and can be attributed to four compelling causes:

- incompatible leadership style and lack of commitment of the president
- inability to develop an appropriate change-planning process
- fear of committing to deep organizational and architectural changes
- failure to engage in strategic thinking throughout the organization

### *CEO's Leadership Style*

The Vanguard colleges' leaders represent diverse experiences, backgrounds, and leadership styles. CEO styles directly affect strategic change and culture management.

The force of momentum toward transformation to the learning college depends to a great extent on the the CEO's style. The appropriate CEO style for the college depends on the institutional culture.

My investigation revealed diverse executive approaches and levels of commitment to the transformation. Several presidents personally managed the strategic planning process and immersed themselves in intricate details, whereas others delegated the oversight, relying on feedback mechanisms established by the stakeholders. Keller (1983) argued that "few governing boards have the competence or the inclination to be innovative, experimental, or chart a new course. Thus, the planning effectiveness of the institution depends on the planning effectiveness of the presidential leaders" (p. 156). Actions must be clearly focused on the practices that will support or create a learning college. Creating and sustaining a learning college to a great extent depends on the ability of the leader to articulate a learning-college vision and mission that support the learning-college propositions, as well as the leader's willingness to embrace and encourage stakeholders from all constituent groups to actively participate in developing and implementing change strategies. The learning-college principles must be understood and accepted when the community college embarks upon the learning-college journey. To effect change, boards as well as the college stakeholders must recruit presidents with a leadership style and approach that are appropriate for the organizational culture.

Successful learning-college leaders take the time to assess the institutional culture to ensure the right fit and develop strategies that are appropriate for the environment. This requirement forces leaders to have a sense of the stakeholders' acceptance, rejection, or resistance to change before beginning the formidable process of leading toward change. To adjust to the institutional culture, the leadership may implement timelines and systems that are designed to slow down the process or advance the process by involving the stakeholders and sharing the decision-making process. Learning-college leaders were not surprised by the pockets of resistance they uncovered. Rewards, incentives, training, and involvement have proven to be magnets for the buy-in of some resisters.

### *Supporting the Change-Planning Process*

Most of the Vanguard colleges conducted an assessment of their strengths and weaknesses, including a formal analysis of the colleges' external environments. In creating their strategic plan, these colleges strongly emphasized the inclusion of all internal stakeholder groups. Leaders among the staff, instructors, students, and alumni served on committees, provided input, and received valuable information regarding the transformation process. To provide flexibility, the colleges established a process for reviewing and modifying the plan continually. Generally, stakeholders supported strategic planning as an appropriate vehicle for change, but there appears to be little evidence that the college community at-large accepted or understood the actual process of transformation to the learning college. According to stakeholders, too often decisions did not support the strategic direction established during the planning process.

### Involvement of Stakeholders

My observations revealed that the transformation process requires that stakeholders be continually involved and supportive of the strategic direction of the college. The extent to which the decisions supporting the plan are made organization-wide depends on the level of resistance or acceptance of the plan within the institutional culture. Haines's (2000) method of empowering the organization requires colleges to create a strategic-management system that motivates and empower people. Based on my findings, a major impediment to implementing the strategic plan was a lack of strategic thinking within the organization. Early intervention and involvement of all constituency groups are keys to successfully implementing any strategic plan; leaders must develop strategies that are designed to gain the support of all stakeholders. They must address people's fear and their perception that the strategic planning efforts are temporary. A balanced approach is more effective in changing attitudes and perceptions about change. Moving structural barriers and empowering and training people will help effect the requisite cultural changes (Kotter, 1996).

To effect change, a complete understanding of the organization is paramount. An institutional assessment will provide fundamental information that should serve as a basis for the next step in the planning process. Cultural change efforts must start with sharing the vision and must be followed with extensive training and information about the college's direction. A college's climate, norms, tradition, and values, as well as its different constituent groups, must be included in the institutional assessment. My research suggests that colleges must focus on efforts to facilitate the transformation process and change organizational behaviors and attitudes. The goal is to implement strategies—providing information, involvement, rewards, and continuous extensive training—that will encourage the buy-in of all stakeholders.

### Decision Support

Although most of the Vanguard colleges have literature-based strategic plans, their decisions and activities have not always supported the strategic plan. To successfully implement the strategic plan the college leadership must be willing to make decisions in support of it. The colleges revealed that throughout the organization, decisions were made that were not clearly linked to strategic-plan goals and objectives. Segments or groups working outside of the plan severely hampered the transformation to the learning college. The change process requires a commitment from the top to ensure that decisions support activities, processes, and systems identified in the strategic plan.

### *Commitment to Deep Organizational Changes*

Proponents of the learning-college revolution did not underestimate the magnitude of the learning-college transformation. This shift has been described by the leaders of the Vanguard colleges as a drastic, complex process that demands visionary thinking and a systematic process of permanent change. O'Banion and Milliron (2001) noted that a "series of extensive and intensive conversations on learning can anchor an institutional effort to place learning as the first priority" (p. 5). The colleges making the shift will face a lengthy, comprehensive, and complex redesign and restructure of educational academic, and student services. The change process is more difficult in a college environment than in other organizations because of the need to involve many internal and external stakeholder groups. Diverse players with different attitudes, skills, interests, and backgrounds create a difficult-to-change and manage organizational culture.

Most community colleges require deep organizational and architectural changes that will force college stakeholders to reject traditional systems. The transformation calls for a shift in education delivery and will require major changes in values, policies, procedures, practices, curricular, behaviors, and attitudes of each constituent group. Putting the student in the center of the education process—shifting from a passive to an active education process—has been a difficult concept for many to understand and for traditionalists to accept. Generally, education leaders have been skeptical about the need to overhaul the traditional education delivery system. My research indicates that resistant instructors, who play an important role in developing new instructional system, often disregard the call for change and hamper the institution's efforts for deep organizational change.

### *Managing the Culture and Encouraging Strategic Thinking*

Managing the culture is the most difficult challenge when implementing the strategic plan. Implementing the plan goes beyond changing policies, procedures, practices, and curricula. It requires changes in human behavior that have developed over decades in a traditional education environment. The failure of several Vanguard colleges to develop strategies for changing the culture has hindered their ability to implement the strategic plan. Although they empowered mid- and upper-level managers and used training programs to prepare employees for the change, their efforts were neither deep enough nor continuous, and many did not issue mandates. They invited—instead of required—administrators and staff to participate.

A Vanguard college's size or location did not significantly affect its ability to communicate with the college community. Whether urban, suburban, or rural, community colleges struggle with the same issues of cultural change. Vanguard colleges, with campuses located on diverse sites, used many strategies to collaborate and communicated campuses-wide to involve people in strategic planning and in implementing the learning college. Most colleges attempted to change the institutional culture via committee structures or the use of department heads and managers as messengers to carry information back to subordinates. Despite these strategies, there continued to be groups, departments, and instructors who have no interest in changing and who operate outside of the plan. These stakeholders did not embrace the vision and often resisted the efforts of the president to bring about change.

My study revealed that instructors are the most difficult stakeholder group to change. Shifting the focus from the teacher to the student—putting the student in the center of the education process—has proven to be a difficult process for instructors to implement. Furthermore, the change process becomes more complicated because of instructors' schedules and the large number of adjunct instructors and part-time staff in need of training. As Barr and Tagg (1995) suggested, the transition is not instantaneous, but "a process of gradual modification and experimentation through which we alter many organizational parts in light of the new vision" (p. 5).

Shifting from teaching to learning requires a comprehensive plan with intervention strategies for bringing all stakeholders into the change process. Developing such a plan requires a complete understanding of institutional culture and stakeholders' expectations. To effect permanent change, colleges must assess and evaluate the culture continuously and thoroughly, implementing corrective measures throughout the change process. The strategic plan must be so well defined that it institutionalizes the goals and develops strategic thinking throughout the culture. My research suggests that a receptive environment to transformation expresses itself on six levels. Figure 4.1 describes the sequential process of environmental analysis and change strategies based on my findings as well as those observed at many of the Vanguard colleges. The following summarizes the goals of each stage of the process:

- Level One—The leader fully understands the institutional culture, as well as the inevitable challenges and opportunities of preparing the organization for a major transformation.
- Level Two—Change agents must involve stakeholders early in the process. Colleges must increase awareness and understanding of where the institution is going and why the change is needed to gain trust and buy-in during the planning and implementation stages.
- Level Three—Stakeholders need to understand the vision or destination, the strategic-planning process, and their role individually and collectively in bringing about the desired results.
- Level Four—Colleges need to provide continuous training programs and culture reassessments to ensure that stakeholders stay connected and understand where the institution is going and what it will take to get there.
- Level Five—Decision makers need to demonstrate their commitment to the plan by making decisions in support of the goals and objectives established during the strategic planning process.

## Table 4.1  Developing an Environment Receptive to Change

| Levels | Action | Results |
|---|---|---|
| Level One | Conduct extensive research internal and external to the organization to assess and diagnosis the cultural climate<br><br>Examine formal and informal networks<br><br>Develop change strategies appropriate for the organizational culture<br><br>Establish partnerships and collaboration | Gain understating of the tradition, moral, ethics, values, and expectation of the stakeholders at the institutions |
| Level Two | Share the vision<br><br>Empower and involve people early in the planning process<br><br>Encourage risk and creativity<br><br>Seek input at all levels in the decision-making process | Establish trust and open lines of communication<br><br>Gain acceptance and involvement |
| Level Three | Implement comprehensive training and awareness programs that are pervasive<br><br>Provide feedback and reward systems<br><br>Share decision making | Increase knowledge and understanding of the change process and the learning college<br><br>Reduce frustration and complacency<br><br>Increase stakeholders' acceptance and participation |
| Level Four | Encourage strategic thinking<br><br>Continue culture assessment and training programs<br><br>Provide options for those unwilling to change | Increase knowledge and awareness while providing alternatives for those not interested in the change |
| Level Five | Provide decision support<br><br>Link decisions to the strategic plan<br><br>Continue awareness and training programs<br><br>Assess effectiveness of training programs | Support the strategic plan and improve the level of confidence in the planning process<br><br>Provide opportunity for training programs for all stakeholders |
| Level Six | Provide rewards and celebration for learning-college programs and initiatives | Expand awareness and encourage wider participation<br><br>Re-energize and increase optimism |

- Level Six—Leaders are more likely to win over resisters and encourage creativity when positive results are apparent and rewarded.

Despite the slow progress in transforming a community college, the strategic plan remains the appropriate vehicle for institutional transformation, a fact supported by my study. The Vanguard colleges had been able to implement strategic-plan components at varying levels, as follows:

- Eleven (all but one) of the Vanguard colleges' mission statements reflect a commitment to learning and have been approved by their governing boards.
- Nine of the Vanguard colleges strongly agreed that their college leaders are sufficiently knowledgeable in learning-college principles to lead the college toward becoming more learning-centered.
- Eight respondents indicated that staff development programs were designed to prepare all staff to help the college become more learning-centered.
- Seven respondents strongly agreed that the strategic plan influenced decisions about developing new programs, setting enrollment targets, and conducting marketing and promotional efforts.
- Less than 50% of the respondents strongly agreed that budget allocation decisions are based on the strategic plan.

The Vanguard colleges indicated a commitment to the learning-college principles, yet only 50% of the institutions strongly agreed that the following activities in support of the learning organization exist:

- The college offered job descriptions for all employees that reflected staff behaviors and outcomes that promote learning.
- The college consistently used information technology to support key learning-college principles in all areas of the college.
- The college used collaborative processes to plan for and promote student and organizational learning.
- The college instructors and staff agreed on the value of identifying, assessing, and documenting student-learning outcomes.

The weakest planning components at the Vanguard Learning Colleges fell into two major areas. Only two colleges indicated that business, industry, and the community are involved in conversation about learning, and only three colleges strongly agreed that the college had a technology plan linked to the overall strategic plan.

Most of the colleges were in the planning stage of implementing the key learning-college elements, which include organizational culture, staff recruitment and development, information technology, learning, and learning outcomes. Although these institutions recognized the need for change, not all are prepared

## Table 4.2   Implementation Stages of Key Learning-College Components

| Elements | Implemented | Planning | Discussion |
|---|---|---|---|
| Organizational culture | 3 | 7 | 1 |
| Staff recruitment & development | 1 | 8 | 2 |
| Information technology | 2 | 6 | 3 |
| Student learning | 0 | 7 | 4 |
| Learning outcomes | 2 | 7 | 2 |

*Note.* Eleven Vanguard Learning Colleges responded to this question.

to begin the difficult process of complete transformation. Table 4.2 reflects the stage of implementation of key learning-college elements for the participating Vanguard colleges.

- Most respondents indicated that the college is in the planning stage of implementing the key learning-college components.
- Three respondents indicated that they have fully implemented strategies to change organizational culture.
- Only two colleges indicated that they have fully implemented learning outcomes.
- Four colleges are discussing proposed changes in students' learning.
- Seven respondents indicated that they somewhat agreed (five strongly agreed ) that the college was committed to overhauling the education delivery structure to include anytime, anywhere, anyplace learning.

These factors suggest that the Vanguard colleges have committed to transforming their institutions; however, at least 50% of the colleges have neither committed to overhauling the education delivery system nor embraced the concept that learning be available at times and locations convenient for the students. Conversely, the colleges' responses indicate greater success in implementing strategies designed to change organizational culture than in implementing activities that support learning.

My investigation revealed that the pace of implementing the strategic plan depends largely on the leadership style of the president and the approach the college uses to win stakeholder buy-in. Two leadership styles were prominent, servant and transformational.

- Servant leaders who prefer to push decision making down in the organization may find it difficult to achieve appropriate changes in an organization where stakeholders are committed to tradition and maintaining the status quo. These leaders must establish critical timelines and feedback mechanisms to ensure adherence to established goals and objectives.

- Transformational leaders, who are often described as creative, innovative, and skilled in the area of managing change, found the change process to be eased by integrating new talent—those receptive to change—throughout the organization.

Leaders at the Vanguard colleges indicated the following concerns and challenges that limited them from fully implementing of learning-college principles and key components:

- the time and energy required by the transformation process
- the difficulty in accomplishing change while dealing with day-to-day operations
- the lack of development and training opportunities for instructors and staff
- the need for a clearer understanding of a learning-centered college
- a high percentage of adjunct instructors
- inadequate funding
- shrinking public support, especially in the area of technology integration
- the need for a follow-up process
- the need for a system of measuring the success of the learning college
- the need for activities that focus more on outcomes for students

## Strategic Planning as a Vehicle for Change

The leaders at the Vanguard college voiced the following observations about strategic planning as a vehicle for change in the transformation to the learning college:

- Our use of key performance indicators following from our mission through strategic priorities for learning has taken the planning to a new level throughout the college.
- Our decentralized planning process has allowed some departments to move forward at a faster pace in becoming a true learning environment without waiting for the entire college to take a few small steps.
- We began our process before O'Banion's (1997) emphasis on learning-college principles, so we have adjusted along the way.
- We have completed the framework and involved all constituent groups including governance structure and evaluation criteria.
- The evolution of our collaborative learning-centered initiative evolved first by systematic and intentional building on previous work products. Participants saw the fruit of their labors.
- Collaboration and decision making that are embedded deep in the organization, based on learning-centered principles, are essential for institutional transformation.
- The institutional planning process is an extremely important way of introducing transformation and change into a mature, academic institution and affecting change of attitude in instructors and staff.
- Top leadership is the key.

- The plan is the beginning of the work. Planning never ends as one adjusts to internal and external changes.
- Our eyes were bigger than our stomach. Our plans overwhelmed us at times because we have set such high ones.
- Planning is much easier than implementation. Talk is easier than doing.
- We are addressing many issues of learning architecture from governance to scheduling to organization and performance review. These changes take time.
- It is not the Bible. It must be flexible and short-term enough to be amended regularly to adapt the changing circumstances in a fast-moving world.

These observations point to an active involvement in the strategic planning process and a commitment to using the strategic plan as a vehicle for change. These colleges focused on collaboration and inclusion as they began to develop and implement learning-college activities. My study revealed that the Vanguard colleges consistently recognized the difficulty in effecting change even with a systematic collaborative planning process. The following are participants' responses to a survey question about their experiences with strategic planning as a vehicle for change.

- As we modified our mission statement, then developed the strategic priorities for learning, most employees gained a greater understanding of the role of planning in moving the college toward our shared vision.
- Opportunity to bring the broad college community together on the mission of our institution; opportunity to dream together on how we might best serve; opportunity to reinvigorate college and its staff and community; great tool for accountability for results.
- It has been extremely valuable to our college and our stakeholders. We are viewed as a college that has done significant work on planning, stakeholder dialogue, and board monitoring, and—to a lesser degree—learning effectiveness.
- Planning is our most powerful tool for bringing the changes from the fringe into the center of the institution.
- Strategic planning serves as an ongoing forum for extensive conversation about what the college should do and how it should be done. Without substantial and genuine engagement of college staff and students, strategic planning can become just another report-generating activity.
- Vision, resources (or projections thereof), and the environment to transfer vision throughout the institution are more important than a burdensome, mechanical planning process.
- It's how we do it, but we are in a constant state of change here.
- Great for focus and measurement; hard to get everyone on board; lots of communication required; can't do too much listening.

- We have been working on our learning-centered initiative since 1995 focusing on collaborative decision making that leads toward significant improvements in learning outcomes.
- Mixed experience—there is more success in understanding than successfully implementing.
- Based on governing board, accreditation, and staff assessments, I was successful as a college president in bringing about planned changes through strategic planning. I am using my experience within a very different environment to achieve changes through strategic planning.

Generally, the Vanguard colleges support strategic planning as a tool in effecting change. Although stressing the importance of having a visionary leader, participants indicated that changing the institutional culture and developing strategic thinking throughout the organization are the greatest challenges in transforming the college.

## Conclusion

Notwithstanding 21st-century pressures and public sector demands, community colleges are not making dramatic changes in their education delivery systems. Although community colleges have embraced learning-college principles and most are implementing significant changes, few have committed to completely overhauling the academic structure. The Vanguard Learning Colleges, pioneers in the learning revolution, have developed strategic plans designed to be the vehicle for change. They are in different stages of implementing literature-based strategic plans. Although all of these strategic plans have plan and process components (mission, vision, values), several of these colleges are not making the tough decisions regarding allocating resources, altering existing programs, and changing processes and systems in support of the strategic plan. Community colleges can examine the Vanguard colleges' best practices and learn from their challenges and successes.

The transformation to the learning college is extremely difficult and has been hampered at the Vanguard colleges by funding cuts, difficulty in managing the organizational culture, lack of time commitment, fast-paced changes in technology, difficult decision making, type of leadership style, limited institutional strategic thinking, and the need for a comprehensive professional development and training program. Given the collegiality of the environment, institutionalizing the strategic plan can be an arduous process; it depends largely on stakeholder buy-in-especially that of instructors-of the vision and the implementation strategies. The leadership style and experience of college leaders in using strategic-planning models improves the chances of obtaining stakeholders' acceptance and participation. Stakeholders must see strategic planning as a permanent commitment, not just a new, temporary wave. Unless these challenges are addressed, activities in support of the learning college may be held in abeyance or abandoned forever.

In implementing key learning-college components (League for Innovation, 2001), the Vanguard colleges have moved from the discussion stage to the planning stage. They are slowly moving toward the fully implemented phase. Yet few have agreed to completely abandon the current academic and student support structures. Supporters at the Vanguard colleges suggest that unless their leaders understand the attitudes, values, and traditions of the existing culture, pockets of resistance and counter-productive activities and systems will continue within the organization, despite the best efforts of the leadership to transform the institution.

Colleges that have achieved the most success in their transformation have centered their entire strategic planning process on the implementation of the learning college. These colleges have adopted strategic priorities, values, goals, and objectives and have outlined step-by-step activities in the operational plan that will achieve the learning-focused vision. They understand that the strategic planning process is merely the beginning of the transformation. Implementation strategies and assessment measurements are the greatest challenges to management.

The challenges of implementing a new educational paradigm call for highly skilled leaders in higher education who can manage the change process. Academic and professional leadership programs must develop and nurture these leaders in great numbers so that they will be prepared to respond to the crises at hand. In transforming community colleges, educators must move with a sense of urgency against a complacent institutional culture that is resistant to change. A leader's style must be appropriate for transforming the organization, and he or she must be cognizant of the institutional culture—the traditions, values, and the subcultures within the organization.

The CEOs at the Vanguard colleges use different approaches to change management, depending on their style and understanding of the institutional culture. The progress of the transformation at these colleges varies greatly, depending on the leadership's ability to manage the culture. Their experiences dovetail with research data suggesting that higher education policymakers and leaders need to do more to disturb the status quo and challenge community colleges to be creative and innovative in effecting deep architectural changes. Community college leaders must commit to using a systematic, inclusive literature-based planning process that will facilitate change. They must be willing to make the difficult decisions that will transform the institution to create a learning-centered environment.

## References

Altbach, P. G., Berdahl, R. O., & Gumport, P. (1999). *Higher education in the twenty-first century.* Baltimore: John Hopkins University Press.

Barr, R., & Tagg, J. (1995, November/December). From teaching to learning: A new paradigm for undergraduate education. *Change, 27*(6), 13–25.

Haines, S. G. (2000). *The systems thinking approach to strategic planning and management.* New York: St. Lucie Press.

Hooker, M. (1997). The transformation of higher education. In D. Oblinger & S. S. Rush (Eds.), *The learning revolution.* Boston: Anker.

Keller, G. (1983). *Academic strategy: The management revolution in American higher education.* Baltimore: John Hopkins University Press.

Keller, G. (1999-2000). The emerging third stage in higher education planning. *Planning for Higher Education, 28,* 1–8.

Kotler, P., & Murphy, P. (1981). Strategic planning for higher education. *Journal of Higher Education, 52*(5), 470–489.

Kotter, J. P. (1996). *Leading change.* Boston: Harvard Business School Press.

League for Innovation. (2001). *Learning college project: Vanguard colleges.* Retrieved August 17, 2004, from www.league.org/league/projects/lcp/vanguard.htm

McClenney, K. (1999). Forces shaping the community college agenda: A view from the states. *Trustee Quarterly, Convention Issue,* 11–13.

O'Banion, T. (1997). *A learning college for the 21st century.* San Francisco: AACC and ACE/Oryx Press.

O'Banion, T., & Milliron, M. (2001). College conversation on learning. *Learning Abstracts, 4.* Available from http://www.league.org/publication/abstract/ learning /lelabs0109.htm

Sheridan, D. H. (1998). *An analysis of strategic planning practices at Ontario College of Applied Arts and Technology.* Unpublished doctoral dissertation, University of Toronto, Canada.

# CHAPTER 5

# The Learning-Outcomes Approach

MARK BATTERSBY

The success of Barr and Tagg's article on the learning paradigm reveals widespread agreement about the kind of change needed in postsecondary education, that is, a shift to learning-centered education (Barr & Tagg, 1995). The idea is that educators have placed undue focus on inputs as a measure of educational success rather than on what the students have actually learned. Although this admission is welcome, most instructors are already concerned with what students are learning and do make considerable efforts to evaluate students' learning.

Nonetheless, Barr and Tagg's basic critique is valid, especially for colleges that base their institutional-effectiveness assessments solely on inputs to measure quality: library books, computer availability, instructors with doctorates, SAT scores of entering students, grants awarded, and so on. The classroom paints a more mixed picture. Many, perhaps most, instructors think of their courses in terms of what material they believe should be covered (e.g., English poetry from Donne to Shelley). Course objectives are typically ambiguous when it comes to inputs (students will be introduced to the basic concepts of biology) and outcomes (students will be able to solve quadratic equations). Assessment procedures also reveal ambiguity. Some methods are clearly designed to test students' understanding and their ability to apply their learning; others merely check that students have memorized the covered material.

As Barr and Tagg rightly note, the key to becoming learning-centered is emphasizing clear and relevant learning outcomes. As the college community fully endorses the learning-centered movement, instructors must devote sufficient attention to this fundamental question: What should students be learning? The discussion generated by the Barr and Tagg article has tended to focus on how to achieve more efficient learning, avoiding fundamental questions about the goals of learning. This omission is largely due to the power of tradition at colleges. Disciplinary tradition often determines curricula. Individual departments have primary authority to establish courses and curricula. Barr and Tagg rightly argue that education institutions are often not well designed to ensure students' learning. In my view, they are also not well designed for shared reflection on the outcomes of learning.

Many who adopt a learning-outcomes approach also ignore the importance of ascertaining students' needs before determining learning outcomes. Taking a narrow view of the learning-outcomes approach, they treat it merely as an improvement in pedagogy that focuses on clarifying the existing goals of a course, which are often implicit or poorly articulated. The theory is that the more clear and explicit instructors are about what they want students to learn, the more likely it is that students will succeed in learning. No doubt this is true and commendable. But instructors cannot assume, without careful and continuous review, that current courses and programs are directed at the appropriate learning goals, whether implicit or explicit. Preliminary reflection on what students need to know and be able to do is an essential part of the learning-outcomes approach. The resulting learning outcomes from such reflection will often differ from the goals of traditional curricula.

My colleagues and I have spent considerable time over the last three years discussing with instructors the concept of learning outcomes and their significance for postsecondary education. Many instructors, particularly those in academia, are suspicious and hostile to this concept (Barr, 1998). Much of this hostility is based on a misunderstanding either of the concept itself or the reason that change is being promoted. In this chapter, I address these concerns and show how the learning-outcomes approach provides a useful tool, a kind of heuristic, for reflecting on and implementing curricular and pedagogic improvements.

What is the concept of the learning-outcomes approach? Curriculum goals should be based on an analysis of what is essential for students to know or be able to do after a course or program. The word essential underlines the need to pare down courses so that sufficient time is available for students to achieve real understanding and learning. Simply covering material is no guarantee of learning. Although focusing a course on essentials is difficult, the alternative is to cover more than students can realistically be expected to learn and be able to use. The usual result of covering too much material is that students study to succeed on tests and assignments rather than work for deeper (useable, transferable) understanding. For understanding or an ability to be a real learning outcome, students must have a level of mastery that ensures that what is learned is something that students can make use of long after the course.

In thinking about what students need to know and be able to do, consider the use students could make of their learning to enhance their lives and to more effectively contribute to society. This use could include enriching their lives through aesthetic experiences, empowering their political understanding, or increasing their job skills. Such reflection leads to a focus on abilities that combine knowledge, skills, and values that provide the basis for the way that people actually use their knowledge.

## Learning-Outcomes Approaches to Teaching and Learning

To explain the learning-outcomes approach, it is useful to contrast this approach with a variety of current theories and practices. Unfortunately, such contrasts inevitably lead to simplification. Educators use a wide range of approaches for designing curricula and assessing outcomes, and the approaches of most instructors overlap the categories described in this chapter. Of course, seeing the big picture comes at the expense of small-scale precision.

### *Learning Outcomes and Competencies*

The learning-outcomes approach emphasizes the application of knowledge, a feature it shares with the instructional approach in career and vocational programs, commonly called competency-based education. But it differs from the competency approach in that it focuses more on integration. The competency approach focuses on the distinct job-specific skills that a graduate of a program needs for success on the job. Skills are usually represented by specific tasks (e.g., being able to format business letters). In contrast, the learning-outcomes approach emphasizes that for competencies to be useable, they must be integrated. For example, competencies such as being able to punctuate correctly or knowing appropriate vocabulary are essential to the learning outcome of writing and communicating effectively. In practice, this means assessing vocabulary in usage context, not by some short-answer or multiple-choice test.

Outcomes are not discrete skills or mere collections of knowledge, but an integrated complex of knowledge, abilities, and attitudes. Instruction and assessment should enable students to attain an effective level of integration. This idea is strikingly difficult to express in English—we seem to have no term for the synthesis of knowledge, abilities, and values that will characterize most outcomes.

The learning-outcomes approach also shares with the competency approach the need for clarity about instruction goals. Both approaches focus on what the student should be able to do at the end of a course or program. This is in contrast to approaches to curricula that emphasize coverage without any clear indication of what a student should be able to do with the material covered. Many studies have shown that students have difficulty in transferring knowledge between courses and between school and life (Perkins & Salomon, 1989). To promote transfer of knowledge, instruction, and especially assessment, must help students practice applying their new knowledge to a variety of situations. If knowledge is acquired and assessed as discrete items of information or skills, students will probably not make integrated use of it outside of school.

### *Learning Outcomes and Course Objectives*

Although competencies are common in career and vocational programs, in academic classes, the course objectives tend to express educational aims in terms of course objectives, and learning outcomes may stand in contrast. Because the notion of course objectives has no fixed meaning, objectives commonly include statements about what the instructor intends to do (provide a basic introduction to. . . , expose the student to. . .); statements about what both the instructor and student will do (there will be daily class discussions); and, often, outcome-type statements about what the student should know or be able to do at the end of the course. Such course objectives are a mixture of instructional intentions, inputs, and learning outcomes.

Although this mélange is understandable, clear statements of learning outcomes are more useful. Statements about what the instructor intends to cover (as opposed to what the students are supposed to learn) fail to clarify for the students what they are to gain from such an exposure. Instructors obviously intend exposure to certain material to have outcomes, but mere reference to exposure or introduction leaves unclear what the student should know or be able to do as a result of this experience. Compare "the student will be introduced to the essentials of good writing" with "the student should be able to write effectively for different audiences and different purposes." Although course-objective statements express what the instructors think are central to their intentions for a course, such objectives are not required to describe the learning that students should achieve. Both the teacher and the student should be much clearer about the goals of the educational project when course outlines clearly express what students should understand and be able to do as the result of the course.

### Learning Outcomes and Assessment

The educational value of a learning outcome depends on how it is assessed; this is widely recognized. An instructor's choice of assignment or assessment instrument reveals the concept of instruction and learning that he or she is using. Instructors need to ask themselves what kind of performance would give them confidence that the student has understood and can apply the material learned.

Articulating the kind of performance that would demonstrate that a student has the desired knowledge and abilities is a useful method for unpacking a learning outcome. Because outcome statements are general and somewhat abstract, instructors usually must give examples of assignments and performances that illustrate the level and content of the outcome. For example, if an outcome involves effective communication, an example of a successful essay or memo with an accompanying grading rubric is needed to give real content to the type and level of performance expected. Revisiting learning outcomes after developing and critiquing illustrative examples helps instructors to refine and clarify the learning outcome.

Key to the learning-outcomes approach to assessment is the use of authentic assessment. Authentic assessments are assignments and assessments that simulate as much as possible the situations in which students would make integrated use of the knowledge, skills, and values developed in the course. By focusing assessment in this way, instructors emphasize the intention that students use their learning outside of class.

Authentic assessment activities usually involve applying course material and concepts to problems and issues not directly covered. Instructors often report that students find such assignments challenging, even daunting. This is not surprising because such performances test both depth of understanding and the ability to transfer learning. Students' reactions underscore the difficulty of developing true understanding, not the inappropriateness of such assignments. The reactions further support the need to teach for transfer and application. Instructors should not assume that students who have mastered course material will necessarily be able to apply the material outside the course context.

The implications of this approach are significant. Standard written tests are seldom appropriate for assessing outcomes because students rarely use their knowledge and skills to write tests. Even the academic essay, which as an assessment tool has many advantages over short-answer testing, is a specialized genre and is limited in preparing students for writing effectively for a wide variety of audiences. This is not to say that the common assessment tools (tests, quizzes, and essays) have no place in a learning-outcomes-based curriculum. Rather, they should be used only to the extent that the feedback and practice they provide contribute to instead of detract from a student's attainment of the course learning outcomes.

Ideally, assessment should allow students to practice the integration of their learning and to receive meaningful feedback. Instructors should view assessments not merely for evaluation purposes, but also as a primary means of learning. However, because learning is greatly facilitated by doing, creating and using meaningful and rich assignments are key components of good instruction. In this context, assessment is directly related to learning, not merely to evaluation or certification.

An outcome need not be readily measured. Yes, outcomes should be assessable—both instructors and students need to know whether the outcomes are being realized. However, because outcomes must be assessed in a realistic context, evaluation will usually require the instructor's judgment rather than measurement. Measurement tends to oversimplify the assessment process to easily quantify what is assessed. Multiple-choice tests, although highly reliable and easily graded, usually have low validity because they fail to assess whether students can use (or even really understand) the knowledge that they are able to recall on an exam. Furthermore, such tests send the dangerous message to students that the point of the course is to acquire testable, rather than useable, knowledge.

While collecting appropriate evidence of a student's understanding, instructors should not confuse such evidence with its related learning outcomes. Often instructors introduce outcomes statements with the phrase "the student will demonstrate. . . ." But surely the course aims for the students to achieve a certain ability; the demonstration merely provides evidence that they have achieved the ability. Confusing outcomes with their demonstration suggests a misunderstanding of the educational project. Instructors should be clear with students that their learning is not preparing them to produce successful demonstrations in college, but rather helping them to acquire knowledge and abilities that they can make effective use of in their lives. Although this point is obvious, it is often lost on many students who, because of their educational experiences, have come to view school as alienated labor—something done to satisfy what appear to be (and often are) the arbitrary demands of school.

### *Learning Outcomes and Generic Abilities*

Learning outcomes express what students should know or be able to do at the end of a course. Colleges should base the delineation of appropriate knowledge and abilities on the needs of students and society. Such reflection leads us not only to clearly articulate the knowledge, abilities, and attitudes that are germane to the immediate subject matter or discipline, but also to recognize the importance of related general knowledge and abilities. The constantly changing nature of knowledge and work-specific abilities requires that all people have the general understanding and generic abilities they need for continual learning and for engaging the world thoughtfully after their formal education.

To prepare students for life-long learning, instructors must teach more than the immediate knowledge that most programs and disciplinary courses offer. Such preparation requires a focus on intellectual abilities such as research and learning strategies, reflective judgment, critical thinking, and communication-recognizing that these abilities are necessary for the specific discipline and for other key life activities. The use of the term ability to describe this kind of learning does not imply that knowledge has no place. Consider, for example, the kind of general knowledge anyone needs to do effective research: a basic understanding of the intellectual landscape and knowledge of concepts and terminology relevant to the particular topic. The crucial point is that students should know how to enter areas where they have had not instruction and be able to acquire the necessary missing knowledge.

Reflecting about students' roles in life will have and the uses they might make of their learning emphasizes the need for general understanding and generic abilities. Course or program learning outcomes (and their means of assessment) should reflect this concern for longer-term learning and should contain an appropriate emphasis on general and course-specific abilities. Consider, then, where the development of discipline-specific abilities fits in this approach.

Obviously, students need to develop specific abilities, and even generic abilities are usually best developed in the context of meaningful course content. Generic abilities are by nature widely applicable. Consider the subject of history, for example. To teach students to think like a historian or to understand the causes of World War I, the instructor must teach students to think critically about historical evidence and theories. In this context, critical thinking is an ability that is both specific and generic to the discipline. When an instructor emphasizes the generic nature of assessing historical evidence, he or she can help students understand how they can apply such reflection to areas outside of historical analysis (i.e., to help students see how their learning can transfer).

In developing the learning outcomes for a course, instructors must ask what the student should be able to do (or do better) as a result of this course (and why). Such reflections should naturally lead one to identify both subject-specific and relevant generic knowledge and abilities. The emphasis on generic abilities follows naturally from any reasonable analysis of students' learning needs, but instructors should not use the centrality of generic abilities to deny the importance of discipline-specific, relevant knowledge and understanding.

### *Learning Outcomes and the Disciplines*

Generic abilities are not the only important outcomes of postsecondary education. Familiarity with, and knowledge of, a variety of disciplines is a pre-condition for transfer and integration of knowledge. Successful university graduates must know their way around the intellectual world. They need to know how to acquire and evaluate discipline-based knowledge. The challenge is to create the breadth of understanding and the desire and ability for inquiry that enables a student to make widespread use of the vast learning produced by disciplinary research.

A common approach to developing a curriculum is to begin by asking what the discipline traditionally covers at this level. Instructors also consider whether their courses will adequately prepare students for subsequent courses in the discipline. Colleges that are preparing students for transfer must also consider whether their curricula will be acceptable to the receiving institutions.

The learning-outcomes approach suggests a different leading question: What do students need to know and be able to do after they graduate (from this course, from this program, from the university. . . )? In directing instructors' attention to what students are likely to do with the knowledge and abilities they acquire, the learning-outcomes approach requires looking beyond the strict boundaries of disciplinary tradition and demands. Such an approach highlights the tension in many introductory courses between serving the short-term preparatory needs of the majors and the longer-term needs of the majority of students. But how much of this tension is necessary?

The major in a discipline needs the kind of general understanding that the non-major should take from an introductory course. One of the ironies of postsecondary education is that a broad overview of one's discipline or area of study is often acquired in graduate school rather than at the beginning of one's studies. This is not unlike being handed a map of a city after living in it for 4 years—useful but belated.

## Challenges to Implementing the Learning-Outcomes Approach

Applying knowledge usually requires that one integrate knowledge from a variety of disciplines. The learning-outcomes approach, with its emphasis on using knowledge and designing down the curricula from the broadest consideration of students' learning needs, naturally focuses on the integration of knowledge. How students are brought to integrate their knowledge is a complex educational and institutional question. Interdisciplinary courses and programs are one way of realizing the learning-outcomes approach to designing curricula, as they can embody the kind of integration students must achieve. They can also provide intellectually stimulating opportunities for instructors to work together to identify and promote shared outcomes. Colleges that adopt a learning-outcomes approach should use this change as an occasion to reflect on shared educational goals and to create institutional processes for encouraging such reflection.

### Attitudes

Many instructors are skeptical and suspicious about the learning-outcomes approach. Many feel that they already are taking a learning-outcomes (and learning-centered) approach to education; the learning-outcomes approach merely changes some terminology on their course outlines (Barr, 1998). To them, it is an unfortunate waste of time. Others fear the imposition of an industrial model with outcomes being centrally imposed, courses being modularized, and instructors being replaced with assessors and facilitators, and perhaps even computers. Many instructors further see the emphasis on outcomes as pressure to make education more directly serve the short-term needs of the economy and the business community, rather than to develop a student's thoughtfulness and intellectual independence.

The learning-outcomes approach is not a change of terminology; to focus on terminology is to miss the point entirely. Learning outcomes are neither learning objectives nor competencies in a new guise. For a variety of understandable reasons, many students approach education as alienated intellectual labor, rather than something that is empowering and a source of learning that will enhance their lives. If education requirements are clearly based on students' post-education learning needs, students should acquire a sense of education as enabling them to lead richer and more empowered lives rather than as a set of hurdles placed between themselves and their vocational goals.

Building a curriculum based on learning outcomes helps ensure that both students and instructors focus on what they need to achieve through a course. The worst thing for this effort would be for it to become mired in word games. Because the learning-outcomes approach emphasizes application, and application requires understanding, it should be seen as another call to place understanding in the center of the educational project, an understanding that enables students to make use of their new knowledge and abilities.

### The Influence of Business

These are times of increased economic anxiety and increased political power in the hands of business. It also appears that the business sector has an increasing influence in establishing social goals and government policy. Thus, it is understandable that any political or educational change might well have business roots. Some of the pressure for a learning-outcomes approach does come from business interests. Those who are skeptical of the effectiveness of postsecondary education and wish to see it made more accountable also support the call for learning outcomes. Measuring learning outcomes can be conceived of as a means for realizing accountability. Although there are grounds for these concerns, they should not unduly trouble educators.

Instructors usually determine curricula and have the professional responsibility to determine what curricular outcomes should be. Nonetheless, in many applied fields, employers have considerable say as to curricular outcomes through their advisory groups, the establishment of credential criteria (e.g., bar exams), and the purchase of instruction. This is not new. It certainly does not arise as a result of the learning-outcomes approach to education. On the contrary, those instructors in applied fields who reflect on what students really need to know and need to be able to do, keeping in mind the rapidly changing demands of the workplace, realize that a learning-outcomes approach requires increasing emphasis on generic skills and less emphasis on job-specific skills. In applied areas, an increased emphasis on generic abilities may well require discussing the importance of these abilities with advisory and employer groups and consequent revamping of curricula, pedagogy, and credential criteria. Nurse educators, for example, committed to making critical thinking an essential part of nurse education, have had some success in getting the nursing credentialing exam changed to reflect the new emphasis on critical thinking.

In the less applied areas, a move to a learning-outcomes approach to education does not mean primarily serving business interests unless, in the professional judgment of the instructors, what the student needs to know would also serve that interest. Ironically, many academic courses suffer from being (academic) job preparation courses in the sense that their curriculum is determined by what is necessary for entrance to graduate school and academic employment. If academic courses are not meant to be job preparation courses, then they should not primarily serve the student going on to post-graduate work and a job in the discipline. Particularly in introductory courses, learning outcomes should be determined by the long-term needs of a broad range of students rather than the few who might go on in the major.

Courses should be designed to realize outcomes that empower students to make sense of the world they live in, to enhance their appreciation of nature and culture, and to function effectively and thoughtfully in their lives. Such courses should help graduates acquire knowledge that can be used in their lives, not only in their work. It is no secret that students often approach postsecondary education as a means to obtaining a good job, rather than as a means to live a richer and more informed life. Responsible educators can not ignore the fact that much of the support for postsecondary education is based on its role in promoting the economic well-being of both the graduate and society. However, the abilities needed to do well in a knowledge-based economy are also those needed to be effective as a citizen and a deeply thoughtful person.

Generic abilities, such as critical thinking and effective communication, as well as abilities such as aesthetic appreciation, empower students whether they are at work, at home, in the public forum, or in the woods. For example, learning to identify assumptions (a basic critical-thinking skill) is enormously useful in any activity. Accounting students need to understand the assumptions of their enterprise, as do citizens, artists, biologists, and economists. Not recognizing one's assumptions limits reflection and creativity in any enterprise. Instructors should respect students' concerns about employment but emphasize to them the wide use and value of what they are learning. Such an emphasis (backed by appropriate pedagogy and assessment) will provide the best and most valuable education for all students.

## Conclusion

Despite the foregoing discussion, some will still want a more precise notion of the learning-outcomes approach. The idea of the learning-outcomes approach is to change the way educators think about curricula and teaching, not simply to change to new buzz words. With apologies for oversimplification, the following definitions and brief statements represent current thinking and may be of some use.

- Learning outcomes are the essential and enduring knowledge, abilities (skills), and attitudes (values, dispositions) that constitute the integrated learning needed by a graduate of a course or program.
- The learning-outcomes approach to education means basing program and curriculum design, content, delivery, and assessment on an analysis of the integrated knowledge, skills, and values needed by both students and society.

This approach differs from competency-based approaches in its emphasis on integration and the development of more general abilities that are often overlooked in a competency approach. It differs from more traditional academic approaches that emphasize coverage by its emphasis on

- basing curricula on what students need to know and need to be able to do as determined by the student's and society's needs, not disciplinary tradition
- focusing on what students should be able to do rather than merely what knowledge they should possess as a result of completing a course or program
- making explicit the development and assessment of generic abilities

Educators should determine learning outcomes based on a careful and broad analysis of what a competent graduate of the program should be able to do. Educators have the social responsibility to ensure that the education available serves the long-term needs of students and society. A thoughtful needs analysis recognizes that learning can and should be relevant to the variety of roles graduates play in their working, civic, and personal lives. Learning outcomes should be the basis for choosing curriculum content and instructional strategies. Curricula should be developed down from the learning outcome ends to the curricular, pedagogic, and assessment means.

A key element in the learning-outcomes approach is the role of assessment. Assessment choices give clear meaning to the more abstract formulations of the learning outcomes. Stating learning outcomes clearly and providing evaluation based on explicit standards greatly facilitates students' learning. Assessment tasks (assignments) should also be seen as the primary means of instruction and learning. Assessment methods should enable students to practice and demonstrate the learning outcomes in as integrated and realistic a manner as possible.

## References

Barr, R. B., & Tagg, J. (1995, November/December). A new paradigm for undergraduate education. *Change, 27*(6), 13–25.

Barr, R. B. (1998, September/October). Obstacles to implementing the learning paradigm: What it takes to overcome them. *About Campus,* 18–25.

Perkins, D. N., & Salomon, G. (1989, January/February). Are cognitive skills context-bound? *Educational Researcher,* 16–25.

CHAPTER 6

# Learning-Outcomes Assessment at the Community College of Baltimore County

HENRY F. LINCK, ROSALIE V. MINCE,
AND TARA E. EBERSOLE

Over the past several years, an interest in learning-outcomes assessment has emerged slowly but decisively at the national level. Accreditation agencies are the primary drivers of learning-outcomes assessment activities. The Middle States Commission on Higher Education, for example, revised its *Characteristics of Excellence* in 2002 to include a new "Standard 14" focusing on the assessment of students' learning: "Assessment of student learning demonstrates that the institution's students have knowledge, skills, and competencies consistent with institutional goals and that students at graduation have achieved appropriate higher education goals" (p. 50). The commission further stated:

> In order to carry out meaningful assessment activities, institutions must articulate statements of expected student learning at the institutional, program, and individual course levels, although the level of specificity will be greater at the course level. Course syllabi or guidelines should include expected learning outcomes. (p. 50)

This new standard imposes significant changes on member colleges. Standard 14 embodies what Barr and Tagg called the new paradigm for higher education—student learning. In their seminal 1995 article in *Change* magazine, Barr and Tagg challenged all of higher education to recognize that a paradigm shift was taking hold.

> A paradigm shift is taking hold in American higher education. In its briefest form, the paradigm that has governed our colleges is this: A college is an institution that exists to *provide instruction*. Subtly but profoundly we are shifting to a new paradigm: A college is an institution that exists to *produce learning*. This shift changes everything. It is both needed and wanted. (1995, p. 13)

Community colleges, in particular, have embraced the learning paradigm shift. O'Banion's work through the League for Innovation in the Community College became the driving force that embedded learning-centered language into the culture of the institution. In his book, *A Learning College for the 21st Century* (1997), O'Banion posed two central questions that are at the core of the learning college philosophy: What does this student know? and What can this student do? For O'Banion, "the learning college succeeds only when improved and expanded learning can be documented for its learners" (p. 60). The operative word here is documented. Although seemingly simple, answers to these two questions, along with the requisite documentation, are difficult to obtain; without clearly documented answers, however, we cannot know that we are truly placing learning first.

This chapter provides a detailed description about how administrators and instructors developed a learning-outcomes assessment process at The Community College of Baltimore County (CCBC). These concepts are communicated most effectively via real-world examples of how processes were designed and implemented. It is with this mindset that the college shares its learning-outcomes assessment process.

## The Community College of Baltimore County

The Community College of Baltimore County is a learning-centered public college that anticipates and responds to the educational needs of the communities it serves through its three major campuses and numerous extension centers. As part of the college's strategic plan, LearningFIRST 2.0, CCBC is committed to making learning its central focus, making students active partners in the learning process, and focusing on learning outcomes to assess the success of students' learning. Evaluating the effectiveness of instruction is an instructor's responsibility that is necessary for the improvement and verification of learning. The college is dedicated to providing instructors with substantial assistance in developing learning-outcomes assessment, programs-outcomes assessment, and classroom learning-assessment processes, as well as in revising instructional practices that may follow from outcomes assessment (Linck, 2004).

Using as its foundation the concept of the learning college as defined by O'Banion (1997) and Barr and Tagg (1995), the LearningFIRST Strategic Plan (McPhail, 1999; see also McPhail, Heacock, & Linck, 2001) was created by Chancellor Irving Pressley McPhail to guide the evolution of CCBC into a premier learning college of the 21st century. The current plan, LearningFIRST 2.0 (McPhail, 2003), is the second iteration of the plan that will guide the college during the next 5 years. The philosophy driving the plan is embodied in the college's statement of beliefs:

As a learning-centered community college, CCBC

• makes learning its central focus.
• makes students active partners in the learning process.

- assumes final responsibility for producing student learning.
- focuses on learning outcomes to assess student learning and success.
- creates a holistic environment that supports student learning.
- ensures that every member of the college community is a learner.
- evaluates all areas of the college by the ways they foster student learning.
- assesses student learning at the institutional, program, and course levels.
- focuses on two questions to guide all institutional decisions:
  - How does this action improve and expand student learning?
  - How do we know this action improves and expands student learning?
  (McPhail, 2003)

LearningFIRST 2.0 establishes the vision of the college as a student-centered learning environment that places learning as its core strategic direction. In addition, the plan identifies nine supporting strategic directions.

- Student learning establishes learning as the core value and direction of CCBC. All other actions are evaluated and judged on the basis of this proposition. CCBC's goal is to provide a high-quality, learning-centered education that maximizes student learning and makes students partners in their education. Students must be able to frame and achieve their educational goals and develop skills that are appropriate for the 21st century.
- Learning support provides a comprehensive and responsive support system that increases student access to learning opportunities and recognizes that the student is central to the learning process. CCBC's learning support goals are to increase student retention and success, create seamless instructional and student support services, improve student skills assessment and course placement, and increase community access to programs and services.
- The concept of the learning college provides the impetus for CCBC's transformation into a learning college, that is, promoting the free exchange of ideas, encouraging innovation, emphasizing continuous improvement through organizational learning, and focusing on assessment through a comprehensive institutional effectiveness and evaluation system.
- Infusing technology recognizes and advances the use of new instructional technologies to enhance student learning, as well as the general use of technology to improve the effectiveness and efficiency of college operations.
- Organizational excellence promotes continual improvement in the college's organizational structure, policies, and practices to focus support on a learning-centered environment. This strategy promotes low-cost access to the college by ensuring efficient operations and focusing on generating additional resources.
- By embracing diversity, CCBC focuses on attracting and retaining a diverse

instructors, staff, and student community. This goal is accomplished through initiatives that (a) advance a learning environment that encourages and values diversity, (b) incorporate diversity into the curriculum, and (c) recognize and address diverse learning styles.

- Community development and institutional advancement defines CCBC as an active member of the larger community. As such, CCBC takes a leading role in improving access to learning for the disadvantaged, delivers workforce training, forms partnerships to support economic and community development, and increases resources through a vigorous institutional advancement effort.

- Strategic Enrollment Management (SEM) is designed to maximize enrollment in a manner that balances access to student learning and the development of a learning college. Central to enrollment management are programs and services that anticipate the changing needs of the college's various communities and that maximize access to learners.

- Strategic communication recognizes the importance of effective internal and external communications to the advancement of the learning college. (McPhail, 2003)

LearningFIRST 2.0 defines CCBC as a learning-centered institution and illustrates a clear commitment to making learning the institution's central focus, making students active partners in the learning process, and focusing on learning outcomes to assess the success of students' learning. The focus on assessing learning outcomes is at the heart of the learning college philosophy and embodies the shift from teaching to learning (Linck, 2004). In addition to this institutional focus on learning outcomes in the strategic plan, CCBC is actively engaged in assessing students' learning throughout the college at the program and course levels.

## Instructors As Partners in Learning-Outcomes Assessment

The accountability movement is connected to and empowered by the need for evidence of high academic achievement. Few instructors would argue with that rationale, yet instructors' resistance to assessing students' learning is a significant issue. Many are convinced that grades are an acceptable means of assessing students' progress and do not realize that grades, which tend to be subjective, are not always based solely on learning outcomes. A learning college succeeds when improved and expanded learning can be documented and when continuous curriculum improvement reflects valid and reliable data.

Thus, instructors must be full participants in any learning-outcomes project from the planning through the implementation phases. The college-wide committee that formulates the institution's assessment plan and acts as the advisory board to assessment should include instructors. Direct advisory assistance to those developing assessment projects should be given by instructors who are well versed in education research and in the language and processes of learning-outcomes assessment. The role of this learning-outcomes associate can be diverse-educating all instructors and staff on the importance of assessing whether students are achieving the desired outcomes, acting as a liaison between instructors and their department chairs and deans, and providing orientations and templates for instructors' project proposals.

## Program-Level Assessment

The Middle States Commission on Higher Education clearly states that assessment of students' learning must take place at the program level as well as at the course and institutional levels. A program can be defined as a college-wide grouping or sequences of courses, as with a general education or developmental education program, or as a specific pattern or collection of courses that lead to a certificate or degree. Regardless of the type of program being reviewed, the assessment process always begins with identification of measurable program outcomes. For a career or transfer program, three to five measurable program outcomes are usually sufficient to clearly and completely define the knowledge and skills that students have mastered upon completion of the program of study. More outcomes may be necessary to adequately capture the essence of a college-wide program, such as general education or developmental education.

At the program level there is a need to verify that students can successfully retain, integrate, and apply outcomes derived from individual courses in a final set of comprehensive competencies that would be expected of program graduates. These program outcomes define what students know or will be able to do at the end of a program. With input from a variety of sources such as advisory committees, employer surveys, DACUM activities, four-year institutions, national or local skill standards, and focus groups, program coordinators at CCBC are responsible for identifying a complete set of workplace-relevant program outcomes that are clearly stated, specific in nature, and, most of all, measurable.

When writing program outcomes, the focus should be on what students need to be able to do to successfully function in their next level of academic study or in the world of work. Program outcomes are more than the simple accumulation of all of the objectives from the courses included in the program. They are the over-arching tasks that students will be able to demonstrate when they synthesize major portions of what they have learned and apply them to what they need to do outside of the classroom. They define in a comprehensive and measurable way what students are able to do as a result of completing the learning outcomes in their courses.

Program outcomes should be identified before course-level learning objectives are written. They should be written at the highest level of learning that students will master in the program. A few examples from CCBC follow:

- Office administration program—Students will be able to produce first-time mailable copy using state-of-the-art software from a variety of input.

- Health and fitness studies program—Students will be able to conduct various laboratory and field tests to evaluate cardiovascular respiratory endurance, muscular fitness, flexibility, and body composition and analyze the results to develop individualized exercise prescriptions.
- Massage therapy program—Students will be able to perform a full-body massage using a combination of Swedish, deep tissue, and myofascial techniques.
- Leisure studies program—Students will be able to assess, plan, implement, and evaluate leisure activities in three or more programmatic areas.
- Surveying technology program—Students will be able to analyze field data collected through the use of global positioning systems and apply that data to establish initial survey control stations.

As with other levels and types of assessment, the purpose of assessing program outcomes is to gather feedback to guide programmatic changes that will improve and expand students' learning. Program assessment may be included as part of the college's program review process. Many colleges already have such a process in place and review each program of study every 3 to 5 years.

The five stages of a learning-outcomes assessment project, whether at the course or program level, include a design component, an implementation component, data collection, data analysis, and development of program improvements. CCBC's *Guide for Learning Outcomes Assessment and Classroom Learning Assessment* (2003), available from CCBC's Web site, describes each stage of an assessment project.

### *Project Requirements*

Program coordinators formulate and draft a project plan to assess learning related to approved major program outcomes, present the project plan to instructors in the program, and elicit timely feedback. The draft plan is next formalized in the form of a request for proposal (RFP) and a timeline that outlines when each step of the RFP will be completed. The RFP includes the following components:

- Outcomes to be measured
- Method(s) to assess the identified program outcomes
- External validation to ensure that the identified outcomes are what the college should be assessing and that the method for doing so will result in valid and reliable data. External validation is included in the project plan when selecting the instrument and analyzing the results, to provide a measure of validity for program outcomes. Benchmarking may be determined by comparing the performance of students to other college students on normed tests, comparing students to criterion-referenced measures, analyzing student performance using inside or outside experts, or other appropriate methods determined by the project leader.

- Data analysis to determine areas in need of improvement
- Program improvement is based on the data analysis. Program revisions are designed and subsequently implemented
- Reassessment is conducted after one to two semesters of implementation of recommended revisions to determine the impact of the revisions
- Dissemination of the results of the assessment project

## Project Design

Many techniques can be used to assess program outcomes and a variety of appropriate points at which assessment can occur. Assessment may be embedded in course assignments or activities or may occur in a capstone course near the end of a program of study. Assessment can also take place in well-defined practicum, internship, or field experiences. Portfolio assessment and standardized tests can also be used at the program level. Many programs employ a variety of methods for assessing program-level outcomes. Accreditation for some programs requires certification exams, which may be used to document students' attainment of program outcomes, and many programs require a capstone course or some type of field experience to assess students' knowledge and skills.

After the data are collected, the most important part of the assessment project begins—determining the appropriate curricular changes to enhance learning. The purpose of all assessment initiatives is to determine what is working well and what needs to be changed. Instructors are the experts who can identify areas for improvement and implement the recommended changes. Most instructors, however, are not experts in the area of research design and data analysis, and thus it is very important to provide adequate and appropriate support throughout the entire assessment project.

## Project Assistance

A college must be committed to outcomes assessment and must provide assistance in all phases of designing, implementing, and evaluating a project. Among the resources colleges should provide to assist instructors in planning, implementing, and evaluating projects are a planning, research, and evaluation office; testing centers; a learning and teaching excellence center; staff development workshops; and faculty peer mentors. Additional assistance may be necessary for project design; technical assistance for data collection, design, and analysis; information about external validation tools; project management; scorers for essays and portfolios; access to student records; access to external resources and existing data about the project; access to external agencies that provide support and validation of existing tools and tests; and access to consultants or experts from other colleges.

## Sample Program Assessment Project: General Education Assessment

The Community College of Baltimore County has been recognized as a national leader in learning-outcomes assessment, particularly in general education assessment. One common method of assessing general education outcomes is to use a standardized, commercially developed test. The benefits of standardized tests include external validity and reliability and the ability to compare results to other colleges. The weaknesses of using an externally developed instrument include the fact that the test was not designed to measure the specific goals of the college's general education program, the expense of purchasing and processing the tests, and the difficulty of encouraging students to put forth their best effort on the test (Bers, 2000).

Another popular approach to general education assessment involves instructors developing their own assessments to directly or indirectly assess learning. Examples of direct assessments include course-embedded essays, research papers, tests, group projects, fieldwork, and final examinations (Bers, 2000). Instructors can use scoring rubrics to determine the level of students' achievement on institutionally developed assignments. One benefit of locally developed assessments is that they can be designed to match an institution's culture, objectives, expectations, and level of students' performance. "They can also be organized in such a way that they permit instructors from many disciplines to participate in developing and scoring assignments, thus bringing a cross-disciplinary perspective to the assessments" (Bers, 2000, p. 184). The assessments, which can be built into regular classroom assignments, have relatively low administrative costs, although they may lack the reliability and validity of standardized tests.

Perhaps the best approach is to use a variety or combination of tools to assess a general education program. This approach, which CCBC adopted, allows for external validation and comparison via a standardized test and also allows instructors to use their own assignments and assessment instruments to measure learning in their courses. Prior to implementing the General Education Assessment Project, the General Education Review Board spent more than a year gathering assessment information from two- and four-year colleges in Maryland and across the country to review what other colleges were doing in learning-outcomes assessment in general education. The results of this research prompted the review board to design a multi-dimensional assessment plan to include feedback from three primary sources: the SIR II evaluation instrument (a standardized, nationally normed evaluation instrument); the Academic Profile (a standardized, nationally normed general education test); and common graded assignments (CGAs) in specific discipline areas, known as the GREAT (General Education Assessment Teams) Project. The purpose of the GREAT Project is to implement CGAs and accompanying scoring rubrics designed by teams of instructors in general education courses across disciplines to gather data to assess CCBC's general education program goals.

Colleges must ensure that all general education instructors are working to help students achieve all of the general education program goals. Many colleges allow instructors to select only one or two outcomes for assessment. This approach provides a very scattered and haphazard look at what is happening in general education classes. Although instructors should always maintain control over how their courses are taught, if their courses are general education courses, they should address all of the college-wide, approved outcomes that encompass skills such as critical thinking or problem-solving, oral and written communication, independent research and learning, information literacy and technology, and collaborative learning and diversity appreciation. Most colleges' general education program goals are built around these types of transferable skills. For students to truly master these higher-level learning skills, they must have the opportunity to practice and refine them in all of their general education classes. It is important, therefore, to design a comprehensive general education assessment plan that includes all courses and students within the general education program.

Because the purpose of general education assessment is to improve students' learning at the program level, it is not necessary to gather and report data for individual courses. What is important is to have an overall look at the strengths and weaknesses of the general education program. One particular course is not sufficient for students to master any of the general education program goals. It is the composite view that must be kept in mind. For example, students cannot be expected to master all of the writing skills that they will need in one English composition course; rather, they need to refine and practice these skills in each of their general education courses. It is the collective result from successfully completing many or all of the required general education courses that will provide students with the greatest benefits, most knowledge, and strongest skills. Because most general education programs include many high-enrollment courses, in most cases, assessing a sample of students will suffice.

Developing an assessment plan and collecting the data are just the beginnings of general education assessment. The most important component is to review the data and determine what curricular changes are necessary to improve students' learning. An instructors' committee composed of representatives from every major area of the college should participate in determining what changes should be recommended and how those changes should be put into place. The assessment data that have been collected at CCBC via the Academic Profile, the GREAT Project, and the SIR II have provided the instructors' committee with the direction it needed regarding the changes necessary for the general education program. At CCBC, general education program assessment is ongoing—it contributes to the continuous feedback cycle that ensures improved and expanded learning at the program level.

## Course-Level Assessment

An important step toward integrating instructors into the assessment process at the course level is to ask for volunteers. Unlike program-level assessment, where one person may be responsible for a program, course-level teaching and corresponding assessment are shared by many instructors. As instructors become more knowledgeable and comfortable with educational research methods, the culture of evidence will spread through the college. In addition, a thorough orientation meeting for all those involved in assessment projects is essential. The mandate from the Middle States Commission on Higher Education is a good starting point when introducing the concept of assessment to instructors. It provides a commonality to the problem and opens up lines of communication through the problem-solving process. But it is also important to go beyond the requirements to conduct assessment and initiate a dialogue about the intent of a learning-outcomes assessment project.

Instructors are often familiar with the summative approach to assessment as witnessed in the public schools through standardized testing, which is an acceptable approach for colleges as well. But learning college proponents believe that assessment instruments should be formative, assessing learning strengths and weakness for the purpose of making accommodations, rather than a final, summative evaluation of what students have learned. Instructors are more responsive to the formative approach because they find it meaningful, less restrictive, and relatively risk-free.

Providing instructors with options for project methodology will increase their sense of ownership. Both the pre/post-test and post-test-only design are acceptable educational tools. The choice of which one to use will be discipline-specific and based on the objectives to be measured. For example, for a health course in which students have been exposed to previous health-related courses in high school, the use of a pre/post-test design may be helpful in shaping the curriculum. In a math course in which students have been placed based on ability, a pre-test may be unnecessary, because the students presumably lack many of the skills that the course is intended to teach. But in a course such as sociology, instructors must decide whether using a pre/post-test design brings advantages to their course that are greater than the possible bias and subsequent impact on post-test results.

In addition, alternative assessment assignments such as portfolios, writing samples, and authentic assignments are legitimate options to a standardized exam. Multiple-choice exams are often used for assessment because of their objectivity and clarity. But in an English course, where the goal is to improve the writing skills of the students, assessing writing samples is a more logical approach to assessment.

As was mentioned previously, instructors must understand the need to validate their chosen instrument. Standardized exams are generally classified as to whether they are norm-referenced, with scores compared between students, or criterion-referenced, based on subject mastery. Either way they are inherently valid instruments. If instructors wish to use their own in-house designed exam, they will need to look for other means to validate the instrument. Just conversing with and sharing ideas with a team of colleagues will provide some content validity. Sending the instrument out to other experts in the field or academic discipline for review and feedback adds additional validity to the instrument.

But the choice of assessment tool and the use of external validation are meaningless without clear, measurable objectives to assess. This is a challenge to many instructors; it may not be the first item discussed at an orientation meeting, but it will be one of the first things addressed by the learning-outcomes assessment (LOA) team. Instructors may resist the concept of having common objectives for all sections of a course. They may see it as an infringement on their academic freedom. But most will agree that it is academically responsible to ensure that some common core objectives will be mastered by all students who complete the same course.

The solution is for a team of instructors to determine the common core objectives that they can all agree on and allow for instructors to individualize their courses with additional objectives of their own design. The LOA instrument can then be embedded as simply one graded assignment within the course or embedded within a larger instrument. For example, an LOA team may decide on 50 multiple-choice questions that will assess their common core objectives; then each instructor may add 50 multiple-choice questions of his or her own choosing. The instructor can then use the entire exam for a grade and only the first half of the exam for assessment.

## Support for Instructors

Instructors may respond well to support services that extend beyond an orientation meeting. Although they may be clear on their responsibilities and direction following an orientation meeting, they may find having all the procedures clearly listed and assessable very helpful. As with program-level assessments, there are five separate stages of a complete, formative assessment project. The LOA checklist should indicate detailed steps for each of those five stages.

As instructors are engaged in the first stage-designing and proposing a learning-outcomes project-they should consider picking a team leader, carefully reviewing their course objectives, determining their LOA instrument, and matching their instrument to their objectives. To ensure a good match between instrument and objectives without internal bias, instructors can use a form or a list of questions when working with external consultants. Questions should include the following:

- Do the test questions (assignment, rubric) match the course objectives?
- Are there a sufficient number of questions per topic/objective?
- Is there a balance of questions per topic/objective?
- Does the test (assignment, rubric) create or indicate any biases based on gender, ethnicity, or cultural background?
- How much value (percentage of course grade) should this test be given?

The last question can frustrate instructors because they will want to have a say as to the assessment tool's value in the total class grade. Providing a range for instructors is acceptable, but if students sense that the assessment has little or no value toward their grade and is strictly being used for research purposes, they may not give their full attention or effort toward completing the assessment.

Before moving into the second stage of the process, instructors should carefully write a proposal that thoroughly describes their project. The proposal should include which course objectives they are intending to measure, the methodology they have chosen, how they will get their instrument externally validated, a clear timeline for completing the five stages of the project, and specific needs and conditions for completing the project. Instructors engaged in a learning-outcomes assessment project may wish to have a template for developing and reporting on their proposal.

The second stage of the process will require instructors to implement their assessment design and collect and analyze data. Few instructors are in a position to collect and analyze their own data, and the institution will want to keep this process consistent. Therefore, a partnership with the institutional research (IR) department is essential. This department can offer a range of support options such as developing opti-scan forms that can allow for data to be scanned directly into the computer without time and energy lost on data entry. The IR department can also establish a template for analyzing and disaggregating the data according to the needs of the LOA team, considering subsets of such data as day or evening students, English as a second language students from native English-speaking students, students with or without prerequisites, ethnicity of students, and results in classes taught by adjunct versus full-time instructors. However, to prevent this process from being punitive, it is not recommended that data be disaggregated according to individual instructors.

Once the initial data are in, the team is now in a position to redesign the course to improve students' learning. Instructors need to identify strengths and weaknesses through item analysis, to recommend curricular interventions, and to determine whether the benefit of administrative-level interventions. Curricular interventions would include such steps as increasing collaborative learning opportunities, redirecting the focus to specific content areas, and using computer-assisted instruction. Redesigning a course to improve students' learning is all a part of stage three. As instructors try to determine the appropriate intervention, they can turn to the results of data-driven research, or they can rely on conversations and articles that focus on best practices in their field.

Stage four involves implementing course revisions and reassessing. In a sense, the first group of students to be assessed in stage two is the control group, as the data collected become the baseline. The group of students that is assessed after interventions are implemented could be viewed as the treatment group in classic experimental design. Final analysis and reporting results constitute the final stage of the process, stage five. A report should be submitted not only to the academic administrators but also to the entire college community.

It would be difficult, although not impossible, to achieve a successful learning-outcomes assessment program without some financial resources. Standardized exams command a significant fee per student and there are the costs of copying, test forms, and consultant fees. Stipends to instructor participants provide encouragement and recognize them for the time and effort that a full LOA project requires.

Shifting emphasis from supporting learning anecdotally to establishing a culture of evidence that fully documents the successful mastery of learning outcomes is at the core of learning-outcomes assessment. Instructors at CCBC have continued to assess informally and continuously even after they have concluded their formal learning-outcomes assessment projects.

## Sample Project Results: Developmental Reading

The high-impact reading project, Developmental Reading (RDNG 052), is one of the first projects at CCBC to have completed all five standard project stages: developing the instrument, collecting and analyzing the data, determining recommendations for interventions to improve learning, reassessing, and completing a final analysis and report. The program assessment tools included two standardized instruments: the Nelson-Denny

**Figure 6.1   Fall 2003 RDNG 052 Learning Outcomes Assessment Project, Pre- and Post-Test Total Score Comparisons at CCBC**

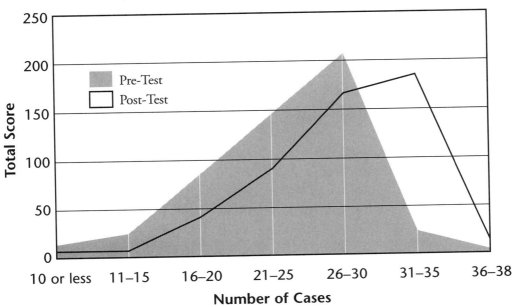

Reading Test (Forms G and H) and the Learning Attitudes and Study Skills Inventory. The primary interventions included a highly interactive lab component and challenging reading assignments.

The data analysis provided by the CCBC Planning, Research, and Evaluation Office demonstrates that the interventions have significantly improved students' reading levels, as is shown in Figure 6.1. The mean 2003 pre-score on the Nelson-Denny for all CCBC students was 24.2 (8.1 grade level equivalent), and the mean post-test score was 28 (10.1 grade level equivalent). The mean difference from pre-test to post-test was 3.7 points, which was statistically significant at the .001 level. In 75% of the cases, the post-test score was greater than the pre-test score. This resulted in an overall grade level increase of one (1.3) grade level for CCBC RDNG 052 students in fall 2003.

## References

Barr, R., & Tagg, J. (1995, November/December). From teaching to learning: A new paradigm for undergraduate education. *Change, 27*(6), 13–25.

Bers, T. (2000). Assessing the achievement of general education objectives: A college-wide approach. *The Journal of General Education, 49*(3), 182–210.

Community College of Baltimore County. (2003). *Guide for learning outcomes assessment and classroom learning assessment.* Baltimore, MD: Author. Available from http://www.ccbcmd.edu/loa/index_t.html

Linck, H. F. (2004). Creating a culture of evidence: Learning assessment at the Community College of Baltimore County. In B. Keith (Ed.), *Contexts for learning: Institutional strategies for managing curricular change through assessment.* Stillwater, OK: New Forums Press.

McPhail, I. P. (1998). *LearningFIRST: Strategic plan,* 1999–2003. Baltimore, MD: The Community College of Baltimore County.

McPhail, I. P. (1999, September). Launching LearningFIRST at the Community College of Baltimore County. *Learning Abstracts, 2*(6).

McPhail, I. P. (2003). *LearningFIRST 2.0 strategic plan: The next five years 2004–2008.* Baltimore, MD: The Community College of Baltimore County.

McPhail, I. P., Heacock, R. C., & Linck, H. F. (2001, January). LearningFIRST: Creating and leading the learning college. *Community College Journal of Research and Practice, 25*(1), 17–28.

The Middle States Commission on Higher Education. (2002). *Characteristics of excellence in higher education: Eligibility requirements and standards for accreditation.* Philadelphia, PA: Author. Retrieved April 12, 2004, from http://www.msache.org

O'Banion, T. (1997). *A learning college for the 21st century.* San Francisco: AACC and ACE/Oryx Press.

# PART 3

# Implications for Expanding the Learning Paradigm

CHAPTER 7

# The Role of Student
# Development in the
# Learning College

EVELYN CLEMENTS, ALICIA B. HARVEY-SMITH,
AND TED JAMES

Over the past decade, higher education in North American has shifted in practice from an institutional approach, directed at instruction, to a greater focus on learning outcomes. This era, "the century of the learning revolution" (Dolence, 2000, p. 2; O'Banion, 1997), is moving colleges toward environments that enhance learning, where students and learning come first and students' success becomes the primary focus of the institution (Barr & Tagg, 1995; Boggs, 1999; Eckel, Green, Hill, & Mallon, 2001; Flynn, 2000; O'Banion, 2000).

As many colleges seize the opportunity to redefine themselves based on students' learning, often absent from the dialogue is the voice of student affairs. Student affairs divisions must be active partners in the learning process and, under a learning paradigm, may need to realign programs, practices, and policies to enhance learning and document their impact (Harvey-Smith, 2003a; O'Banion, 2000). Authentic learning institutions must examine and support the involvement of student affairs leadership in institution-wide change efforts, particularly because the philosophy and values of student affairs are highly compatible with learning-centered change (Dungy, 1988).

The higher education landscape is providing new opportunities to improve and expand learning, by establishing connected systems and blended partnerships with academic affairs and other college communities (Harvey-Smith, 2003a; James, 2002). As colleges seek to understand and implement learning-centered approaches, they are discovering that student development plays an essential role in leading and sustaining organizational change.

Student development programs on community college campuses provide a complex array of support services and staff to meet the needs of diverse student populations and to contribute to students' learning and academic success. In response to the learning-college movement, student affairs professionals need to better articulate their role and continue to design functions to promote and increase learning, self-reflection, and personal development as central goals of undergraduate education.

The learning-centered college has emerged as a catalytic force that recognizes the role of student development in learning organizations. As student affairs divisions continue to examine services and to develop programs to enhance students' learning, the way practices are aligned in support of the learning is critical. O'Banion (1997) addressed the need for higher education to examine its practices and "overhaul its outdated traditional framework" (p. 1). Certainly, as community colleges continue to develop more effective learning environments, student affairs personnel need to be fully engaged.

Colleges should expect student development professionals to more effectively demonstrate what they contribute to students' learning and to assertively partner with instructors in the goal of achieving positive learning outcomes for students (Newton & Smith, 1996). To demonstrate enhanced learning, student affairs divisions need to monitor progress, measure outcomes, and evaluate the overall effectiveness of programs and services, which should promote a highly involved and interactive student body in all aspects of college life.

Colleges must use the expertise of student development personnel to guide and direct institutional resources to a comprehensive understanding of learning experiences and offer ongoing staff development opportunities to train student affairs professionals. Woodard, Love, and Komives (2000) viewed it as essential that student affairs divisions map the learning and developmental agenda for students and delineate the educational strategies identified as necessary in helping learners find real understanding and wisdom. Student development's leading role in the learning college is to develop comprehensive systems initiated from entry to exit. To aid in learning enhancement, these systems should incorporate career planning and placement programs, as well as educational planning and intervention strategies such as degree audits, early warning systems, and minimum academic progress checks (Harvey-Smith, 2002).

Within learning organizations, student affairs professionals can serve effectively in the role of campus consultants on learning, and they can take the lead in developing systematic planned change efforts and comprehensive strategies to integrate long-range planning into effective organizational change (Caple, 1996; Dungy, 1988; Harvey-Smith, 2003b; Pope, 1993). They can also become actively involved in engaging students as full partners in the learning process.

The learning-college movement confirms a transition of student affairs divisions toward assuming greater leadership in institutional change. Student development is not necessarily centralized into academic affairs units but integrated skillfully into the total college function, with clear systematic links between these areas. At the core of this new role is the measurement of learning outcomes and the documentation of improved and expanded learning. These outcomes can be measured through student retention and success rates, out-of-class involvement with resources such as student activities, tutoring, assessment of orientation experiences, advising, counseling, and deliberately creating a campus climate with increased instructor-student interactions.

## From Quantity of Learning to Quality of Learning

Student development professionals have traditionally provided service to students, from enrollment processes, financial aid, career services, and job placement to supportive activities such as activities and recreation and fitness programs. Traditionally, these programs supported learning activities in the classroom and provided ancillary programs that engaged students in the college community. In the learning college, however, the role of student development professionals shifts dramatically. Student development professionals are no longer supportive players, but now are core members of the learning team.

That shift from supportive player to learning-team member brings a new level of responsibility in student development. As a player on the learning team, student development professionals now need to ask these questions: What are we trying to accomplish? What are the learning outcomes we are trying to achieve? Are these learning outcomes ours alone, or do they fit into the mission and learning goals of the college learning community? Often, student development professionals are so busy helping students that they rarely have the time to reflect on their role in the learning process.

Learning goals and outcomes are actually not a new concept in student development. The social and emotional growth of students, their development as citizens, their self-awareness, and their increased understanding of their own goals and aspirations are all part of the traditional work of student development. The difference is that the learning-college model allows these goals to become part of the learning process for all students.

In the traditional college model, it is accepted that learning occurs throughout a student's experience on campus: in social interactions, student activities, and other experiences the students may have outside the classroom. However, the only measurement of learning that is formally recognized in the traditional college model is the academic, classroom experience evaluated by grades and listed on the college transcript. The learning college changes the notion that student learning occurs only in the classroom. In the learning college, the evaluation of student learning shifts from classroom grades to documented learning outcomes in a variety of settings, from mentoring with a student development professional to completing a series of experiences designed to fulfill a predetermined learning goal.

The task of measuring these learning outcomes goes beyond the standard academic transcript to a student portfolio that includes documentation of the student's learning outcomes and competencies. Student development professionals, then, can play an active role, both as facilitators assisting students to determine their learning goals and outcomes and as true players in the learning team that provides learning experiences and determines learning outcomes. The portfolio process provides credible documentation of learning beyond the classroom experience and moves the student development professional from playing an ancillary role to being a key member of the learning team.

## From Quantity to Quality Assessment

Student development professionals have an increased level of responsibility if they become active members of the learning team. In addition to determining the learning outcomes as a part of the learning team, they must be able to measure these outcomes, and measurement often has been a challenge in student development. Student development is easier to measure by quantity; for example, a career counselor had 600 student appointments, gave 25 class presentations, and conducted 50 workshops. A more difficult assessment is whether that career counselor had an effect on the learning outcomes of the students who participated in the career services. Do the students who participated in those career services have a better understanding of their career and life goals? Are they less likely to change majors than are students who have not used career services? These are the critical questions that address learning outcomes and move the measurement of career services from outcomes by quantity to outcomes by quality.

Data collection in student development must move beyond counting numbers (the counselor had X number of appointments) to measurement that is based on clear learning objectives. Such data collection is essential for student development professionals if they are to become active players in the learning-college movement, although it is not easy and requires a new way of looking at student development. The data collection may focus on learning outcomes in a particular activity such as the impact of career counseling on students' career awareness or the effect that students' participation in leadership activities has had on leadership skills. It also may focus on a broader impact across the college, including the effect specific student service interventions have had on student course completion, retention rates, or grade point averages (GPAs).

At Middlesex Community College in Massachusetts, for example, student development professionals work directly with instructors in a number of classrooms. They may give class presentations on related topics, meet with students outside class, or assist instructors in classroom activities. This program, called the Collaborative Intervention Team program, has been in place for more than 5 years. Is it successful? Careful measurement using control groups and examining course completion rates, retention, and GPAs, shows that it is. Although the process of data collection is time-consuming, the results provide specific information about the value of a program and its impact on learning (National Association of Student Personnel Administrators [NASPA], 2003).

Freshman seminar courses, now used in many community colleges nationwide, are another ideal vehicle for such research. These courses often meet specific learning outcomes and can be measured in terms of student growth in meeting predetermined course objectives. On a broader scale, students' participation in freshman seminar courses often increases retention rates and GPAs as students learn critical skills necessary for success.

## From Separation to Integration

In the past, student development services have been routinely relegated to a secondary role. Almost everywhere, colleges primarily value instructors and the instructional role. Instruction earns tuition revenue, generates full-time equivalent production, and awards credit leading to credentials. Student development services, in contrast, usually do not produce revenue, are labor intensive, and support rather than provide the core curriculum. Although the role of student development services in facilitating intake and students' success is not altogether ignored-the services are clearly needed to help meet the access missions of community colleges-student development professionals know they are the Cinderellas of academia whose work is less valued (James, 2002) or the Rodney Dangerfields who "get no respect" (Hudgins, 2002).

However, the shift toward the learning college is eroding this devaluation and bringing student development services into a more central role. First, the skills traditionally possessed by student development professionals—being client-friendly, goal-focused, and individualized—are becoming more critical to the success of colleges. Second, student development professionals work in more flexible, less role-bound organizational units that are easier to realign. Third, student development has embraced technology to deliver information and interactivity with less time-bound or place-bound media. But, perhaps most important, student development theory and practice is grounded in focusing on the needs of the whole learner rather than in compartmentalizing a program or discipline.

Moreover, in the learning college, the differences between services and instruction are blurring, with profound implications for the separation between academic and student affairs. Content is becoming uncoupled from delivery as educational technology allows learners to access information and curriculum electronically from anywhere in the world. As the role of instructor shifts from content presenter to learning mentor or facilitator, instructors will need to use many of the skills and strategies traditionally found in student development divisions. As performance indicators and learning outcomes documentation infiltrate student development areas, the professionals working in these areas will need to develop some formal assessment procedures for their services and activities.

The colleges of the future are likely to become "learning support centers which are skilled in supporting learners who get information from a variety of sources" (Doucette, 1998). In the process, the traditional roles of those working within colleges must converge. The inescapable conclusion is that to create a learner-centered campus, these two groups—instructors and student affairs staff—must work closely together to arrange students' in-class and out-of-class experiments, so that they are consistent with the research on college student development and effective educational practices (Kuh & Hinkle, 2002).

Calls for a common partnership between instructors and student affairs are not new. Twenty years ago or more, observers lamented the separation of roles and the resulting fragmentation of effort (Caple, 1996). Throughout the past decade, student affairs leaders have explored and recommended ways in which partnerships and collaboration can grow (AAHE, ACPA, & NASPA, 1998; ACPA, 1994; ACPA & NASPA, 1997), and handbooks on leadership development in higher education regularly include chapters on the need to bridge organizational gaps (Barr, Desler, & Associates, 2000; Diamond, 2002).

Unfortunately, previous efforts have often been unsuccessful, partly because institutional support has been low and innovations became unsustainable when energies or resources dwindled (Tagg, 2003). But previous attempts have occurred mainly within a paradigm that still divides service functions from instructional ones and houses them in separate organizational units (Engstrom & Tinto, 2000). Adopting a learning college approach, however, not only provides a blueprint for developing better partnerships but also emphasizes how they are achieved through the common mission of being learning-focused rather than through the separate roles of being instruction-focused and support-focused. Barr called this being driven by "a commitment to a mission or purpose rather than [to] maintain a role identity" (1998, p. 23).

If the key lies in an integrated approach, what are some features of this approach and how are they linked to the characteristics of the learning college? The following examples are drawn from exemplary practices and programs of community colleges recently showcased in publications from the National Council on Student Development (NCSD, 2000; NCSD, 2002); the National Association of Student Personnel Administrators (NASPA, 2003); and the Canadian Association of College and University Student Services (CACUSS).

### Integrated Intake

The integrated approach begins at home. Student development services need to desegregate more of their functions and unify around a common goal. Too often, learners complain of getting the run-around, being shunted from one office to another across campus as they seek to complete admission processes, apply for financial aid, meet with academic advisors, take assessment tests, and clarify career goals with counselors (James, 1999). Many colleges have responded by developing one-stop shops that integrate student development functions into a single location.

Central Florida Community College developed three initiatives to integrate services (NCSD, 2000). First, a new Enrollment Services Center linked the departments of counseling, admissions, records, and financial aid and cross-trained all employees to perform a variety of common services. Second, a team of peer educators, paid as part-time employees, was selected and trained to deliver to students a comprehensive series of workshops to help them navigate the intake process. Third, a SALT team (an acronym for skills, assessment, learning, and testing) was trained to perform any role in the Learning Support Center and the Academic and Career Assessment Center. These changes resulted in reduced waiting time for students trying to access information and assistance and increased self-reliance of students.

Similarly, orientation to college life or academic expectations is often left entirely to student development personnel—especially at commuter colleges with no student residences—or is fragmented among academic departments. In response, many colleges have actively sought the integration of instructors and student development to redesign their orientation activities. For instance, Northern Essex Community College in Massachusetts grouped together several formerly sporadic approaches into a comprehensive orientation program (NCSD, 2002). The new orientation program was really a four-stage procedure that every student encountered:

1. pre-enrollment workshop
2. one-stop registration process
3. welcome week activities
4. student success seminars

This orientation procedure was developed through deliberate consultation with departments across the college to identify ways to help students make smoother transitions to college through direct connection with a broad cross section of college personnel, a factor often identified as crucial for student retention.

### Integrated Programming

Many student support functions ordinarily offered in workshop formats or other noncredit activities can be integrated into the mainstream of college credit programming. Students success seminars, for example, rather than being offered by learning counselors through a separate series of seminars, are often best taught within a program format where they can be tailored to meet specific needs of students, instructors' expectations, and discipline cultures. Where students earn college credit, these courses can gain additional credibility in the eyes of students and instructors.

This occurred at Moraine Valley Community College in Illinois where a one-semester hour course, College: Changes, Challenges, Choices (COL 101) was developed by a cross-college group of instructors and administrators who teach the course each semester. These instructors are drawn from across the college and are trained in the same pedagogy. During the first couple of years, more than 100 instructors and administrators have taught the course one or more times, and the college has struggled to offer enough sections of the course to meet the demand from incoming students.

Interdisciplinary approaches toward co-curricular teaching are another way in which integration can occur in educational programming within colleges. Typically, these approaches involve some form of team teaching where student development professionals act as guest lecturers in classes, but more successful strategies aim to blend the service and instructional roles in more creative and complex ways. Such a blending of roles can be seen in the partnership between the speech department and career development center at the Community College of Baltimore County in (NCSD, 2002). On the Essex campus, these departments developed an interdisciplinary learning experience that helped students with career planning as well as with developing a research speech for Fundamentals of Communication (SPCM 101). The joint enterprise arose from a mutual need to make previous activities more relevant and interesting to students. The initiative was structured around seven elements:

1. classroom lecture by career development
2. occupational assessment of students
3. career library visit
4. an individualized report profiling occupational interests
5. supervised research
6. completion of an informational interview
7. completion of the research speech.

Feedback from participants was overwhelmingly positive, with 95% stating they had acquired knowledge that was crucial to assisting their decision about a career.

### Integrated Resources

Other ways of integrating services and instruction may involve creating new types of learning delivery through newly created resources. These resources can assume various forms, often taking advantage of emerging educational technology to deliver information or services online. One innovative approach taken by Humber College Institute of Technology and Advanced Learning in Toronto, Canada, seeks to enhance students' success by soliciting information from new students about their needs and then identifying areas within the college that can serve these needs.

Called the Freshman Integrated Tracking System (FITS), this software program compares students' records data and self-reported questionnaire data. New students receive a Partners in Education report outlining which student services they may need and how to access them. The report is based on information collected at the students' first class. A second report based on student responses to a second survey administered around the midterm point helps to highlight the new students' experiences to date in their first semester and whether they have made use of services available. These FITS reports act as early warning devices for instructors and student development professionals and help them to identify at-risk students. Rather than waiting for students to access services by themselves, these professionals can consult FITS reports and can make contact with students whose data match the profile of students needing help. FITS provides academic affairs and student affairs professionals with common information about their students and a common language to facilitate dialogue.

Not all examples of integrated resources are electronically based. Some rely on other types of collaborations. For instance, the Learning Centre at Douglas College in British Columbia was deliberately established by the student development unit in collaboration with instructors. Aiming to provide tutoring services to students in need of additional learning support outside of class, the Learning Centre staff appreciated from the outset the need to ensure instructional support. The center staff created an instructor's referral form so that not only did students inform their instructors that they were seeking help, but also instructors were able to give advice on what help would be suitable.

The Learning Centre then employed peer tutors who were trained to provide appropriate help and not do the work for the students. Within this structured environment, students received timely and valuable learning support that helped them achieve grades higher than they would have otherwise received. The framework did not compromise the integrity of instruction. Over time, instructors throughout the college became the most vociferous supporters of the work of the Centre when budgets threatened its continued existence.

Such examples illuminate the path forward. As community colleges move to become learning-centered, they face challenges to trying to integrate the service and instructional sides of their operation. But these examples highlight some of the innovative and adventurous approaches that are possible, especially when academic and student affairs focus on a common role and purpose.

## From Delivering to Developing

The learning-college paradigm provides a catalyst for change and innovation and a mechanism by which student development practitioners can be proactive in developing a college climate that supports learning. As student development practice shifts from the delivery of services to the development of systems that address students' learning and success from orientation until graduation or goal completion, student affairs divisions can be change agents, transforming institutional cultures into ones that are more open and responsive to learning. The need to create an empowerment culture is particularly important as institutions address the needs of nontraditional learners (McPhail & McPhail, 1999). What follows is a road map for change and the creation of an open organizational culture used by two exemplary colleges undergoing learning-centered transformation as revealed through a recent study (Harvey-Smith, 2003a).

### *Two Examples and a Blueprint for Transformation*

Southeast Community College (SCC) and North Community College (NCC), pseudonyms for actual institutions, are the largest and fastest-growing colleges in their regions and are guided by clearly defined institutional change strategies. SCC used a systems-design approach to strategic ' and NCC used an institutional-effectiveness model as the foundation of its strategic initiatives. Both institutions experienced dissatisfaction with the performance of specific student populations. This dissatisfaction provided the "urgency" (Kotter, 1996, p. 5) that led each college to begin the process of self-evaluation to examine programs and services and to explore research and conceptual models. As a result, each college engaged in extensive discussion about change and how to become more learning-centered with the goal of improving student performance and success.

The changes evolved over several years and were precipitated by expansive discussions with stakeholders about transformation and learning. From these initial discussions and research the colleges established broad-based teams, integrated change strategies and strategic planning, and propelled change efforts more extensively into the organization with a focus on students' success, improved collaboration, and enhanced learning. Neither college attempted to fully implement the learning paradigm without first identifying specific areas of concern and undertaking a comprehensive study of preexisting systems, structures, programs, and processes. They also evaluated intended outcomes and their impact on learning. These actions allowed for increased support from institutional stakeholders and an opportunity to properly fit the paradigm to the environment. The change process was forged through collaboration between student affairs divisions and other units of the college, with the student affairs divisions taking the lead in initiating and adopting learning-centered change.

Both institutional cultures allowed for risk taking, and both encouraged and supported innovation. Before arriving at their current student development delivery systems, each institution assessed its readiness for change and strategically reallocated, reorganized, or functionally realigned operations to support learning outcomes. A senior student affairs administrator captured the feeling of readiness for change that could be applied across sites when he said, "It was the right time for change. Everything came together. Not moving forward was not an option. The stage was set for transformation."

### *Processes of Change*

The processes of adoption and change within these student affairs divisions were initiated after a period of individual and collective learning that provided a framework for further assessing the divisions' potential and readiness for change (Harvey-Smith, 2004). Throughout this period of acquisition of new knowledge, the colleges conducted a literature review to heighten awareness of what it means to be a learning college, evaluated existing models, and explored meaningful ways to collaborate. During this period, the foundation was laid for transformational change in student affairs. Comprehensive student support delivery systems were designed to generate improved student performance and learning.

One college adjusted its mixed-matrix organizational structure and realigned all student affairs functions under one administrator. Similarly, the other implemented a new reporting system and functionally realigned outreach and retention units under one administrator. Both institutions sought to shift the work of student development away from special projects and elevate it as a core component of strategic planning. In addition, administrative structures supported change by recognizing student affairs leadership and by providing the necessary human and fiscal resources.

### Influences on Change

The elements of leadership, communication, institutional support, organizational culture, and institutionalization were identified in the literature as having most influenced the complex process of adopting the learning paradigm into student development practice.

**Leadership.** Leadership is a central element in intentional and successful organizational change; the characteristics and qualities of leaders are vital to bringing about effective transformations. The institution encouraged leadership, and it emerged from various levels of the college, particularly the student affairs divisions. This appreciation of diverse leadership was seen within the organization as essential in providing a foundation for implementing change and accelerating the change process.

These college leaders played consistent roles in enabling positive change. For example, both the president at SCC and the provost at NCC determined it was vital to approach the change process holistically and to plan for the integration of the change that emerged. At SCC, the president emphasized the importance of having a structure that allowed the student affairs division to have an equal voice at the table. In fact, leadership for all of student affairs at this multi-campus college was placed under the senior student affairs officer, who also had the responsibility of co-leading the institution's learning-centered initiative.

**Communication.** Communication is vital to initiating and sustaining change. Both colleges created and aggressively maintained a continuous system of communication and feedback, arriving at a mutual understanding about the change process in student affairs, which involved high levels of openness and responsiveness. SCC established multiple feedback opportunities for stakeholders, both within and outside the student affairs division.

The most frequent feedback mechanisms used were cross-functional learning dialogues, which provided the opportunity for college communities to participate in committees, roundtables, and workshops and to solicit feedback through surveys. Both colleges allowed the input and feedback received to shape the change process. SCC used concentric circles in the student affairs division to communicate the change process to the broader college community and allowed for increased numbers of stakeholders to acquire knowledge regarding change. SCC also allowed for greater college-wide support of the process and initiatives that emerged from the student development area, ultimately resulting in a sizeable budget allocation to fund a total student affairs redesign. NCC used process mapping to communicate the need for change in student affairs; SCC used multiple layers of communication and influenced many from outside student affairs to become involved in and to support the change process.

**Institutional support.** The student affairs divisions described the support that was received from the college as being critical to their success in the change process. This support was demonstrated through measures such as providing the financial and human capital to sponsor staff development training, shifts in governance and administrative structures to facilitate change, and visibly valuing the voice of student affairs by placing leadership for change within the division. Support initially provided in the form of grants for new initiatives evolved to refocus and move this work from the edge to the center of the colleges' missions and strategic planning efforts. At SCC, traditional grant work in student affairs was integrated into practice and became the impetus for developing core competencies and a developmental advising model. An SCC student affairs administrator had this to say about grant integration:

> The grants we sought were always to enhance the total college and were not isolated. We received tremendous institutional support because the college in general could see how it would benefit and how the learning in student affairs was to be shared.

Efforts to innovate within the student affairs division were also supported by introducing changes in structure, integrating initiatives, evaluating outcomes, and hiring personnel who supported the paradigm shift.

**Institutional culture.** Institutional culture is critical in aiding community members to understand changes taking place. Much as Schein (1992) posited, the cultures at both SCC and NCC influenced how community members received the change and how experiences were viewed and evaluated. The complexity of organizational culture is a crucial element that wields tremendous influence on successful change. As organizations continue to evolve, there will continue to be challenges to be overcome when community members periodically revert to old mental models based on history and tradition. SCC's student affairs division led a cultural transformation that created a synergy in response to the institutional inertia that had been part of the traditional architecture. The new culture eagerly developed practices to support the division's new learning goals.

Both institutions readily took risks and applied innovative approaches, abandoning excuses as to why an approach could not be tried. Over time, the development of trust with larger numbers of stakeholders enabled the change process to take hold and reduced the level of resistance to change. As a further result, greater integration of innovation became possible as acceptance grew. This change in culture aided in breaking down what was called faculty/administration suspicion. A senior instructor at SCC made this observation: "Our culture now recognizes and supports the good work emerging from student affairs. The differences in style and approach are readily accepted and appreciated."

The results underscored the importance of including a seventh learning-college principle: Create and nurture an organizational culture that is open and responsive to change and learning. These student affairs divisions assertively worked to change institutional environments both inside and outside of the classroom to embrace and value the learning of all the organization's members.

**Institutionalization.** Colleges must institutionalize change in order to sustain it. Each college expected that new student affairs initiatives would be integrated into the life of the college and took steps to build coalitions in support of change integration. Specifically, changes were fused into core competencies, strategic planning, and the ongoing processes and practices in student affairs.

A common strategy was to plan for the integration of initiatives as innovative ideas were introduced and proven to be successful. At SCC, the student affairs division successfully institutionalized major changes by using a comprehensive advising system, undertaking significant collaborations with academic affairs, and redesigning all business systems. Institutionalization of change was rapid because of the college's earnest commitment to transform practice to improve learning. A senior instructor shared these feelings: "The initiatives that emerged from student affairs were designed with the end in mind, and the end was institutionalization. That's what made change worth it. As a principle-based learning-centered organization, this is expected." A student affairs staff member described the innovative processes that were integrated into practice at NCC as a "significant part of a natural evolution in student affairs that attempts to respond to the many needs students have and is a means of supporting their learning."

The reactions to change at the two colleges resulted in greater levels of collaboration with academic affairs and other stakeholders, higher levels of trust, and increased and open dialogues and systems that empowered change. Mechanisms were developed to reward risk taking, and internal and external support networks were established to provide ongoing feedback. These new processes led to transformed student affairs practice and the development of comprehensive data systems that allowed for the collecting and analysis of quantitative and qualitative data. Process mapping and clarifying new procedures aided in transforming practice more rapidly and building stakeholders' support. Parallel data systems increased technology and expanded systems of collaboration, communication, and division redesign to accelerate transformation. Expanding the student affairs team to include instructors and others external to the division—and rigorously assessing the division's impact on learning and general outcomes—will aid successful change, specifically when it is approached from a student and an institutional perspective.

The real learning transformation began as each institution let go of old mental models and approaches. This ending of traditional approaches to learning allowed for real change and transformation to occur, as Bridges (1991) indicated: "The starting point for transition is not the outcome but the ending that you will have to make to leave the old situation behind" (p. 4). Further examples of the change in student affairs practices and processes at the two colleges to successfully align with learning=college principles are demonstrated in the Cross Case Dynamics Matrix, shown in Table 7.1. The matrix displays the specific structural, procedural, and cultural shifts that took place at the colleges participating in Harvey-Smith's (2003a) study.

Research indicates that change takes on many forms. Miles and Huberman (1994) identified three aspects of change: structural, procedural, and cultural. Using Miles and Huberman's Cross Case Dynamics Matrix, Harvey-Smith (2003a) illustrated how the two colleges' student affairs divisions adopted learning-college principles in their student affairs division.

## Implementing Learning-College Principles in Student Affairs

Both colleges made significant progress in addressing the first core principle of creating substantive change in learners. They achieved this progress through a major redesign effort that allowed the student affairs division to focus more fully on learning outcomes and developing and implementing a comprehensive retention system that provided the catalyst for change. The institutional environments were considered learning communities, where all members of the community were learning and transforming together.

The colleges made significant attempts to engage learners as full partners in the learning process, in response to the second principle. Strategies included instituting a developmental advising model, which engages students in the planning process and incorporates self-sufficiency as a core element, and establishing partnerships with students that involved increased dialogue and interaction through orientations and learning communities.

Each college created and offered a variety of learning options within the student affairs divisions. These included expanded presentations, student success courses, dual enrollment, pre-college programs, distance learning, exploration of learning styles, services for students with disabilities, and weekend and summer programs. Expanded co-curricular programming efforts, expanded learning options for high-risk students, and interactive learning camps were also provided.

Assisting learners in forming and participating in collaborative learning activities took the form of leadership experiences in co-curricular programs and learning

## Table 7.1  Alignment of Practices With Learning College Principles

| Principle | College | Realignment | Type of Change |
|---|---|---|---|
| 1. Create substantive change in learner | SCC | Major redesign to focus on outcomes | S, P |
| | NCC | Implementation of comprehensive retention system | S, P |
| 2. Engage learners as full partners | SCC | Developmental advising model—with goal of self-sufficiency | S, P, C |
| | NCC | Increased dialogue and interactions through orientations and learning communities | P, C |
| 3. Create and offer a variety of learning options | SCC | Expanded presentations, student success courses, dual enrollment, pre-college programs, distance learning, weekend and summer programs | P, C |
| | NCC | Expanded co-curricular programs, expanded options for high-risk students, learning camps | P |
| 4. Assist learners in forming and participating in collaborative learning activities | SCC | Student life co-curricular programming, learning communities, internships, service learning, varied course offerings, chat rooms | P |
| | NCC | Student life co-curricular programming, learning communities, collaborative approach embedded throughout programs and services | P, C |
| 5. Define roles in response to needs of learners | SCC | Reexamination of role culminating in redesign; transitioned from independent role to integrated role | S, P, C |
| | NCC | Reexamination of role culminating in realignment; transitioned from independent role to integrated role | S, P, C |

## Table 7.1   Alignment of Practices With Learning College Principles (cont'd)

| Principle | College | Realignment | Type of Change |
|---|---|---|---|
| 6. Document improved and expanded learning | SCC | Building culture of evidence through cyber-portfolios, goal team reports, internal and external assessments, placement, success, retention rates | P, C |
| | NCC | Building culture of evidence through internal and external assessments, placement, success, retention rates | P, C |

*Note.* S = structural change; P = procedural change; C = cultural change. Adapted from Harvey-Smith (2003a).

communities, as well as internship opportunities, varied course offerings, and service learning opportunities. These divisions incorporated technology at a significant level to provide chat rooms and other opportunities for students to exchange information to enhance learning. Collaborative learning activities were strategically embedded within all programs and services.

The study revealed an emerging role for student affairs within learning organizations. The role was derived from an in-depth examination of student affairs, related systems, and business practices as they related to the outcomes of expanding and measuring learning. The result at both colleges was a redesign or a realignment of the student affairs structure. Before the change process, the role of student affairs was more traditional, with the division operating independently of the other institutional units. After the change, the role became highly integrated into total college functioning with clearer ties to the academic and instructional areas. The role and function of student affairs was described as connecting students with the appropriate supports to achieve self-sufficiency and enhanced learning and was described as critical in leading the learning transformation at both institutions.

The sixth learning-college principle focused on the student affairs divisions' ability to document improved and expanded learning in order to build a culture of evidence. This principle was demonstrated by documenting outcomes through the use of instruments such as cyber portfolios and student success course portfolios to assess student learning, goal team reports, and other internal and external assessment and evaluation instruments.

The journeys undertaken by these exemplary institutions are instructional and have broader implications beyond the work of student affairs. The lessons learned provide a blueprint for transformation for others wishing to take a leading role in the learning college through improved and expanded learning, quality program development and service delivery, and the effective integration of efforts for sustainability.

## References

American Association for Higher Education, American College Personnel Association, & National Association of Student Personnel Administrators (AAHE, ACPA, & NASPA). (1998). *Powerful partnerships: A shared responsibility for learning.* Washington, DC: Author.

American College Personnel Association (ACPA). (1994). *The student learning imperative: Implications for student affairs.* Washington, DC: Author.

American College Personnel Association & National Association of Student Personnel Administrators (ACPA & NASPA). (1997). *Defining principles of good practice for student affairs.* Washington, DC: Author.

Barr, M. J., Desler, M. K., & Associates (2000). *The handbook of student affairs administration* (2nd ed.). San Francisco: Jossey-Bass.

Barr, R. (1998). Obstacles to implementing the learning paradigm: What it takes to overcome them. *About Campus, 2*(3), 18–25.

Barr, R. B., & Tagg, J. (1995). From teaching to learning: A new paradigm for undergraduate education. *Change, 27*(6), 13–25.

Boggs, G. (1999). What the learning paradigm means for faculty. *Learning Abstracts, 2*(4). Available from http://www.league.org/publication/abstracts/learning/lelabs9906.html

Bridges, W. (1991). *Managing transitions: Making the most of change.* Cambridge, MA: Perseus Books.

Caple, R. B. (1996). Student affairs professionals as learning consultants. In S. C. Ender, F. B. Newton, & R. B. Caple (Eds.), *Contributing to learning: The role of student affairs* (pp. 33–43). (New Directions for Student Services: No. 75) San Francisco: Jossey-Bass.

Caple, R. B. (1996). The learning debate: A historical perspective. *Journal of College Student Development, 37*(2), 193–202.

Diamond, R. M. (Ed.). (2002). *Field guide to academic leadership.* San Francisco: Jossey-Bass.

Dolence, M. G. (2000). *Strategic planning for enrollment growth.* Presentation at Sinclair Community College, Dayton, OH.

Dungy, G. (1988). Thanks, we needed this. *Journal of College Student Development, 29,* 11–13.

Eckel, P., Green, M., Hill, B, & Mallon, W. (2001). *On change III: Taking charge of change: A primer for colleges and universities.* Washington, DC: American Council on Education.

Engstrom, C. M., & Tinto, T. (2000). Developing partnerships with academic affairs to enhance student learning. In M. J. Barr, M. K. Dresler, & Associates (Eds.), *The handbook of student affairs administration* (2nd ed., pp. 425–452). San Francisco: Jossey-Bass.

Flynn, W. J. (2000). *The search for the learning-centered college* (New Expeditions Issues Paper No. 9: Charting the Second Century of Community Colleges). Washington, DC: American Association of Community Colleges.

Harvey-Smith, A. B. (2002, November). An examination of the retention literature and application in student success. In *Promoting inclusion: Research–based strategies for access & equity* (pp. 14–26). Washington, DC: Community College Press.

Harvey-Smith, A. B. (2003a). *The adoption of the learning paradigm in student affairs divisions in Vanguard community colleges.* Unpublished doctoral dissertation, University of Maryland, College Park.

Harvey-Smith, A. B. (2003b). A framework for transforming learning organizations: Proposing a new learning college principle. *Learning Abstracts, 6*(7). Available from http://www.league.org/publication/abstracts/learning/lelabs0307.htm

Harvey-Smith. A. B. (2004). Transforming the first-year experience using the learning paradigm. In J. Henscheid (Ed), *The integrative role of first-year seminars in learning communities.* Columbia, SC: University of South Carolina Press.

Hudgins, J. (2002). The role of student development services in the new millennium. *NASPA2002,* 1–6.

James, T. (1999). *Learner support and success: Determining the educational support needs for learners into the 21st century.* Report prepared for the British Columbia Senior Educational Officers Committee and Senior Instructional Officers Committee.

James, T. (2002, April). *No longer Cinderella: The future of student development services.* Paper presented at the annual meeting of the American Association of Community Colleges, Seattle, WA.

Kotter, J. P. (1996). *Leading change.* Boston: Harvard Business School Press.

Kuh, G. D., & Hinkle, S. E. (2002). Enhancing student learning through collaboration between academic affairs and student affairs. In R. M. Diamond (Ed.), *Field guide to academic leadership* (pp. 311–327). San Francisco: Jossey-Bass.

McPhail, I. P., & McPhail, C. J. (1999). Transforming classroom practice for African-American learners: Implications for the learning paradigm. In *Removing vestiges: Research–based strategies to promote inclusion.* Washington, DC: Community College Press.

Miles, M. B., & Huberman, A. M. (1994). *Qualitative data analyses: An expanded sourcebook* (2nd ed.). Thousand Oaks, CA: Sage.

National Association of Student Personnel Administrators (NASPA). (2003). Bridges to student success. In G. J. Dungy & E. Clements (Eds.), *NASPA and NCSD 2003 Exemplary Programs: Special Community College Edition.* Washington, DC: Author.

National Council on Student Development (NCSD). (2000). Revolutionizing student development: New waves for student development professionals. In A. M. James & T. James (Eds.), *Summary report of the second annual conference of the National Council on Student Development.* Washington, DC: Author.

National Council on Student Development (NCSD). (2002, October). New directions in student development. In E. Clements & C. Dukes (Eds.), *Summary report of the fourth annual conference of the National Council on Student Development.* Washington, DC: Author.

Newton, F. B., & Smith, J. H. (1996). Principles and strategies for enhancing student learning. In S. C. Ender, F. B. Newton, & R. B. Caple (Eds.), *Contributing to learning: The role of student affairs* (New Directions for Student Services: No. 75, 19–32). San Francisco: Jossey-Bass.

O'Banion, T. (1997). *A learning college for the 21st century.* San Francisco: AACC and ACE/Oryx Press.

O'Banion, T. (2000). An inventory for learning-centered colleges. *Community College Journal, 71*(1), 114.

Pope, R. L. (1993). Multi-cultural organization development in student affairs. *Journal of College Student Development, 34,* 201–205.

Schein, E. H. (1992). *Organizational culture in leadership.* San Francisco: Jossey-Bass.

Tagg, J. (2003). *The learning paradigm college.* Bolton, MA: Anker Publishing.

Woodard, D. B., Love, P., Jr., & Komives, S. (2000). Learning and development. In D. B. Woodard, P. Love, Jr., & S. Komives (Eds.), *Leadership and management issues for a new century* (New Directions for Student Services: No. 92, pp. 49–60). San Francisco: Jossey-Bass.

CHAPTER 8

# Technology in the
# Learning College

MARK DAVID MILLIRON AND MARY PRENTICE

Since the 1997 publication of O'Banion's *A Learning College for the 21st Century,* educators and policymakers have been grappling with how to recognize and create a learning college. Some colleges took immediate steps to assess the things they were doing well and the policies, practices, and procedures that were blocking improved and expanded learning. Others were unconvinced. Often, they reacted to nonsensical arguments about teaching versus learning-centered education labeled red herrings by O'Banion by claiming that they had been placing students' learning first all along. And they were right!

What many of these indignant educators had not realized, however, is that the idea of learning-centered education goes well beyond individual classrooms. A learning college is willing to ask hard questions about every aspect of its operations. Employees in student services, buildings and grounds, maintenance, food services, technology, and finance need to be included when examining the learning-friendly quotient in operations. O'Banion was calling for not only a learning-centered revolution in the classroom but also a college-wide revolution in which every member of the college community participates.

In this spirit, it made perfect sense to begin asking hard questions about technology use. Technology has become an increasingly important aspect of community college education. As O'Banion pointed out, participants in the 1995 Higher Education Roundtable Program mentioned technology frequently as one of the most important issues on their campuses (as cited in O'Banion, 1997, p. 65). Certainly the rate at which colleges are adopting technology bears this out (Green, 2003). Once the realm of early innovation adopters, technology is now used by instructors who, although lacking in technological expertise, nevertheless see what other instructors are doing in and out of the classroom and want to be a part of it.

And when technology is viewed through the learning-college lens, who could blame instructors for wanting to take part in the revolution? Technology is particularly suited to enhancing learning. For example, O'Banion has argued that "the learning college places learning first and provides educational experiences for students anyway, anyplace, anytime" (O'Banion, 1997, p. 70). Technology allows colleges to adopt this type of flexibility. Moreover, "Technology is a time- and place-free medium . . . " (p. 71) so that students who are two counties, two states, or two nations away from a community college can take a class via the Internet when it is convenient for them. Even better, the instruction can be individualized to meet different learning styles and different mastery levels through computer-assisted instruction and computerized placement testing. In addition, "technology can provide access to great amounts of information including the most recently discovered knowledge" (p. 74).

Technology use in the learning college eases the pressure on the instructor to know everything in fields that are exploding with new information. Through the Internet, the information is now available to everyone, and instructors are now liberated to better facilitate learning. If a learning-college goal is to develop "independent, lifelong learners" (O'Banion, 1997, p. 51), then training students to be technologically literate while developing their information literacy is essential to the mission of these colleges (Milliron & Miles, 2000). It is happening in colleges across the nation.

In this chapter we examine the role of technology tools play, anytime, anyplace, in the access, affordability, and outreach of learning colleges. Some of the work that we will discuss comes from outside projects and alliances that are helping colleges to use technology to accomplish learning-focused goals, whereas other work comes directly from the community colleges. In all situations, however, it is the college that has assessed the cultural and climatic readiness of the campus to make sure that changes are coming from within and are not being imposed by others. Some colleges are in an evolutionary process, whereas others are challenging traditional practices. All are deeply committed to learning. We begin by taking a big picture look at more broad initiatives and will then turn to a closer examination of specific institutions. We begin by looking at the best practices of some large projects and national organizations that could well inform those interested in thoughtful, effective, learning-centered technology use.

## The Program in Course Redesign

The Program in Course Redesign, supported by a grant from The Pew Charitable Trusts (Twigg, 2003, 2004) was created in 1999. Its goal was to demonstrate how colleges could use information technology to address the significant academic problems experienced by first-year students. Each of the 30 participating two-year and four-year institutions chose large-enrollment introductory courses to redesign because of the effect of their size on retention and success rates. Evaluators at each college are conducting a rigorous assessment of these classes, comparing the redesigned courses' outcomes with the outcomes of courses with the same content but delivered in a traditional (predesign) format. Of the 30 projects, 22 have shown statistically significant increases in students' learning, and the remaining 8 projects have shown learning equivalent to that achieved in traditional formats. Additionally, 22 of the 24 projects that measured retention have reported a decrease in drop-failure-withdrawal (DWF) rates ranging from 10% to 20%.

What seems to underlie the success of the 30 different projects are six overarching characteristics of course redesign (Twigg, 2004).

1. The whole course (not just a single class or section) is the target of the redesign.

2. All of the redesign projects make the teaching–learning venture more student centered. For example, lectures are replaced with a variety of learning resources that move students into an active learning orientation. Students learn by doing, not by listening to someone talk about the subject.

3. Instructional software and Web-based learning resources become important in engaging students in course content. Computer-assisted learning comes into its own as a course redesign technique providing tutorials, exercises, and low-stakes quizzes for feedback and reinforcement of course content.

4. The redesigned courses provide greater flexibility in how students engage with the course. Pacing and progress are organized around the mastery of specific learning objectives instead of around specific class meetings.

5. Students receive help from an expanded support system. Many of the projects replace lecture time with face-to-face or online individual and small-group activities. Instructors, teaching assistants, or peer tutors are available in the labs or online so that students have one-on-one assistance.

6. Because various kinds of instructional personnel make up the support systems, the projects are designed to offer the right level of human intervention for particular problems. Instructors are thus freed from the responsibility for all aspects of learning and can focus on academic rather than logistical tasks.

### Course Redesign at Rio Salado College and Tallahassee Community College

What would a redesigned project look like? Two community colleges involved in the project are examples of how to apply course redesign at two-year institutions. These two colleges—Rio Salado College (Arizona) and Tallahassee Community College (Florida)—also showcase Twigg's (2004) finding that redesign techniques have been particularly effective with minority and adult students.

For the last 20 years, Rio Salado College in Phoenix has offered distance and alternative format education to adult students who are constrained by work and family commitments. For these students, the removal of learning barriers such as class size and fixed-time instruction is especially important. Rio Salado personnel chose pre-calculus mathematics for redesign because retention and academic success (a grade of C or better) in these courses was only 59%. Even though the college had been using Academic Systems mathematics software to deliver its pre-algebra and college algebra courses, before the redesign most instructors' time was spent troubleshooting technology problems and advising students rather than helping students learn. With the redesign, the college added a nonacademic course assistant to address non-math-related questions, which freed the instructor to focus on academic interactions with students.

Because the Academic Systems software contained a large bank of problems and answers for each topic, the redesign incorporated these as quizzes and assignments as a way to give feedback to students. The software graded quizzes and assignments on the spot. The instructor and course assistant also knew every student's status in each of the four courses through the software's built-in tracking system. The Rio Salado redesign increased completion rates to 65%. As an added benefit, the staff found that students in the redesigned mathematics courses were more consistently prepared when they moved to the next course in the sequence.

Tallahassee Community College (TCC) is another college for which the course redesign process reaped benefits for students (Twigg, 2004). Tallahassee Community College ranks first among Florida community colleges in enrolling Black students and first in the percentage of Black students who complete associate degrees. For example, TCC redesigned its college composition classes. It moved away from the traditional format of combining in-class lecture and writing activities, which had an annual success rate of less than 60%.

The redesign had two major components. First, technology was used to make diagnostic assessments that resulted in individualized learning plans. The college also implemented interactive tutorials in grammar, mechanics, reading comprehension, and basic research skills and online tutorials for feedback on written assignments. Additionally, students submitted drafts to tutors for review, which reduced the amount of time instructors spent grading papers.

The second component involved classroom restructuring to focus on student-centered writing activities. With the addition of available out-of-class technology and tutoring, instructors could now focus the classroom portion of the course on writing. By adding these two components, over a two-year period TCC saw a 13.6% decrease in the DWF decreased to rate in the redesigned college composition classes.

### Collegis, Inc. and Three-A Strategies

Community colleges need to design flexible schedules and flexible education formats to facilitate learning for students who are working adults, commuters, and academically less prepared, as well as those who fit the traditional model. The Program in Course Redesign has shown how colleges can combine information technology with pedagogy to address academic challenges successfully (Twigg, 2004). William Graves, Collegis's chief academic officer, recommended the use of academic service redesign strategies to achieve measurable learning outcomes without spending more on technology. Collegis is arguably the largest consulting service organization in the nation that is solely dedicated to higher education. Based on his work with community colleges and other organizations, Graves (2004) suggested that educators focus their technology use on what he calls the three As—accessibility, affordability, and accountability—in deciding what technology is needed and how existing technology can best be used to achieve the college's goals. Taking Graves's suggestion and applying it to learning colleges, it is easy to see how Web-based technology is increasing the flexibility (accessibility), efficiency (affordability), and effectiveness (accountability) of academic-service design and delivery.

Graves (2004) has made clear that community colleges' technology investments will generate returns only through three-A strategies designed to accommodate mushrooming enrollments while improving instructional learning outcomes. He offered four examples of community colleges that have embraced such three-A strategies in the form of flex instruction. Brookdale Community College in Lincroft, New Jersey; Broward Community College in Fort Lauderdale, Florida; Montgomery College in Rockville, Maryland; and the Tennessee Board of Regents have all implemented academic redesign principles that incorporate three-A strategies.

Brookdale Community College imported a noncredit information technology certification program as one approach to meeting the workforce needs of its community. The flex delivery model for the program includes open enrollment, asynchronous access to online materials, and hands-on work and mentoring housed in a local computer lab, along with intervention strategies to minimize attrition. In its first year, the program sustained a 98% retention rate and an 89% certification success rate.

Broward Community College has been working to address the nursing shortage and other needs in allied health professions in Broward County. To rapidly increase the college's program development capacity, employees outsourced additional capacity to develop flex programs and provide around-the-clock technical support for students and instructors in the allied health programs. The college's instructional technology professionals now work collaboratively with a mix of externally contracted onsite and project professionals. The collaborative effort resulted in grants that enabled instructors to redesign one online nursing degree program into three diverse flex tracks for the community's differentiated nursing needs.

Montgomery College used an approach similar to that of Broward Community College. Its personnel have successfully outsourced course management system infrastructure and related technical and academic support services for the last 3 years. Again, with remotely located around-the-clock systems-administration and help-desk services and the addition of part-time professionals for planning and training, the college is now engaged in a redesign project of a math course focused on the skill development of students who failed the college's math placement exam.

Finally, to showcase what can happen when an entire state focuses on providing anytime, anyplace learning, Graves (2004) reported the Tennessee Board of Regents's (TBR) decision to mandate the creation of the Regents Online Degree Programs (RODP). Overseeing 13 community colleges, 6 universities, and 28 technology centers, the TBR motivated these institutions to offer five fully online degree programs through the RODP. Three of these were associate programs that articulated into two baccalaureate completion programs. RODP enrolls more than 5,000 students who would not be in college today were it not for the RODP flex programs (Graves, 2004).

Accessibility and affordability have always been hallmarks of community college education. Graves (2004) pointed to four examples of academically redesigned programs in which accessibility, affordability, and now accountability have been increased. Each redesign also increased the anytime, anywhere nature of the courses and the levels of students' success through the use of technology paired with instruction.

## The Teaching, Learning, and Technology Group

The Teaching, Learning, and Technology (TLT) Group, under the leadership of Steven Gilbert, has also helped implement learning-college strategies through a focus on technology. Gilbert (2004) has argued that the most important challenge of higher education is enabling instructors, students, and other college professionals to improve students' learning by taking advantage of the new environment that has been created by telecommunications and information technologies. In his work, he has discussed educational challenges, visions, and goals worth working toward, along with principles, strategies, and tools to handle the challenges and achieve the objective of student learning.

Gilbert (2004) has focused his work in higher education with the proposition that colleges are not broken and instructors are not failures. Higher education is facing unavoidable changes, but educators and administrators can make improvements while still respecting what has already been accomplished. Unfortunately, what often happens when colleges integrate technology with academics is that the gains in efficiency increase expectations that even more should be done. Those involved in the changes then have trouble feeling proud of what they have accomplished. More often than not, these change makers are disappointed by what has not been accomplished. Gilbert suggests that to avoid such stress, colleges should encourage instructors to collaborate and help each other take better advantage of new technology resources.

One major hurdle to this goal is the tradition in higher education of rewarding independent achievement and penalizing collaborative work. Most instructors are too busy to independently adopt technology options that will improve the facilitation of learning. They need to become comfortable in collaborating with peers so that each instructor does not have to become a technology expert before using the tools to improve learning. The solution to collaboration resistance, Gilbert (2004) has found, is that collaboration among instructors becomes a nonissue when everyone involved feels confident that they will not lose opportunities to connect meaningfully with students.

The variety of instructor and student combinations that result from such collaborations ensures that a range of learning needs can be met. Certainly, linking different configurations of groups and individuals synchronously and asynchronously is one combination. In a convergence of technology and instruction, instructors have easily accessible options to use in meeting a variety of learning styles and needs. As independent workers, however, few instructors have the skills, time, support, or access to learn the technology tools to respond to students who learn in different modalities. Although many new options have emerged for improving learning, a smaller subset of options will simultaneously increase community, connectedness, and engagement among instructors and students.

Gilbert (2004) has recommended some specific tools that instructors might consider when seeking out methods to meet students' learning needs. First, instructors should consider adopting tools to include their own voices within or attached to other media. Using the human voice adds personality and vitality to instructor-student interactions. Second, instructors can now get constructive feedback about how the learning process is progressing for students by creating an online survey; collecting responses online; and then analyzing, displaying, and sharing results with students online. The immediacy of this approach makes it more likely that the feedback will be used to improve instructional practices that enhance learning.

Finally, instructors can now use tools that enable groups to communicate at a distance synchronously in a variety of media. Some of these tools allow every participant to speak and be heard by all the others; others have mechanisms that allow the teacher to ask questions that students can respond to simultaneously. The results can then be immediately aggregated and displayed for all to see. These specific techniques develop community among students and foster connectedness among students and between students and learning facilitators. Thus, both facilitators and students become engaged in the process of learning.

## The Learning College Project

As Gilbert (2004) has pointed out, often what educators who want to adopt learning-centered strategies need are simply easily accessible ideas and innovations in teaching and technology. In many ways, this was the essential driver behind the launching of the Learning College Project by the League for Innovation in the Community College (McClenney 2001, 2003a, 2003b). The Learning College Project is arguably the most ambitious collective learning-centered education program in North America.

Through this project, 12 colleges, called the Vanguard Learning Colleges, committed to taking on the hard work of asking difficult questions about how to improve and expand learning and, more important, how to document it. Moreover, they committed to sharing this journey publicly. The colleges are as follows:

- Cascadia Community College, Washington
- Community College of Baltimore County, Maryland
- Community College of Denver, Colorado
- Humber College Institute of Technology and Advanced Learning, Ontario, Canada
- Kirkwood Community College, Iowa
- Lane Community College, Oregon
- Madison Area Technical College, Wisconsin
- Moraine Valley Community College, Illinois
- Palomar College, California
- Richland College, Texas
- Sinclair Community College, Ohio
- Valencia Community College, Florida

The project Web site (www.league.org/learningcollege) is a treasure trove of resources for those interested in learning-centered education, and these colleges are also committed to exploring their use of technology as one of the principal project goals. Exciting examples emerged, such as Sinclair Community College's Center for Interactive Learning and its online Individualized Learning Plan (ILP) for at-risk students. The ILP provides detailed information about students' learning and personality styles to instructors to help them better target their instruction. Cascadia Community College is doing extensive work with electronic portfolios (ePortfolios) to document students' learning and employees' professional development. The Community College of Baltimore County created the Virtual Academy to train first-time online teachers. Valencia created an integrated student portal called ATLAS, coupled with a customized advising and career-planning system called LifeMap.

An important concept also emerged as a dominant technology-related theme from this project: Although it plays an important role, technology has to be put in its place. That means ensuring that colleges use technology to serve the greater ends of learning and students, not to gratify ego or impress constituents. Many change agents become so enamored with technology that they end up using it for its novelty, not its utility. The Learning College Project participants were the best teachers in advocating the thoughtful and nonhyperbolic application of technology (Milliron, 2004).

Moreover, colleges must ensure that students learn about, with, and beyond technology—that they develop a love of and appreciation for the liberal arts. Critical thinking, problem solving, communicating, decision making, and community and global awareness will be ever more important as our society becomes increasingly technologically connected (Milliron 2004; Milliron & Miles, 2001). Although the compelling examples of technology use that emerged from the Learning College Project are instructive, what is most striking is learning about the hard work of transformation, culture change, and the essential value of human contribution. It does indeed put technology in its place.

Certainly, collaboration among community colleges and independent organizations working to improve students' learning has become valuable in the quest for learning-college transformation. The Pew Charitable Trusts project, Collegis, the TLT Group, and the League for Innovation in the Community College are clear examples. As college personnel have found, the shift from a centuries-old learning tradition to the new lifelong anytime, anywhere learning methods is a task best handled by all who care about learning, whether they work in a college or not. Yet college personnel, who are on the front lines of these changes, have a distinct voice in what is needed to create such all-encompassing changes. In this spirit, we offer next a more in-depth exploration of the broader efforts of Rio Salado College and El Paso Community College.

## Technology Use at Rio Salado

Although we have already outlined Rio Salado's course redesign efforts, there is much more to the story. Rio Salado is a college without walls that specializes in serving working adults through distance learning and accelerated programs. The college is obviously successful at what it does: Its total 2002–2003 credit-enrollment headcount was 38,419. Additional enrollments come through high school dual enrollment, partnerships with corporations and government agencies for onsite education, and accelerated learning formats.

E-learning is integral to the entire college and is closely tied to its overall mission and growth, rather than existing as a separate division or function (Thor & Scarafiotti, 2004). Thor and Scarafiotti (2004) pointed to four strategies that have allowed Rio Salado to infuse distance delivery throughout every aspect of the college. The strategies began with the adoption of total quality management (TQM). The TQM adoption then evolved into the implementation of a learning-organization model, which led to the introduction of e-learning courses and then culminated in implementing complete online programs.

The first strategy began with an organizational adoption of TQM, a management style traditionally used in businesses. The emphasis on quality, customer service, and process improvement became part of the college's institutional culture. The TQM approach helped college personnel alter many of the college's traditional education practices. After several years, however, college personnel found that TQM's "plan, do, check, act" process and its focus on continuous improvement teams were no longer flexible enough. College personnel needed faster processes to respond to external changes in higher education and internal changes within the college. For its second distance-delivery strategy, Rio Salado adopted of Senge's learning-organization concept (1990), who stated, "A Learning Organization is a place where people continually expand their capacity to create its future, where adaptive learning is joined by generative learning" (p. 14). The learning organization's philosophy was a good fit with the existing TQM foundation.

The philosophy consists of five components. The first is personal mastery. The focus is on increasing an individual's personal capacity to expand and on creating a culture that encourages all members to develop so that they can achieve their goals. The second component, mental models, focuses on continuous reflection on improving the individuals' internal pictures of the world and noticing how they shape actions and decisions.

This is supported by the third component, shared visions. The college builds group commitment by developing shared images of the future that the college seeks and the principles by which the college expects to get there. Team learning is the fourth commitment, and it involves transforming conversational and collective thinking so that groups within the college can develop intelligence and ability that is greater than the sum of their members' talents.

Finally, systems thinking encourages learning a new way of thinking about the forces that shape systems behavior, seeing how to effectively change systems, and acting in harmony with larger processes, such as economic forces. Thor and Scarafiotti (2004) reported that the systems-thinking component ultimately led to some of the greatest innovations in the college's approach to distance learning. Just as Gilbert (2004) reported the need for collaboration through the breakdown of barriers between departments and disciplines, Rio Salado found that with the adoption of systems thinking, employees were encouraged to think beyond their segregated functions and recognize the implications of their work for the larger system. At the same time that the college was adopting and implementing learning-organization principles, the Internet was emerging as a tool that could revolutionize higher education practices. Rio Salado felt it was well positioned to capitalize on this new e-learning strategy for delivering courses.

College personnel recognized early on that the commitment to e-learning would require substantial changes in methods for providing support services. To serve its number-one customer, the student, Rio Salado decided to offer all major college services over the Internet: registration, textbook orders, academic advising and counseling, tutoring, and financial aid applications. This systems-approach integration was modeled after the systems-thinking component of Senge's (1990) model. College personnel identified eight specific functions involved in distance learning delivery and then set up a systems approach to coordinate them. A systems approach was set up for course production and support, student enrollment services, services for adjunct instructors, marketing, online library/media support, instructor and staff development, instructional and technical support, and institutional research. Distance learning was now integrated throughout the college.

The third strategy to infuse distance delivery college-wide emerged naturally out of the transformations that occurred when the college applied the systems approach. Once e-learning had begun and all necessary student support services had been placed online, college personnel then set out to brand Rio Salado's offerings. All the branding factors have the commonalities of convenience, flexibility, and affordability. Three examples of branding techniques intended to create customer astonishment for the college's students include adopting 26 course start dates, which eliminated the traditional semester by initiating course start dates every two weeks for the majority of its Web-based courses; adding 1,800 virtual books to the online support services available to students while providing a technical help desk accessible 7 days a week; and creating the Successful Start program to help those new to online learning. The program guides students from online registration through the first 2 weeks of class.

The final strategy for distance delivery involved the natural move from offering online courses to offering model programs online that had been considered off limits for nontraditional delivery formats (Thor & Scarafiotti, 2004). Programs such as dental assistance, teacher education, and nursing have all been redesigned so that students can take online courses with onsite or at-home practical work. For example, dental assistance students receive a distance lab kit that allows them to practice lessons at home prior to their practicum assignments. Adults with undergraduate degrees can enroll in the Online Post Baccalaureate Teacher Preparation program to earn teacher certification, and licensed practical nurses who want to become registered nurses can enroll in a 25-credit-hour online nursing program that combines online courses and onsite clinical laboratory work.

The latest step in advancing these model programs aligns with the examples of learning-college principles mentioned elsewhere in this chapter. Colleges use collaboration to bring these principles to life. Rio Salado has done the same. In each strategy it adopted to become a learning college, Rio Salado has engaged in partnerships. Recent partnerships the college formed in adopting the fourth strategy of developing model online programs have been with the Arizona Dental Association, the U.S. Army, the Arizona State Board of Nursing, Charter Oak State College in Connecticut, and Walden University, to name a few. Certainly, in reviewing the steps that personnel have undertaken to offer education to unserved and underserved target markets, Rio Salado is clearly learning-college focused. Through its service to the needs of working adults who demand convenience, flexibility, and affordability, the college has made use of collaborations and partnerships.

## Technology Use at El Paso Community College

The same is true for El Paso Community College (EPCC) in its work to close the digital divide. El Paso, Texas, and Ciudad Juarez, Chihuahua, are on opposite sides of the United States–Mexico border. Travel between these two cities is routine and flows back and forth daily as citizens from Mexico cross over to El Paso to work, and shoppers and tourists cross over from the United States to Juarez to take advantage of the devalued peso. Poverty (24%, compared with the national average of 12%) and a lack of education (16% are college graduates, compared with 24% nationally) put this community at risk. According to Rhodes and Walker (2004), however, the greater the risk, the greater the opportunity to make a difference.

EPCC had an opportunity in 2003, when personnel had a vision to take donated fiber optic cable that they had upgraded and "light up" students through enhanced and accessible education. In turn, the college anticipated that the move would light up the El Paso economy through workforce development and light up the community through an educated citizenry. As others striving toward learning-college goals have found, EPCC recognized that collaboration with partners sharing their vision would leverage the fiber asset most strategically.

EPCC approached the University of Texas at El Paso (UTEP) and the El Paso Independent School District (EPISD); these institutions serve collectively more than 100,000 students. In conversations, UTEP and EPISD appeared ready to develop an interconnected high-tech community. In 2003, the three institutions came together and launched the Orion Project. EPCC agreed to light the fiber; UTEP made the connection to the Orion Ring, making Internet 2 accessible; and EPISD contributed video carts.

The project had three major initiatives, each with several specific goals. One initiative focused on teachers, the second focused on students, and the third focused on the community. Goals included complying with the national No Child Left Behind Act, increasing the recruitment and retention of teachers; increasing the quality of dual-credit enrollment; increasing the number of graduates with associate, bachelor's, and master's degrees; bringing dropouts back into the education system; providing a seamless education portal K–16; training a better-educated workforce for economic development; and providing access to health–care resources, to name a few (Rhodes & Walker, 2004).

From the results of this beginning collaboration, Rhodes and Walker (2004) foresaw that future collaborations in the project by other organizations would result in a lower total cost for all through shared development costs; shared operation costs; common delivery of a platform for shared operations; and economies of scale in pricing for connectivity, content, software licenses, and hardware. Rhodes and Walker pointed out that the project's strong educational leadership would facilitate community and economic growth by providing wider access to learning applications, flexible learning opportunities, and consistent and pervasive technology.

By increasing educational attainment and addressing the teacher shortage issue, the Orion Project will become a key to economic development in El Paso. Future project members are possible as surrounding rural independent school districts build high-speed fiber optics rings through e-rate discounts. El Paso County has already budgeted the cost to connect the City of El Paso, Thomason Hospital, and the Texas Tech Health Sciences

Center to increase community access to health care. These represent only the beginning of growth for the Orion Project. With the addition of each new member, the possibilities increase exponentially. When the possibilities increase, all of the Orion Project members immediately benefit from the addition of the service to the project's portfolio. EPCC, UTEP, and EPISD, in coming together in partnership, have made strategic use of technology and asynchronous learning. This has helped not only EPCC adopt additional learning-college principles, but also the city of El Paso to use such principles to transform the community into one where education, employment, and health care are equitably available to all.

## Conclusion

New learning technologies are powerful. They support individual face-to-face classes through supplemental online tools, provide the entire class format online, and create entire programs that can be accessed online. College after college has demonstrated that optimal use of these learning tools occurs when partnerships are encouraged, either within the college or with outside organizations that are devoted to making education richer. This generates excitement about the use of technology in education. And such technology also allows learning-college principles to come to life on a campus. Keller (as cited in O'Banion, 1997, p. 226) believed that "We need an outburst of utopian schemes and inventive thinking" to make the learning college a reality. Certainly, the cases presented in this chapter came from outbursts of creativity in response to the question of how colleges can engage in processes differently so that learning comes first in everything community colleges do.

O'Banion (1997) has said that many colleges will experience a trigger event that will be the catalyst for launching a learning college. After viewing the role that technology is playing in creating learning colleges, the rapid expansion and availability of technology may have just been that trigger event for many community colleges. What could only have been imagined before is now possible. An entire college filled with students learning at their own pace, in their own environments, at a time that is convenient for them, and without having to sacrifice the advantages that students have who are physically on campus, such as access to the library, to financial aid, to student services advisors, or to the bookstore, would have been a dream 10 years ago. Today, it is Rio Salado's reality. O'Banion (1997) offered that external forces can often be such a trigger event. El Paso Community College is using the external gift of fiber optic cable to transform education in its community into a continuous K-16 experience, bringing learning options to people who might otherwise have none.

Clearly, technology and learning-college transformation go hand in hand. Wise leaders realize that such changes need to evolve from the culture of the college, but leaders should also realize that a groundswell in incorporating technology into classes and courses and programs has begun. Instructors are adopting technology to improve learning outcomes in classes at the same time that student services, financial aid, and the library are searching for technological means to do their part to facilitate learning. If the learning college defines the roles of learning facilitators by the needs of the students, and if everyone at the college is a learning facilitator, then technology, by its very ubiquity, is an essential tool for learning-college transformation.

## References

Gilbert, S. W. (2004, February). If it ain't broke, improve it: Thoughts on engaging education for us all, *JALN, 8*(1). Retrieved February 26, 2004, from http://www.aln.org/publications/jaln/v8n1/v8n1_gilbert.asp

Graves, W. H. (2004, February). Academic redesign: Accomplishing more with less, *JALN 8*(1). Retrieved February 26, 2004, from http://www.aln.org/publications/jaln/v8n1/v8n1_graves.asp

Green, K. (2003, October). *The 2003 national survey of information technology in U.S. higher education: Campus policies address copyright issues; wireless networks show big gains.* Retrieved February 26, 2004, from http://www.campuscomputing.net

McClenney, K. (2001, March). Learning from the learning colleges: Observations along the journey. *Learning Abstracts, 4*(2). Retrieved February 26, 2004, from http://www.league.org/publication/abstracts/learning/lelabs0103.html

McClenney, K. (2003a). Becoming a learning college: Milestones on the journey, *Learning Abstracts, 6*(3). Retrieved February 26, 2004, from http://www.league.org/publication/abstracts/learning/lelabs0303.html

McClenney, K. (2003b). Benchmarking best practices in the learning college. *Learning Abstracts, 6*(4). Retrieved February 26, 2004, from http://www.league.org/publication/abstracts/learning/lelabs0304.html

Milliron, M. D. (2004, February). The road to dotcalm in education, *JALN, 8*(1). Retrieved February 26, 2004, from http://www.aln.org/publications/jaln/v8n1/v8n1_milliron2.asp

Milliron, M. D., & Miles, C. L. (2000, November/December). Education in a digital democracy: Leading the change for learning about, with, and beyond technology. *EDUCAUSE Review.* Retrieved February 26, 2004, from http://www.educause.edu/ir/library/pdf/ERM0064.pdf

O'Banion, T. (1997). *A learning college for the 21st century.* San Francisco: AACC and ACE/Oryx Press.

Rhodes, R. M., & Walker, B. (2004, February). The Orion project: Connecting a community, *JALN, 8*(1). Retrieved February 26, 2004, from http://www.aln.org/publications/jaln/v8n1/v8n1_rhodes.asp

Senge, P. M. (1990). *The fifth discipline: The art and practice of the learning organization.* New York: Doubleday.

Thor, L. M., & Scarafiotti, C. (2004, February). Mainstreaming distance learning into the community college. *JALN, 8*(1). Retrieved February 26, 2004, from http://www.aln.org/publications/jaln/v8n1/v8n1_thor.asp

Twigg, C. A. (2003, September/October). Improving learning and reducing costs: New models for online learning. *EDUCAUSE Review.* Retrieved February 26, 2004, from http://www.educause.edu/ir/library/pdf/ERM0352.pdf

Twigg, C. A. (2004, February). Using asynchronous learning in redesign: Reaching and retaining the at-risk student, *JALN 8*(1). Retrieved February 26, 2004, from http://www.aln.org/publications/jaln/v8n1/v8n1_twigg.asp

# PART 4

# Emerging Organizational Changes

# CHAPTER 9

# Architecture and Infrastructure: A Metaphor for Transformation

## WILLIAM J. FLYNN

At the end of 1995, with the publication of Barr and Tagg's article in *Change*, Palomar College suddenly gained national notoriety. As the article became the topic of conversation in education (sometimes heated discussions in the early days), the college was bombarded with phone calls from people wanting more information and asking when teams from other colleges could come to visit such a clearly advanced institution. The problem was that Barr and Tagg had never claimed that Palomar had achieved the learning paradigm, but many early callers assumed that they were writing from first-hand experience.

George Boggs, then president of Palomar, convened a meeting in which a cross section of staff including instructors, deans, students, and trustees discussed strategies to deal with their newly minted national reputation. After lengthy discussion, I jokingly offered a suggestion: "Well, we could do a conference on the topic of the learning paradigm before Terry O'Banion does." Boggs replied, "That's a good idea, Bill, and thanks for volunteering to produce it."

And so, 1 year after the article and 7 months after that meeting, the first conference on the learning paradigm was held in San Diego. And the person who gave the keynote address at that first national conference was none other than Terry O'Banion. The lightning that struck Palomar College because of the Barr and Tagg article caused enough interest in their concept to fuel five successful learning paradigm conferences and subsequent initiatives such as the League for Innovation's Vanguard Learning College project, among others.

In his remarks, O'Banion prominently quoted the Wingspread Group and one particular statement that came from its 1993 report, *An American Imperative: Higher Expectations for Higher Education*. These words resonated with me very strongly: "putting learning at the heart of the academic enterprise will mean overhauling the conceptual, procedural, curricular and other architecture of postsecondary education on most campuses."

## Architecture and Infrastructure

It is noteworthy that the Wingspread Group chose the descriptive term architecture to identify the components of higher education in need of overhaul. Clearly, they did not mean the design of campus buildings, but rather how learning institutions were designed, structured, and organized. Observers of the education scene were quick to pick up on the metaphor and shortly thereafter make insightful analyses of the shortcomings of the status quo.

Discussions on revitalizing higher education architecture covered obvious targets—the Carnegie unit, the semester or quarter system, the 50-minute hour, exam week, funding based on seat time, and other characteristics unique to higher education. But despite the continuing publication of articles and monographs, as well as conferences promoting innovation, change, and transformation, few concrete examples of colleges that have made significant strides to change the traditional architecture emerged. It has been over a decade since the Wingspread Group report, and although a substantial body of literature criticizing the architecture of education has been written, little evidence indicates that meaningful learning colleges have been the result—reformers are still locked in the architecture's embrace.

Toward the late 1990s, Palomar College received a grant from the state of California that resulted in the college spending 2 years digging up the campus. When the project was finally completed, Palomar had a campus capable of efficiently and effectively dealing with the demands of the information age (not to mention close to 30,000 students). Yet when the last bulldozer left the premises, the campus looked remarkably similar to its appearance at the beginning of excavation in 1998. That is because the state funds were used to completely redo, reroute, and replace the water, sewer, gas, electrical, telephone, and data lines. This was infrastructure replacement, not architecture.

During that construction time, when blasting was constant, when electricity disappeared owing to an inadvertently cut line, when parking lots were filled with construction equipment to the chagrin and anger of students who had paid parking fees, I was thinking about this architecture of higher education concept, with O'Banion's voice ringing in my ears. I eventually concluded that the Wingspread Group might have chosen the wrong metaphor. Perhaps it was not the architecture of education that needed change. Perhaps it is the infrastructure. Picture home for a moment, a familiar house or apartment. The outside is recognizable, as are the division into various rooms and spaces on the inside, the size of the rooms, the placement of windows, stairs and doors, the way in which the parts of the edifice relate to each other, the comfort zones of the place. The person or family buys or rents it because the architecture suits the family's needs. As they live in it over time, it becomes personal and comfortable living space—an ideal environment. They inhabit this environment and make it their own with furnishings, decoration, color schemes, and other accoutrements. Although they were not the architects of the facility, they have absorbed its design and made it their own—not unlike the comfort level academics and students have with the architecture of higher education.

Now put on x-ray vision glasses for a moment, and see not just the architecture, but the infrastructure of the dwelling—the plumbing, wiring, HVAC, electrical conduits, framing and foundation—the things that make a house livable, dynamic, and operational. For example, if the thermostat is set to a specified temperature, an electrical impulse sends a signal to the furnace, which functions long enough to reach the desired level of comfort, then automatically shuts off. Ductwork carries the warmed air throughout the house. Electrical, mechanical, and thermal interactions produce a comfortable environment. The infrastructure makes the architecture livable and appealing. But these transactions remain unnoticed until there is a malfunction. No matter how beautifully appointed or intelligently designed, if the infrastructure is unsound or inoperative, the house is incomplete—an empty, dysfunctional shell.

The architects of modern higher education created the blueprints and design scheme for what educators have and do today. From campus to campus, colleges have followed their plans with remarkable similarity. The architecture is identical-semesters or quarters, departments, contact hours, curriculum committees, spring break, student activities, three-credit courses, vice presidents and deans, graduation, and numerous other components of academia. But at the same time, it is safe to say that no two colleges are exactly the same. What makes each college unique is its infrastructure, and if we are serious about transforming colleges into learning organizations, everyone must analyze the infrastructure of higher education, the essential, yet invisible skeleton of colleges that infuses daily activities and at the same time makes campuses unique. Significant changes to the infrastructure will bring changes to the architecture.

And what is the infrastructure of a college? Essentially, it is the sum of its relationships, transactions, and interactions—individually and collectively. It is how instructors deal with each other; how instructors treat students and colleagues; and how instructors have identified and claimed curricular, political, and procedural turf. Eventually, it is how the collective and remembered interactions evolve into that intangible, yet pervasive thing called organizational culture. As Harman described it in *An Incomplete Guide to the Future:* " . . . it is seldom if ever stated explicitly. It exists as a tacit understanding that is transmitted . . . to succeeding generations through direct experience rather than being taught."

## Transforming the Infrastructure

Anyone who has worked at a number of colleges will acknowledge that each had its own culture, its own infrastructure. It cannot be touched or seen or felt, but it was there, beneath the surface, guiding choices, decisions, and behaviors. It is what makes the

University of California at Berkeley significantly different from the University of California at Los Angeles, although both are in the same system and are governed by the same rules. It is the assumptions, values, and norms that lie beneath decisions and behaviors. It is infrastructure that is the real culprit, causing what futurist Joel Barker called "paradigm paralysis," the inability of stakeholders to see all the potential for change and transformation at the college.

How can colleges transform themselves into learning institutions, as opposed to the teaching-centered model often referred to as Barr and Tagg's instruction paradigm? Changing the architecture—reorganizing academic divisions, designing mini-mesters, streamlining work flow, reassigning duties to balance work load, or rewriting job descriptions—adds another layer of paint to the education edifice. To bring true systemic transformation to colleges, the community needs to change the infrastructure, a daunting challenge given the nature of organizational culture in higher education settings. What is needed is a window of opportunity, a magic bullet that will enable all campus constituencies to see in a new light and eventually concur that change must be substantial to allow colleges to become relevant institutions in this new century. The time to do so is now, and the window of opportunity is open.

## Harnessing the Power of New Technology

Attempting to radically transform a complex entity like a college is not an overnight task. The dawning of the information age and its attendant technology offers a lever for change never seen before. If a college's infrastructure is the sum of its relationships, transactions, and interactions, then the technology in use currently, as well as the technology on the horizon, can be the lever that enables colleges to redefine those relationships and thus, the infrastructure. The incredible explosion of information availability, coupled with the phenomenal growth of the Internet and the rapid rise of virtual learning opportunities, has created a unique opportunity. Instead of nervously eyeing technology as a necessary evil, colleges can use it to redefine the basic relationships developed and maintained on campus. Colleges can use it to create a new infrastructure, and in the process, commit to making the institutions truly student-centered and learning-driven.

Consider how much teaching and learning have been recently transformed by technology in the areas of communication and personal interaction. Ten years ago, the in basket would contain little pink message slips noting missed phone calls. There were memos to type (yes, type!), duplicate, and stuff in interoffice envelopes; meetings to schedule on desk calendars; and numerous opportunities to play telephone tag. Instructors were comfortable in departmental enclaves, venturing forth to occasionally serve on a college committee. There were parts of the campus some instructors may never have seen, colleagues they had never met. Students came for instruction at times and in places that suited the college. Instructors and their departments chose what to teach and how to teach it; it was the student's responsibility to learn just what was presented. Colleges could do it because that was the only game in town.

All that is gone. The pervasive influx of e-mail and voice mail messages has moved everyone to a different, asynchronous way of communicating, making a profound impact on relations among colleagues, staff, and students. Fast communications happen over the campus intranet, adjusted in text and tone because e-mail deprives the users of the rich dimension of human interaction experienced in vocal expression, nuance, and intimation. Materials can be purchased through e-commerce, thus changing the way consumers relate to suppliers and vendors. Instructors still teach students in classrooms, but they also interact with them in chat rooms, online, and via fax and interactive video. Administrators market their colleges differently, knowing that students now view each college as one choice among a myriad of education providers offering a variety of delivery formats. College must either redesign these interactions or risk being designed by them.

## The Effect of Technology on Relationships

Colleges can now redesign basic relationships left unchanged for generations—the basic pedagogical interaction between teacher and student, the often turbulent tension between instructors and administration, the caste system relationship that has existed between instructors and support staff, the patriarchal relationship between administration and students. By consciously and systematically examining the many ways in which different groups relate to each other in a college environment, and by analyzing how technology can liberate those groups to redefine these relationships, colleges can devise a new infrastructure that will inevitably drive the transformation of the architecture, thus making colleges competitive, accountable, and liberated from the structural and organizational limitations so long accepted as the norm.

Some basic relationships are already changing. The earliest online courses were text-based replications of course syllabi. As instructors learned the technology of presentation software and knowledge navigation tools, they began to design, not just new courses, but new learning environments, thus changing the ways in which they related to students. As this phenomenon grows, instructors will adopt new roles, and access to information and multiple learning sources will become generally available to students and instructors alike. Rather than allowing students to surf randomly to find information relevant to a course of study, instructors will become researchers and developers of Web sites relevant to their courses, synthesizing the information, making it into a cohesive body of knowledge, skills, and competencies that may be accessed by the student in a variety of learning modalities. This in turn will make the more traditional means of relating—even lecture—more meaningful, because there will be so much more to analyze, synthesize, and discuss in class meetings.

If the basic pedagogical relationship between teacher and student changes, other dimensions of the education environment can change as well to support students' learning.

Instructors will need instructional design assistance, as well as technical support, to maintain ongoing asynchronous communication with students. The nature of academic advisement will change as well. Freed of the constraints of the Carnegie unit and fueled by the limitless research potential of the Internet, instructors can begin to fully explore the multidisciplinary dimensions of their subject matter, an approach previously limited by the constraints of the classroom and the limited resources of the college library. Instructors will develop new collaborative initiatives with colleagues in other disciplines, possibly leading to the end of the traditional academic department. Would that be such a bad thing?

Another changing relationship is the one initiated by the student with the teacher. The Internet opens to the student a vast array of data, information, and knowledge. The physical limitation of the brick-and-mortar library is gone, replaced by limitless opportunities for primary source research that will increasingly become self-directed. Thus the role of the instructor is changed from the traditional model—lecture, assign, and evaluate—to one of critiquing students' progress and learning with the student throughout the research process. In time, the student, sensing this independence, will become more proactive in negotiating grade expectations and conditions of evaluation. The basic relationship between student and teacher will change, and ultimately the architecture that contains that relationship will be forced to adapt to accommodate the new interactions.

The relationship between a college administration and the student is another area where technology has radically changed the equation. In the past, the rules of the game were determined by the administration, and students had little recourse other than to obey. If students wanted to register for classes, they could stand in long lines to receive computer punch cards that allowed access to a class. In some cases, they had to get permission to enroll. Today, registration is asynchronous, online, and driven by e-commerce, and colleges actively compete for enrollments without regard to geographical borders or district boundaries.

The administration was also the keeper of transcripts—paper documents that conveyed progress in, and completion of, a prescribed course of study—along with other estimates of academic accomplishment documented in a letter grade format, and the time period within which the student completed residency at the college. It was succinct, accurate, and probably had a raised seal or official signature of the college registrar for authentication.

But traditional transcripts and the grades they record do not accurately reflect the wide range of complex knowledge, skills, and abilities that students are asked to demonstrate during their collegiate career. Again, technology can provide new tools to record and organize evidence of scholarship and competency. Electronic portfolios, which can document academic achievement plus professional growth, reflective practice, and demonstrated competencies, are such tools. Electronic portfolios can be constructive instruments for authentic documentation and assessment, providing evidence of outcomes attainment, competency, and readiness for work. The content can include papers, presentations, projects, or research, much of it in multimedia format, enabling users to share their accomplishments with instructors, peers, and family as well as potential employers and education providers. Access to the electronic portfolio is controlled by the student, not the college. With such content-rich documentation of knowledge, skills, and abilities now a possibility for students, colleges must rethink how they collect and document students' progress and attainment of learning outcomes. As the relationship changes, the architecture will follow.

College administrators will experience other significant shifts in their basic relationship with the student. As the technology infrastructure becomes pervasive, colleges will become responsible for detailed management of a student's education plan. Using learning management software, administrators can implement a networked system designed to assess the learning needs of its students, employees, and suppliers; provide multiple offerings asynchronously; track progress for individuals and cohorts; and manage assessment initiatives that help document successful learning.

This approach—when combined with developing extensive articulation agreements with real and virtual institutions to ensure accepted, accredited, and seamless transfer of credits; competency certification; or whatever will become the desired credential of the future—mean that transcripts will take on new dimensions. Administrative support of academic, personal, and professional advising, combined with management of virtual learning environments, will ultimately affect how colleges assign personnel. Job descriptions and categories will change to support the new learning environment. The redesigned relationships will drive the change of the infrastructure. If the infrastructure changes, so will the architecture.

The division of responsibility among major administrative components will also be changed. The traditional big three—instruction, student services, and administrative services—are being confronted with a new player with a huge appetite for funding-information technology (IT). Many colleges are still struggling to find the proper niche for technology development and support, often grafting it onto existing organizational charts. The result? Dueling administrative and academic technology entities competing for precious resources, newly hired IT managers trying to apply corporate systems and approaches to Byzantine academic structures, dual reporting lines, and unclear accountability clouding purpose and causing tension. Viewed with unease, hostility, or outright fear, IT is perceived as the black hole into which precious funds flow, diverted from traditional recipients. But technology will not simply go away, and colleges must find the appropriate place for IT within the organization, so that everyone can explore its rich potential. Once that place is found, how all college personnel use technology will cause seismic changes in behavior, performance, and collaboration.

Internal relationships and interactions also require reexamination. What about the relationship between colleges and the community? Much has been made in recent years of the threat—or opportunity—called credentialing and certification. Colleges for the most part have been skeptical about certification programs in IT, as they come from a different part of the education universe that has little if anything to do with the traditional credit apparatus. On closer examination, the entire credentialing and certification movement is almost the opposite of the academic architecture. Because of Internet learning opportunities, colleges no longer possess the local knowledge monopoly. Adults, particularly those in the transitional workforce, want a new relationship with their local college, one that is mutually beneficial, producing learning on demand with tangible results in a short time frame and with a process that fits into a busy work schedule. What colleges offer in return—associate degrees (or certificates carved out of those degrees), usually offered in a semester-length format—is often simply not a good match for what the adult student needs. It is a different ballgame, and colleges that play by the old rules miss an opportunity to substantially serve their local citizenry.

As certification of skills and competencies grows in value, more individualized programs of study will emerge, supported by the technology infrastructure. Ultimately, the instructor–student relationship becomes a co-designed course of study, in which the student contracts for a learning experience with mutually agreed on outcomes, and the instructor monitors, assesses, and certifies student progress. The idea of the student as customer, proactively designing a course of study with the instructor, is heresy among many instructors. But just as society is becoming a service economy—the manufacturing and services sectors of the economy have essentially reversed their positions of importance in the past 50 years—so will the academic community come to be seen as a service-oriented institution, rather than a knowledge factory. And ultimately, if a student sees himself or herself as a customer—paying the bills and having high expectations of receiving educational value for money—it really does not matter what any instructor thinks. The student will go—or log on—to the college that fulfills a learning need. To be competitive, instructors must accept these new realities.

If these changes in the infrastructure occur—if the essential relationships and transactions between and among instructors, students, and staff are significantly transformed to what was only a dream years ago—colleges will see their architecture change, raising some interesting questions. Will it be the end of academic departments as presently construed, to be replaced by configurations driven by the new pedagogical transactions? Will there be a détente between administrators and instructors, as each group recognizes the mutually supportive relationship that has evolved because technology binds them together? Will support staff be fully treated as equals in the complex process of creating, maintaining, and evolving the learning college? Would it be so bad if instructors, staff, and administrators treated each other with respect born of mutual needs, goals, and a shared commitment to helping students learn?

Colleges often use the term learning communities to describe an approach to interdisciplinary studies in which instructors and students work together to tackle complex issues unaddressed by individual three-credit classes. The experience changes the way in which instructors and students interact with each other and the way in which instructors traditionally work with each other. The result has been proven gains in learning and comprehension-changing the infrastructure of the teaching and learning experience improves the bottom line. But learning communities are still not widely accepted, because the architecture of the institutions—the teaching-load calculation, the room-scheduling system, the departmental imperative—inhibits innovation, collaboration, and ultimately learning.

Infusing technology into decision-making processes, and making it a full partner in driving the strategic planning of the college, will cause a fundamental rethinking of daily life on campus. Instead of the micro-level learning community that brings groups of students and teachers together infrequently, look at colleges on the macro level—as connected learning communities in the most expansive and innovative sense—communities of employees connected through technology and united in purpose to produce learning.

## Conclusion

In real estate, the conventional wisdom holds that when a house goes on the market, the owner spruces it up with a thorough cleaning, adds a coat of paint, touches up the landscaping, perhaps even adds a porch or a pool. The goal is to showcase the architecture, the look and feel of the dwelling. The savvy buyer, impressed with the exterior appearance and design of the house, nevertheless commissions a professional inspector to do a thorough analysis of the plumbing, wiring, foundation, and other invisible components that make the house livable. The discerning customer wants a guarantee that both the architecture is pleasing and the infrastructure functional. The new generation of students has the means and capability to do some serious shopping for their educational house. How many colleges can guarantee their institutions will meet students' standards?

The architecture of higher education goes back many generations and is showing its age. Given the choices of education providers that students have today, the increasing calls for accountability and return on investment, and the new breed of competitor already well-funded and technologically savvy, a cosmetic touch-up is not enough to ensure a college's viability in the coming years. To keep an educational house in order, the college must be transformed from the inside out.

## References

Barr, R. B., & Tagg, J. (1995, November/December). From teaching to learning: A new paradigm for undergraduate education, *Change, 27*(6), 13–25.

Harman, W. S. (1976). *An incomplete guide to the future.* New York: Simon & Schuster.

Wingspread Group on Higher Education. (1993). *An American imperative: Higher expectations for higher education.* Racine, WI: The Johnson Foundation.

# CHAPTER 10

# Learning-Centered Governance in Community Colleges

## CHRISTINE JOHNSON MCPHAIL

The American community college is expected to change in response to major historical, economic, political, and philosophical developments within society (Cohen & Brawer, 1999). These external and internal forces serve as benchmarks by which community colleges justify and evaluate themselves. In general, knowledge about problems has not always led to the right action. For example, the commonly accepted dichotomy in education leadership—administration versus governance—takes governance for granted. Community college educators focus so much on the importance of administration in community colleges that the role of governance in leadership too often is overlooked. The leadership role of trustees is a topic worthy of deeper consideration among community college leaders, especially within the learning college movement.

In this chapter, I provide a compelling perspective for involving trustees in the learning college movement and offer practical guidelines that will allow trustees to examine their own beliefs, question traditional governance practices, and understand more deeply how the principles of the learning college can transform the way trustees govern community colleges. Despite the popularity of the movement among community college leaders, it has failed to create sufficient urgency for action among community college trustees. In community colleges, a trustee is usually understood to be a person who is given legal responsibility to hold property in the best interest of or for the benefit of the institution. I do not believe the term *trustee* is broad enough to describe the responsibilities community college trustees must assume. A community college trustee is much more than a person entrusted with the property or the fiscal resources of the college. Community college trustees are responsible for building an institution that can serve both today's and tomorrow's students with increasing accountability. This key function makes community college trustees' role vital to sustaining and facilitating the continued evolution of learning-centered initiatives in community colleges.

When trustees assume their roles, many are relatively inexperienced with issues that confront community colleges, even though they themselves may be college graduates. Consequently, many new trustees are initially uncertain about their duties and responsibilities. At the beginning of their jobs, community college trustees must attend orientation training and trustee meetings. An untrained or absent board member offers little help to the institution. Trustees need to know the origin, purpose, and programs of their community colleges. They must also understand how the learning college movement is directly connected to the historical mission of the community college. Many education leaders view community colleges as being more flexible than other education institutions because they keep in touch with local needs and have the ability to adjust more readily to rapid change (Roueche, Taber, & Roueche, 1995).

President Harry S. Truman described the role of the community college in higher education in the landmark Truman Commission Report (Zook, 1947). This report indicated that 49% of the population of the United States had the mental ability to complete 14 years of schooling and promoted the establishment of a network of publicly supported 2-year colleges. The report stated that whatever form the community college would take, its purpose would be providing education services to the entire community, and this purpose would require a variety of functions and programs.

Effective community college trustees also need to understand the historical mission of the community college to understand the current demands for change and reorganization. Nowhere is this need greater than in trustees' involvement in facilitating learning-centered college initiatives in community colleges. Despite the growing interest in the learning college movement among community colleges, a significant number of boards of trustees throughout the United States are not involved in the movement, and some question its relevance to their roles. The learning college has been heralded as an answer to many of the problems that plague community colleges today—accountability, institutional effectiveness, student outcomes, and so on. The learning college movement has created a new environment for many American community colleges. However, although many community colleges have made significant changes in the delivery systems of their academic and support programs in an effort to become learning-centered environments, only minor shifts in this direction appear to be taking place within the governance of these institutions.

## Trustees in the Learning College

Much of the discussion about learning-centered colleges appears to be focused on experiences within the organization or in the classroom: teaching and learning, curriculum, organizational culture, staff recruitment and development, underprepared students, technology, and student outcomes. To date, few education leaders have proclaimed the importance of understanding the role of trustees related to the learning college movement, and little has been done to involve community college trustees in the movement (McKay, 2004). The pace and scale of the evolution of the learning revolution in community colleges is enormous. O'Banion (1997) stated that "community colleges that begin the journey to become more learner-centered will almost always reorganize their current structure to ensure more collaboration and teamwork among institutional members." O'Banion called for a deep and meaningful involvement of the whole organization.

I have studied the evolution of the learning college movement for the past 8 years. During the past several years, I have paid special attention to the 12 Vanguard Learning Colleges that were established to serve as incubators and catalysts for the learning college concept by working to build on values that place learning first throughout their institutions. According to the League for Innovation in the Community Colleges, these colleges are developing and strengthening policies, programs, and practices throughout their institutions by focusing on the five project objectives: organizational culture, staff recruitment and development, technology, learning outcomes, and underprepared students. After conducting a close review of the activities, programs, and services of the Vanguard colleges, as well as other learning-centered colleges, I am convinced that most learning-centered colleges have not operationalized the involvement of trustees in their learning college initiatives. These are not a few isolated cases: The majority of learning colleges show little or no visible evidence that the role of trustees has been identified or that they are involved in the learning college initiatives at their institutions (McKay, 2004).

The truth about the learning college revolution is that we still have a lot of unfinished business related to the involvement of community college trustees. Although there might be some disagreement about the role of trustees in the governance of institutions, trustees are ultimately responsible for rethinking, redefining, and restructuring their institutions. In trying to understand the transition of community colleges from teaching to learning institutions, we need to ask the following question: Where are the trustees in this learning revolution?

## A Single Direction and a Uniform Vision

Carver and Mayhew (1994) suggested that boards explicitly design their own products and processes. They stated that boards rarely enunciate and hold fast to the principles that guide their own operations, making these boards appear directionless and even, at times, capricious. The learning-centered college is a strategic mechanism that focuses trustees on placing learning at the forefront of their decisions. In other words, learning-centered governance is a single direction that can crystallize a uniform vision for community college trustees.

I believe this notion might be one of the most challenging aspects of institutional governance for the next several decades. Making the shift to learning-centered governance, however, is not a one-size-fits-all proposition. Each trustee in each system will need to interpret the learning college concept in a form that applies to his or her own institution and the overall mission of the college. The beauty of the learning college movement is that it continues to be defined as it unfolds. The evolutionary process allows for a certain amount of creativity on the part of institutions that embrace the movement.

The role assigned to trustees at any particular community college depends on the principles and protocols accepted for community college trustees in general. A stable and democratic board of trustees is impossible without widespread acceptance of a common set of values and without a minimum degree of competency and knowledge on the part of the trustees. In general, the Association of Community College Trustees (ACCT) assumes a leading role in educating trustees by promoting effective board governance through advocacy and education.

A quick review of the duties for trustees should suggest that learning-centered governance does not detract from the roles and responsibilities of the administration or the board; rather, it enhances them. According to ACCT (2004), the general duties for trustees include a wide range of functions:

- Act as a unit (to promote learning)
- Represent the common good (to promote learning)
- Set policy direction (to promote learning)
- Employ, support, and evaluate the chief executive officers (CEOs) (to promote learning)
- Define policy standards for college operations (to promote learning)
- Monitor institutional performance (to promote learning)
- Create a positive climate (to promote learning)
- Support and advocate the interests of the institution (to promote learning)
- Lead as a thoughtful, educated team (to promote learning)

Notice how the roles of the trustee change with the addition of the words to promote learning to the basic duties identified by ACCT. When learning drives governance, discrete patterns begin to emerge. Involving trustees in the learning college revolution is critical in helping to move the learning college impetus beyond the paradigm shift and beyond a popular trend to a transformation of how community colleges respond to the needs of their students. In a learning-centered college, the members of the governing board, as education leaders charged with the responsibility of the institution, rely on the learning college principles to frame their policymaking, and decisions evolve from this foundation. The focus of the community college will still be on multiple missions, but it will be viewed through a single lens.

## Cultural Context of Governing Boards

Trustees have different backgrounds (Smith, 2000), face issues differently, and need to learn different concepts. I am not proposing drastic changes in the fundamental way that community colleges are governed. However, I do want trustees to change their minds about what is important and to enhance governance on the behalf of students. Specifically, I would like to identify and close the gap between how trustees currently govern their institutions and the shift to learning-centered governance to improve learning for all students. The properties of the learning college could serve as the foundation to close this gap.

An examination of colleges that have made the shift from teaching to learning reveals that the commonalities of what trustees must do to be in step with this process and to move toward learning-centered governance are strikingly similar. Trustees have their own culture, structure, and politics, however, and many of these attributes make it difficult for trustees to change the way they govern community colleges. Some trustees have a limited vision that impedes their ability to understand and respond to the transformation potential of the learning college. In the December 12, 2000, issue of the *Community College Times* (McPhail, 2000, p. 3), I posed two key questions about trustee involvement in the learning college movement:

1. What transformation is taking place in the way trustees govern learning-centered institutions?
2. Are trustees committed to and knowledgeable about the changes necessary to governing learning colleges in the 21st century?

In this article, I suggested that governance of the learning-centered college cannot be business as usual and that the manner in which decisions and policies are made must be changed. Some trustees were offended by the following statement about their responsibilities: "Yet many trustees understand neither the concept of the Learning College nor their responsibilities to ensure that policies are made to provide adequate resources for learning to take place."

I believe that many community college trustees are interested in educating themselves about the learning college. The paradigm shift suggested by Barr and Tagg (1995) is connected to issues related to governance. Just as the learning college creates substantial change in the student, it also should create change in the way the college is governed. The success of the learning college is intricately interwoven with the vision and leadership of its board of trustees. Governing boards must have both the vision and capacity to forego their individual interests to advocate for the needs of the institution on behalf of the student.

## Transcending Traditional Boundaries

In my years of studying learning colleges I have not seen substantial change in the way trustees in the learning colleges conducted their business. All trustee organizations have goals, boundaries, levels of authority, communications systems, coordinating mechanisms, and distinctive procedures (Bolman & Deal, 1991). The traditional paradigm of governance has, at best, resulted in compliance with rules, regulations, and policies. In many cases, however, it has produced mediocre to competent governance. The traditional paradigm of governance often results in boards with narrow thinking, dependency on the

CEO, and a focus on processes and procedures rather than outcomes and results. Learning-centered governance requires the board to transcend the boundaries of the traditional governance model.

Traditional governance often results in stagnation and burnout for trustees who are eager to become involved with the learning college movement in a more meaningful way. A good example is the following case study of a fictionalized trustee who is searching for a way to make a meaningful contribution to the organization:

> Karen Battles has been on the board of trustees at Paradise River Community College for 7 years. She has served as the chair of the board for the past year and lives within walking distance of the college. Her children learned how to drive in the college's parking lot. Karen usually walks to the board meeting. As board chair, she usually arrives at the boardroom early so that she can get a few things done before other board members arrive.
>
> When she reaches the college, she drops her bags in her chair in the board room; each board member has an informally designated place to sit. It does not take long for new board members to discover where not to sit. Karen drops by the president's office to let her know she has arrived. The president's secretary gives Karen a pile of letters and folders and a special packet from the president. From where she is standing, Karen can see that the president is still in a meeting with her cabinet. The president spots Karen and nods as she continues her meeting.
>
> Karen returns to the boardroom, glancing at the various pieces of mail. When she reaches the boardroom, she places all of the materials in a pile, trying to decide what to read first. She thumbs through the red confidential file from the president. The other material can wait until she gets home.
>
> Other board members trickle into the room; one or two show little or no enthusiasm. Karen smiles and greets each of them in a high-energy fashion. She pauses for a minute and removes a sheet from the red file. She walks over to one of the board members who has been absent for the last two board meetings and gives her the form. The board member, familiar with the routine, takes a form, signs it, and hands it back to Karen. Karen smiles and takes the form. Across the room, Brad, the vice president of the board, entertains board members with a story about his golf game. The absentee board member gives Karen the "mean eye," and sways as she walks over to the golfers.
>
> A couple of board members are seated, reading their board packets. The president walks in, initiates brief conversations with some of the board members, and then takes her seat next to Karen. Some of the board members take their seats and begin to thumb through their board packets. Brad and the absentee board member continue caucusing in the corner, glancing at Karen

and the president. Karen talks casually with the president and waits patiently for the two board members to take their seats. The president's administrative assistant enters the room and begins to distribute more papers to the board as the executive board session gets under way.

Meanwhile, the president explains the various documents that are being distributed. The board members ask no questions. Karen reminds the board about the National Trustee meeting. About half of the board members indicate that they have a problem with the date. Karen reminds the board that the national convention is very informative and important to board development. When Karen quickly reviews the items in the board packet, some board members do not even pretend to be interested.

The president interjects a statement about the district's strategic plan document in the board packet. With the planning retreat for the college coming up next week, the president wants to be certain that the board knows about the planning activity. She pulls an attractive document from the board packet and waves it in the air. She spends 5 minutes telling the board about the lodge where the administrative retreat is being held. Brad, the board's representative on the strategic planning committee, asks a question about the golf course.

The president's behavior is familiar: She brings the plan to the board members a few days before the planning retreat, reminds them that the strategic planning retreat is scheduled, and asks if they have any questions about the document. The board members look at her intently but do not engage the president in any dialogue about the strategic plan. Karen asks the president a few questions and politely admonishes the president for providing the planning document on such short notice. Other board members are not actively listening to the dialogue between Karen and the president. They are back to thumbing through the other documents in their board packet. Karen's disappointment shows on her face. Two hours have passed, the executive session is over, and other administrators and interested parties saunter into the room for the regular board meeting. As the room fills, Karen tells the president that she would like to discuss the strategic plan before it is brought to the board for voting. Karen has had several conversations with the president about this situation before, but most of the other board members express little or no interest in the strategic plan.

At a recent board meeting, Karen had encouraged the board members to become more attentive to the scope and depth of the decisions that they make. A couple of the board members acknowledged Karen's concern but indicated that they did not really know as much about planning as the president and her cabinet. Others indicated that they simply did not have the time to plow through all of the materials. In general, most of them do not understand the strategic planning process and question whether the plan serves any meaningful purpose. Nevertheless, Karen had asked the president to schedule a series of workshops for the board on the strategic planning process. Karen had indicated that the workshops should focus largely on the goals, expected outcomes, and projected expenditures of the process.

The room is now full; Karen calls the meeting to order and facilitates the presentations from the president. At times she wants to interrupt and ask the president a few questions about several of the agenda items, but thinks better of doing that after looking at the faces of her fellow board members. The topics under discussion are all related to the reductions being made because of fiscal constraints (including elimination of instructor positions, reduction of classes, deferred maintenance on buildings, reduction in student support offices, and elimination of some academic programs). The board members have discussed all of these matters before, so they wonder why they are being brought up again.

The board looks on as the vice president rattles off the list of cuts one after the other. Karen wonders why she appears to be the only one concerned about the impact of these cuts. She wonders why she does not speak up. She wonders whether any of the other board members share any of her concerns. She also worries about the board's becoming a rubber-stamp board. Unbeknownst to Karen, the rest of the board members feel the same way she does; they just do not know how to bring the subject up or what to do about it.

At the end of the board meeting, Karen walks home wondering why she feels so guilty and depressed. She thinks there is a real gap between her views of governance and those of the president and her fellow board members. Karen decides that it is time for her to step up to the plate or step down from the board. She desperately needs a way to use her time and talents more effectively.

## A Change of Mind and a Change of Rules

In *The Effective Executive,* Drucker (1966), might have referred to the situation of Karen's board as the "gradual erosion of the board of directors as a functioning organ of the [business] enterprise....In reality the Board as conceived by the lawmakers is a tired fiction." Even though Drucker's reference was to business organizations, a question could be asked of community college trustees: Is your board a "tired fiction" or a "rubber stamp"? Unfortunately, in too many instances, the answer to this question may be yes. It is a good sign when trustees like Karen Battles start to reexamine their work and strive to discover ways in which they may use their time, talents, and resources more effectively. The best accountability mechanisms are designed around the assessment of performance and quality rather than around compliance with regulations, administrative procedures, and red tape (Association of Governing Boards of Universities and Colleges, 1996).

Trustees who govern learning-centered colleges should make the shift to learning-centered governance to experience the benefit of putting learning first. Learning-centered trustees must be willing to change the rules and the rituals to relate to the student and to make policies that support substantial change in the student. With this type of decision making, trustees will evolve to become full partners in the learning process. Learning-centered trustees look for ways to integrate learning-centered principles into all aspects of the governance process. They conduct learning-centered board meetings, and their connections with the college become opportunities to learn more about the learning college's impact on the student. Focusing on learning-centered governance has two benefits:

1. Trustees are liberated from roles that no longer serve any meaningful function and that may have outlived their purpose.
2. The outcomes of the learning college are clear and direct—it places learning first. No other education reform initiative has offered governing boards such a strong vehicle for unity.

The notion that the learning college movement will reform governance in community colleges may be far-fetched for some, but it can be seen as a strategic approach to integrating and applying the learning college principles into the art of policymaking of the college. It might enable the board to provide trusteeship at a much deeper level than currently realized under the existing structure of institutional governance. Think back on the situation of Karen Battles, the fictitious trustee. In a learning-centered governance situation, all items on the board's agenda would have a learning-centered focus.

If indeed the learning college puts learning first and provides educational experiences for students anyplace, anyway, and anytime (O'Banion, 1997), boards of trustees must redefine their roles and accept responsibility for changing policies and practices consistent with the principles that undergird the learning college. In the learning college, trustees must understand that the college can no longer be tied to outdated practices and procedures. To place learning first, trustees will need to make expedient decisions that support new programs and delivery systems. When the board makes it clear that learning is the foundation for its policymaking, stakeholders will see that the learning revolution is taking place at the college.

## Transformation to a Learning-Centered College

Leaders of the learning college movement speak with tremendous pride about the transformative power of the learning college in many areas of the institution. Some even suggest that integration of the learning college principles does, in fact, change the culture of the institution. I acknowledge that what I am advocating about trustees' involvement does not lend itself to an immediate change in the governance patterns of trustees. All the same, with carefully crafted orientation, training, and education (including seminars, conferences, retreats, and presentations), trustees could learn a great deal about the learning college principles in a short period of time. Because the board's major responsibility is to assist, guide, and evaluate the progress of the institution, it is critical that trustees know the college—its purpose, its constituencies, its programs, and its physical and financial conditions (Chait, Holland, & Taylor, 1991).

How do trustees acquire information to govern the college? Chait et al. (1991) suggested that governance information has four essential properties:

1. Strategic: The data and performance indicators provided to the board are directly related to issues of corporate strategy.
2. Normative: Performance data are displayed for the board against norms, targets, and anticipated results so that trustees can readily compare actual performance to historical trends and industry standards, and to prompt board action.
3. Selective: Trustees routinely receive only information that is necessary to exercise proper oversight, to monitor institutional and management performance, and to prompt board action.
4. Graphic: Whenever possible, data are displayed in graphic formats that communicate directly and succinctly.

Just as students learn differently, there is no single best way for board members to access and acquire the skills necessary to govern community colleges. Thus, some board members may prefer to acquire knowledge about the learning college through one or more of these modes (i.e., strategic, normative, selective, or graphic). In the fictionalized example, Karen initially struggled to find the best ways to gather and present information to her board. In the end, she decided to work with the president to determine the most effective way to share information with the board. Karen discovered a number of residual benefits from working with the board and the president to present the information. The key benefit was the collaboration that took place among the board members. After collecting information from her board, Karen decided to use an integrated approach that drew on all four of the essential properties of governance information suggested by Chait et al.

Trustees can learn about the community college from several perspectives. The transition from teaching to learning calls for a transformation of the entire college culture—it affects all stakeholders at the institution. Table 10.1 describes two specific ways of approaching governance in the learning-centered environment. The first approach, "the way we do things around here," emphasizes the fact that trustees make decisions on the basis of past procedures, rules, and rituals. The second approach is learning centered and is responsive to the changing and diverse needs of the students. The first approach allows

# Table 10.1 Transitioning to Learning-Centered Governance

| The Way Trustees Govern Now | Learning-Centered Governance |
|---|---|
| Trustees have limited knowledge of the Learning Revolution. | Trustees place learning first in policy adoption. This facilitates a range of options to institutionalize learning principles. |
| Personal interests sometimes interfere with effectiveness. | Trustees act and speak as a board and execute a uniform vision. |
| Trustees have been taught to value and hold on to past political processes. | Trustees change the way they govern—step out of the box and try new ways of governing. |
| Bylaws and numerous standing committees stagnate and restrict the involvement of board members. | Trustees appoint temporary committees to deal with special issues and problems as they arise. |
| Trustees' capacity to make decisions is sometimes held hostage by outdated rules and regulations. | Trustees need a wide range of options to make expedient decisions to facilitate learning options. |
| Trustees are often criticized for micromanagement, so they sometimes become disengaged from the learning process. | Trustees must take risks, become more inquisitive, and actively monitor how their decisions affect learning. |
| The education of the board or board training process is sometimes limited to meetings or one to two training sessions per year. | Trustees must develop and execute ongoing trustee training programs and become full partners in the learning process. |
| The administration sometimes exclusively defines the vision for the board. | Trustees must participate with the administration in designing the vision and evaluation processes. Learning is in the forefront. |
| Search firms and committees assume large responsibility for developing the CEO profile and the selection process. | Trustees take an active leadership role in seeking the CEO. |
| CEO leadership teams create and monitor the organizational culture. | Trustees create the college's climate and work with the leadership team to keep it positive. |

trustees to see their role in a vacuum—separate and apart from the college and the student; the second approach allows trustees to see their role as full partners in the learning process at the institution, which is focused on the student. Trustees are encouraged to evaluate their current situation and to search for ways to make the transition from traditional governance to learning-centered governance. Just as some instructors in learning colleges decide to end old ways of teaching and define new ways of teaching, trustees can work together to define new ways of governing.

## Nine Strategies for Implementing Learning-Centered Governance

How can you promote the idea of learning-centered governance when so few trustees appear to be involved in the learning college revolution? With appropriate information, I believe that trustees can become strong supporters of the learning-centered college. Armed with accurate information, they will be able to see that learning-centered governance is at the core of the shift from teaching to learning and is a transformation that can fundamentally change community college education.

Although I strongly encourage transitioning from the way trustees now govern to a learning-centered focus of governance, some trustees and institutions may not find the departure from the old way to be easy. The learning-centered college affects every aspect of the college, including governance, because the so-called stable understanding about "the way we do things around here" is being challenged and reformed. Nevertheless, for trustees to govern in a manner consistent with the forces that converge on the boardroom, they must change—or risk being ineffective. Just as the students and structures of the colleges are changing, the ways trustees govern must change. The culture of governance is changing, and the definition of effective governance is changing. The learning college presents a logical framework for trustees to change the way they govern.

What does change really mean for trustees who may want to shift from traditional governance to a learning-centered approach? Learning-centered governance provides a vehicle for trustees to focus on the most important issue facing community colleges—students' success. Using Chait et al.'s (1991) essential properties of governance information, I have identified the following nine strategies to illustrate a hands-on process for transitioning trustees to learning-centered governance. These strategies are intended to equip community college trustees with a new tool kit—the strategies, and mind-sets needed to transition to learning-centered governance:

1. Place learning first. Items that promote the learning-centered agenda should be categorized and placed on the agenda first rather than being integrated with other items on the agenda. This tactic provides consistent opportunities to reinforce the learning-centered college focus regularly.

2. Link learning to governance. Designate a specific time on the board agenda for the president or a designee to briefly describe or explain the learning-centered agenda items. The description should explain how this action improves and expands learning at the college. The data and performance indicators will link the board's action to the implementation of the learning-centered functions at the college.

3. Develop learning-centered policies. Trustees should empower the president and the leadership team to provide a written learning-centered preface to each major policy issue related to learning-centered action items. The preface should explain why this issue is coming to the board now and how it improves and expands learning at the college.

4. Reinforce learning-centered governance, anyplace, anytime, anyway. The board's commitment to learning-centered governance can be reinforced in a number of ways. The agenda and work plans can be prominently displayed in graphic formats at each meeting and in the board room. The board's Web site can display information about its learning-centered governance and decisions. These methods can serve as ongoing reminders of the board's commitment to learning-centered governance.

5. Integrate learning-centered governance into local and national learning college initiatives. Trustees can conduct focus groups and presentations to promote and elevate trustees' involvement in the learning college movement. Trustees and constituent groups can engage in regular conversations about the significance of board involvement in the learning college.

6. Create a learning-centered governance vision statement. A learning-centered vision statement serves as the driving force behind the decisions made by the board of trustees. The statement can be placed in prominent positions on the campus, on business cards, and elsewhere.

7. Develop learning-centered governance outcome assessments. Committee work and the board's continuous agenda can be evaluated to assess the extent to which learning-centered decisions are at the forefront of board transactions. Performance data can be displayed for the board against norms, targets, and anticipated results so that trustees can observe relevant trends.

8. Establish professional development training programs. Learning-centered governance preparation programs need to be developed by local colleges and at the national level. Learning-centered governance preparation takes on an action orientation as trustees' critical reflections include supporting and promoting learning-centered governance in the community college. Trustees will acquire skills necessary to exercise proper oversight to monitor institutional management and performance.

9. Communicate results widely whenever possible. Data about board decisions should be displayed in graphic formats that communicate board actions directly and succinctly. Information should be shared with the consent of the board.

Learning-centered governance requires trustees to see the learning college as a way to strengthen the mission of the community college: a system that creates a kaleidoscope of learning options for a diverse population of students. I recommend starting with a few trustees who understand the foundations of the learning college principles. The learning college leaders could work with these trustees to reach out to other trustees on the local and national levels. This core group of trustees will change the image of trustees; they will help build a professional community and a professional culture of learning-centered governance.

National community college associations such as the League for Innovation in the Community College, the American Association of Community Colleges, and ACCT could collaborate with this core group of trustees to launch a national conversation about learning-centered governance in community colleges. A key purpose for involving trustees in the learning college movement is to create a common ground for stimulating, improving, and expanding learning options for community college students. The concept of learning-centered governance should affirm what is fundamentally important to community colleges—the success of students.

In many contexts, the transition from traditional governance to learning-centered governance may be imperceptible—simply a move from traditional rituals, rules, and roles to learning-centered decision making and policy adoption. The challenge is that the results of trustees' governance activities often is confined to the boardroom. Although trustees may take actions that influence learning outcomes for students, these outcomes are rarely articulated to show the larger college community how trustees view the relationship of governance and decision making to outcomes for the student. The trustees themselves are crucial in articulating learning-centered governance. However, the president and campus administrators also need to be included in the process because they need to understand and support the relationship among the governance decisions and learning enactment at the college.

## Evaluating Learning-Centered Governance

What are the effects and outcomes of learning-centered governance? I recommend summative types of evaluations because they address outcomes. In other words, questions such as the following need to be examined:

- To what extent did policies and decisions accomplish what was intended?
- What happened as a result of the decisions?
- Did something happen that was not intended?

- Did the action improve and expand learning and how can that be determined?
- How will decisions about outcomes be communicated to all stakeholders?

For trustees, this evaluation means discovering whether all of the decisions and policies actually facilitated and fostered meaningful learning options for all students. This is the ultimate test of the effectiveness of learning-centered governance. It will probably be concluded that there is no standardized way to assess the effectiveness of learning-centered governance. Thus, strategies to assess the effectiveness of learning-centered governance may be as diverse as the community colleges and the communities they serve.

## References

Association of Governing Boards of Universities and Colleges. (1996). *Renewing the academic presidency: Stronger leadership for tougher times.* Washington, DC: Commission on the Academic Presidency: Author.

Barr, R., & Tagg, J. (1995, November/December). From teaching to learning: A new paradigm for undergraduate education. *Change, 27,* 13–25.

Bolman, L. G., & Deal, T. E. (1991). *Reframing organizations: Artistry, choice, and leadership.* San Francisco: Jossey-Bass.

Carver, J., & Mayhew, M. (1994). *A new vision of board leadership: Governing the community college.* Washington, DC: Association of Community College Trustees.

Chait, R., Holland, T., & Taylor, B. (1991). The effective board of trustees. Phoenix, AZ: AACC and ACE/Oryx Press.

Cohen, A., & Brawer, F. B. (1999). *Managing community colleges: A handbook for effective practice.* San Francisco: Jossey-Bass.

Drucker, P. (1966). *The effective executive.* New York: Harper & Row.

McKay, S. L. (2004). *Chief executive officers' and board of trustees' perceptions and preferences of their levels of involvement in institutional governance activities.* Unpublished doctoral dissertation, Morgan State University, Baltimore, MD.

McPhail, C. J. (2000, December 12). Reframing governance: At a true learning college, trustees have a lot to learn, too. *Community College Times,* pp. 3, 6.

O'Banion, T. (1997). *A learning college for the 21st century.* Phoenix, AZ: AACC and ACE/Oryx Press.

Roueche, J. E., Taber, L. S., & Roueche, S. D. (1995). *The company we keep: Collaboration in the American community college.* Washington, DC: Community College Press.

Smith, C. (2000). *Trustees in community colleges: A guide to effective governance.* Washington, DC: Association of Community College Trustees.

Zook, G. F. (1947). *Higher education for democracy: A report of the President's Commission on Higher Education: Vol. 1. Establishing the goals.* New York: U.S. Government Printing Office.

# CHAPTER 11

# Aligning Strategic Planning, Budgeting, and Resource Allocation in LearningFIRST

IRVING PRESSLEY MCPHAIL

The Community College of Baltimore County in Maryland (CCBC) aligns planning and budgeting with resource allocation in support of the LearningFIRST 1.0 strategic plan agenda. In this chapter, I explore the unique relationship among planning, budgeting, and resource allocation in higher education and analyze some of the impediments to linking planning and budgeting successfully. I continue by discussing the keys to effective resource allocation, reviewing resource allocation problems in higher education, and presenting the critical elements of the unique CCBC approach to linking planning, budgeting, and resource allocation.

In practice, CCBC is strongly committed to a culture of planning as the primary catalyst for leading the organizational transformation toward a more learning-centered institution (McPhail, 1999; McPhail & Heacock, 1999; McPhail, Heacock, & Linck, 2001). CCBC's LearningFIRST 1.0 Strategic Plan, 1999–2003, presents the college's vision as a single college, multi-campus, learning-centered institution and contains the college's vision statement, mission statement, statement of beliefs, and strategic directions (see Table 11.1 and Figure 11.1).

CCBC has made a deliberate effort to link planning, budgeting, and resource allocation. The college's operating budget has been developed incorporating the LearningFIRST 1.0 vision statement, mission statement, statement of beliefs, and strategic directions. The fiscal year 2004 operating budget is the fourth that linked all tier requests (requests for additional funding above the maintenance of effort level) specifically to LearningFIRST 1.0.

## Impediments to Linking Planning and Budgeting

Linking planning, budgeting, and resource allocation has proven difficult in higher education.

Those in higher education who are seeking the perfect relationship between planning and budgeting are like the physicists who are searching for the

## Table 11.1   LearningFIRST 1.0: Vision, Mission, and Statement of Beliefs

### Vision

The Community College of Baltimore County (CCBC) is a premier, learning-centered, single college, multi-campus institution.

### Mission

The Community College of Baltimore County is a learning-centered public college that anticipates and responds to the educational, training, and employment needs of the community by offering a broad array of general education, transfer and career programs, student support services, and economic and community development activities. The College serves its diverse community as a center for lifelong learning to improve the quality of life in Baltimore County and the region in a time of rapid societal and technological change. The Community College of Baltimore County commits to the optimal use of available resources in a responsive and responsible manner.

### Statement of Beliefs

The Community College of Baltimore County acquires its direction through adherence to its Vision and Mission Statements. The implementation of the College's strategic and operational plans is the primary means for focusing the entire organization to this end. The College will achieve institutional excellence from its strategic planning process in concert with a persistently positive attitude on the part of faculty, administration, and staff.

As a learning-centered community college, CCBC will

- make learning its central focus;
- make students active partners in the learning process;
- assume final responsibility for producing student learning;
- focus on learning outcomes to assess student learning and success;
- create a holistic environment that supports student learning;
- ensure that every member of the college community is a learner; and
- evaluate all areas of the College by the ways they support student learning.[1]

---

[1] The statement of beliefs was drawn from a number of authors who have defined learning-centered education. The outline and the beliefs stated were drawn most heavily from principles articulated in the following publication: O'Banion, T. (1997). *Creating more learning centered community colleges*, Phoenix, AZ: Onyx Press. 1997.

**Figure 11.1   LearningFIRST 1.0: Core and Supporting Strategic Directions**

unified theory of forces. Both sides draw closer and closer to eloquent solutions, but are confounded by unexpected complexities in the physical world and the world of organized individuals. (Meisinger, 1990, p. 1)

Meisinger (1990) added that in higher education the theorists call for clearly delineated goals and a set of objectives for which priorities have been established (the strategic plan), an implementation framework that estimates the cost of achieving these goals and objectives (the budget plan), an allocation of funds (resource allocation plan) for these goals and objectives, and a scheme for measuring the success in achieving the goals and objectives (evaluation plan).

Meisinger (1990) admitted that few people would disagree with these prescriptions for linking planning, resource allocation, and budgeting more effectively; but like the Wall Street maxim to buy low and sell high or the real estate maxim location, location, location, the complexities of the real world make this advice too simple to be helpful. Schmidtlein (1990) viewed the situation with similar skepticism. He noted:

Within the field of public administration, the belief that budgets should be derived from well-conceived plans appears to be an unquestioned article of faith. Like the search for the Holy Grail, theorists and practitioners for many years have maintained a quest for the secret to a successful linkage. Some theorists have claimed success, but, like claims for cold hydrogen fusion, the results of their formulations have been inconclusive and controversial. (p. 9)

The observations shared here are largely based on an analysis of budgeting by Schmidtlein's work on planning and budgeting. Schmidtlein's 1990 article, "Why Linking Budgets to Plans Has Proven Difficult in Higher Education" identified many of the impediments to successful planning and budgeting. Schmidtlein is the former director of the Institutional Planning Project at the National Center for Postsecondary Governance and Finance, University of Maryland, College Park. His work suits this discussion because it draws on information obtained from a 3-year national study of higher education institutional planning that presented planning and budgeting typologies and the links among them.

## Types of Planning and Their Links to Budgeting

Planning usually includes several levels and may vary from comprehensive to issue-specific. When colleges examine this connection between planning and budgeting, they must be clear about the type of planning, or which combination of types, they review. Each type of planning has different implications for achieving such a connection. Schmidtlein identified six principal planning types:

1. Strategic planning—determining the nature of the environment in which an institution operates, assessing its internal strengths and weaknesses, and developing a vision of its future character, given these assumptions

2. Program planning—determining the nature of the programs needed to implement the college's vision and the types of structures and processes required to support these programs

3. Operational planning—establishing short-range objectives, determining their relative priorities, and deciding the kinds and levels of resources to be devoted to each objective

4. Issue-specific planning—determining the policies and actions required to resolve issues affecting a specific campus function or limited set of functions

5. Budget planning—determining the goods and services needed to implement desired programs, estimating their costs, determining potential sources of revenue, and reconciling competing claims for resources, given assumptions about revenue limitations

6. Facility planning—determining the character of physical facilities needed to effectively implement an institution's programs

### Strategic Planning's Links to Budgeting

Because planning is a complex process, colleges must establish clear operational definitions when launching a planning process. Schmidtlein defined strategic planning to include determining the nature of the environment in which an institution operates, assessing its internal strengths and weaknesses, and developing a vision of its future character given these assumptions. According to Schmidtlein, strategic planning does not provide program, operational, or budget guidance for decisions on specific priorities or on goods and services a unit should request in budget documents. It does, however, provide a context for a college's vision for a market niche and an institutional mission appropriate to exploit that niche. Consensus on a mission creates a set of shared values and assumptions that in turn create a context for program planning, operational planning, and budget decisions. In practice, strategic planning provides the context but rarely provides explicit guidance for budget decisions. Schmidtlein (1990) advanced the notion that under optional conditions, strategic planning leads to agreement on a college's mission and provides a broad vision of its future directions.

### Program Planning's Links to Budgeting

Program planning, by its very nature, provides somewhat more specific guidance for budgeting than strategic planning. Program planning determines the nature of the programs needed to implement the college's vision and the types of structures and processes required to support these programs. In most colleges, the relative priority of programs fluctuates from year to year. Although operational agreement on programs provides a greater degree of guidance for budget decisions than does strategic planning, a large area remains for discretionary budget decisions.

### Operational Planning's Link to Budgeting

The number of community colleges engaged in the learning process continues to increase. Schmidtlein (1990) stated, "The primary function of Operational Planning is to develop consensus on specific items to be included in a budget, or at least the new items, since most of the items in a budget represent continuing commitments" (p. 12). He observed that operational planning rests on the hope that, through an early planning cycle, analysis can take place and political struggles can be settled, avoiding interference with the technical work involved in costing out elements in the budget, identifying fund sources or accounts, and preparing budget justifications. At many colleges, operational planning often takes place as budgetary decisions are being made.

In practice, organizational units nearly always view planning as an opportunity to enlarge their budgets. As a result, unit plans frequently contain laundry or wish lists of new items for which they seek resources. The politics of reconciling financially unrealistic unit requests with district-wide priorities complicate the development of planners' explicit strategic plans.

Many community colleges will readily admit that plans are often not an adequate guide for budget decisions because units typically are reluctant to document their significant problems. Some may fear that media, governing boards, and the general public will make inaccurate assessments of a problem's magnitude. In addition, adversaries may be able to use such negative information against them in budgetary allocations or other aspects of resource acquisition. As a consequence, plans appear to be a better guide for new initiatives than they are for reductions or reallocations of funds. My observation is that, even in the best of times, departments of divisions tend to view their budget base as an inheritance and seek to limit budget discussions to requests for increases, turning the reduction or reallocation of funds into a highly contested political process.

## Keys to Effective Resource Allocation

There is no one-size-fits-all approach when it comes to resource allocation. Massey's (1996) seminal work, Resource Allocation in Higher Education, suggested to us that institutions are in a battle against a well-established education institution maxim known as Bowen's Law: "Universities will raise all the money they can and spend all the money they raise" (p. 5). Bowen's Law sends a sound message to community colleges and is all the more reason why education institutions must identify and understand the keys to effective resource allocation in higher education.

### *Understanding the System of Incentives*

The first major key identified by Massey (1996) focused on the system of incentives that guides spending in colleges and universities. According to Massey, incentives are based partly on intrinsic values and partly on instrumental ones. A good example is the view that college academic, vocational, and contract education programs with strong job and market values serve to cross-subsidize academic programs with low intrinsic values. Low intrinsic-value programs are ones that have high traditional liberal education value but low job and market value. Massey maintains that an effective resource allocation process will allow the college to achieve an appropriate balance between its identified intrinsic values and those of the marketplace.

### *Recognizing and Managing Complexity*

Higher education institutions generally use incremental or formula concepts to develop their budgets. This process drives the need to be aware of the diversity of intrinsic values of the institution. The diversity springs partly from differences in technical and professional background, partly from differences in educational purposes, and partly from political self-interest. Each group argues for its view in terms of high principles, often reinforced by the fact that success also furthers political self-interest.

The third key to resource allocation reform is the ability and capacity to manage complexity. In higher education institutions, resource allocation reform usually involves decentralizing detailed budgeting responsibility away from central organizational units where it traditionally has been held. According to Massey (1996), and based on my own observations as a CEO, centralization can disempower those who represent the institution's core competencies, undermining the incentives for productivity improvement and making accountability for such improvement impossible. To minimize distraction to resource allocation, it is logical that effective resource allocation in colleges and universities include appropriate decentralization of power.

## Resource Allocation Problems

Careful study of the resource allocation pattern of higher education institutions reveals that efforts to balance values and market forces, cope with value diversity, and manage complexity tend to lead chief executive and business officers to insist on central control over resources. As I mentioned earlier, the most common control method is incremental line-item budgeting. At many institutions, the need to manage complexity drives the allocation process. Attention is focused on additions and deletions because the base budget is too hard to analyze. After using incremental budgeting over a period of time, the incremental character emerges. Various budget centers tend to assert ownership of base funding levels and come to view most of their costs as fixed. Although many institutional leaders may not like the process, they often come into the politics of the situation.

Massey (1996) proposed that the antidote lies in resource allocation reform at several levels. The first priority is to dissolve the operating units' sense of base budget ownership and their belief that cost and quality are synonymous. Unit management needs to understand that resources will flow in relation to market demand and assessed performance. I believe that as the rate of change within a college increases and external demands increase, the willingness and ability to change also increases.

Today's increasingly changing economic environment highlights the importance of the change process and its value to institutional effectiveness, a concept that is demonstrated at CCBC institutions. Another key priority in resolving resource allocation problems is dialogue. Maintaining dialogue about program relevance, quality, and productivity and implementing the processes and data needed to make the dialogue meaningful is critical to addressing the problem. Resources should be invested according to the so-called high-assay principle. According to this principle, if one owned several gold mines, it would make sense to invest in the one with the highest assay or opportunity for growth and values.

In colleges and universities, high assay means quality relative to institutional values, vision, mission, and goals delivered as productively as possible. Massey (1996) described the final priority as the capacity to relax restrictions on how operating units manage resource trade-offs. Cost centers should be free to determine for themselves how to meet the agreed upon objectives within the available budget allocation.

## The Integrated Planning Process

The Integrated Planning Process (IPP), as developed by Below (Below, Morrisey, & Acomb, 1987), presents a total framework for depicting an organization's planning and control system. The IPP has been modified over time by the author to fit the academic planning context. Figure 11.2 presents the current three-tiered model in use at CCBC.

### *Annual Operational Planning Process*

The planning process at CCBC is continuous and intended to achieve real results. It is designed to provide the overall vision, mission, and strategic directions for the college and each of the three campuses. It welcomes and encourages planning at all levels and assumes that planning behavior is a fundamental responsibility of all managers, administrators, and other college leaders.

CCBC is involved in three major types of planning: strategic, operational, and long-range. The operational plan consists of annual objectives for each of the strategic directions in LearningFIRST 1.0: students' learning, learning support, learning college, infusing technology, management excellence, embracing diversity, building community, and enrollment management. CCBC ensures that the strategic plan is carried out consistently in all parts of the college annually. Table 11.2 is an example of the action planning worksheet (APW). The APW ensures that the operational plan will be implemented. Implementation revolves around making the translation from the specific strategic direction in LearningFIRST 1.0 to annual objectives linked to that specific strategic direction to specific actions and results.

## Figure 11.2  The Integrated Planning Process

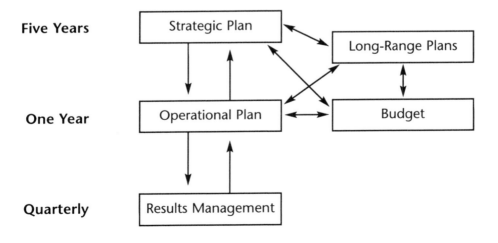

**Table 11.2  Action Planning Worksheet**

KRA: Student Learning    ADMINISTRATOR: Henry Linck

## ACTION PLANNING WORKSHEET

OBJECTIVE 1.2.1: To conduct five high-impact learning outcomes assessment projects

| Actions Steps | Accountability | | Schedule | | Resources | Feedback Mechanisms |
|---|---|---|---|---|---|---|
| | Primary | Others | Start | Complete | | |
| 1. Select courses for inclusion. | Academic Division Deans | R. Mince H. Linck D. McKusick A. MacLellan Instructors | 2/02 | 5/02 | 6 hours of reassigned time for Ann MacLellan; $90,000 (approved 2003 Operational budget for LOA projects.) | Notice to instructors of selected courses |
| 2. Identification of team leaders. | Academic Division Deans | A. MacLellan R. Mince | 3/02 | 6/02 | IR staff hours for data analysis: 60–80 | Instructor-volunteer to serve as project team leaders |
| 3. Budget decisions made by teams (distribution of stipend). | LOA Teams | A. MacLellan R. Mince | 5/02 6/02 | 8/02 | Staff/faculty hours for conducting LOAs: 120–200 | Budget approved by Henry Linck |

**Table 11.2   Action Planning Worksheet (cont'd)**

| Actions Steps | Accountability | | Schedule | | Resources | Feedback Mechanisms |
|---|---|---|---|---|---|---|
| | Primary | Others | Start | Complete | | |
| 4. Project design (instrument, external validation, data collection and analysis, timeline, etc.) approved by Outcomes Associate, Deans, and VCLSD. | LOA Teams A. MacLellan | Academic Division Deans R. Mince H. Linck | 6/02 | 9/02 | | Approval of proposals |
| 5. Collection of data | LOA Teams A.MacLellan G. Fink T. Hirsch | Instructors Deans | Fall 2002 | Spring 2002 | | Data collected for all 5 projects and submitted to Planning, Research, and Evaluation for analysis |
| 6. Analysis of data | LOA Teams A. MacLellan G. Fink T. Hirsch | Instructors Deans R. Mince H. Linck, D. McConochie | Spring 2002 | Fall 2002 | | Data analysis completed and returned to LOA Teams |

**Table 11.2   Action Planning Worksheet (cont'd)**

| Actions Steps | Accountability | | Schedule | | Resources | Feedback Mechanisms |
| --- | --- | --- | --- | --- | --- | --- |
| | Primary | Others | Start | Complete | | |
| 7. Curriculum revision (based on data analysis) | LOA Teams A. MacLellan R. Mince | Instructors Deans H. Linck | Fall 2002 | Spring 2003 | | Curriculum revisions approved and implemented (?) |
| 8. Ongoing updates and revisions, as necessary | LOA Teams A. MacLellan | Instructors Deans R.Mince H. Linck | Spring 2003 | Ongoing | | Post data collection—to compare pre- and post-results |
| 9. Collection of data | LOA Teams A. MacLellan G. Fink T. Hirsch | Instructors Deans | Fall 2003 and beyond | Spring 2004 and beyond | | Post data collection—to compare pre- and post-results |

*Note.* Resource column should include estimated cost, time commitment (in staff FTE or hours), budget area (base, tier, capital), and budget organization.

CCBC begins to construct the annual operational plan by articulating primary issues related to each of the strategic directions. The chancellor's cabinet reviews data to focus discussion on each of the strategic directions and identifies results to address the issues. Next, the cabinet develops a concluding statement, which, along with the results, defines the direction for the operational objectives. The operational plan then takes shape over several months.

Each spring, the chancellor's cabinet participates in a planning retreat devoted to operational planning. During this retreat, the participants develop the operational objectives based on the following:

- a comprehensive analysis of results of the quarterly and annual cabinet-level review of the college's success in achieving the prior year's operational plan
- a review of new and different data related to current objectives that require changes
- the development of new objectives and desired results in accordance with performance indicators

The chancellor's cabinet formulates tentative annual objectives and finalizes the operational plan by July 1.

Next, the cabinet moves to approve the operational plan for the fiscal year just beginning. In September, the operational plan is submitted to the board of trustees and to the college community. Upon presentation, all cabinet-level administrators receive the operational plan for use in their respective areas of responsibility. Each campus president also receives the plan for use in campus-level planning implementation. CCBC determines its budget and spending on the basis of its strategic plan and allocates its resources in order to achieve the objectives determined in its operational plan. In the recently completed planning year (FY2003), the college identified 27 objectives in the operational plan, each of which was addressed by one or more members of the chancellor's cabinet. A comprehensive review of the 27 operational plan objectives indicated that 26 (96%) were completed as originally formulated, and 1 (4%) was completed as revised.

### Annual Budget Development Process

The annual budget is the basic budgetary constraint intended to ensure that a government unit, in this case CCBC, does not spend beyond its means. The college operates within a balanced budget. At a minimum, balance should be defined to ensure that a government's use of resources for operating purposes does not exceed available resources over a defined budget period.

Budgeting is the process of translating the college's plans into an itemized, authorized, and systematic plan of operation, expressed in appropriated dollars, for a given period. The result of this process is a document that serves as a financial blueprint to monitor and control ongoing operations. Budgeting provides an opportunity to examine the composition and viability of the college's resources and current or anticipated program activities. This examination allows for the most efficient allocation of available resources to the college's priorities.

The mission of the budget process is to help decision makers come to informed choices about the provision of services and assets and to promote stakeholders' participation in the process. The budgeting process is far more than the preparation of a legal document that appropriates funds for a series of line items. Budgeting is a broadly defined process that has political, managerial, planning, communication, and financial dimensions (see Wildavsky, 1979). The operating budget has many essential features. The budget process

- incorporates a long-term perspective (prior, actual, and adopted budgets)
- establishes linkage to organizational goals (LearningFIRST 1.0 Strategic Plan)
- focuses budget decisions on results and outcomes (allocation to new or expanding programs)
- involves and promotes effective communication with stakeholders (cost-center managers, campus governance, chancellor's cabinet, county government, and constituents)
- provides flexibility to cost-center managers (budget transfers)

Formulating the CCBC's operating budget is the responsibility of the director of budgeting, who reports to the assistant vice chancellor for finance and administration. The director of budgeting is also responsible for ensuring that the budget is subject to the controls established within the accounting system and that expenditures by organizational managers remain within appropriation balances by category and by function.

The formulation process begins with the setting of budget parameters by the chancellor's cabinet. During an August retreat, my cabinet members and I review and approve the budget parameters. The approved parameters are incorporated into an operating budget development instruction letter and sent to all organization managers. During September, the organization managers develop their operating budgets based on these parameters and forward their budget requests, along with detailed line-item justifications, to the director of budgeting.

All organization requests are consolidated into a working operating budget by program and category. October is dedicated to the cabinet's review, prioritization, and transition of a working operating budget into the administration's proposed operating budget. The administration's proposed operating budget is presented to the board of trustees in November for review and is approved by the board in December. The board of trustees' operating budget is forwarded to the Baltimore County office of budget and finance (executive branch) in January. During February and March, the county office of budget and finance reviews, verifies, and revises the operating budget. The office may increase, decrease, or delete any items in the budget.

The final product of this process, presented in April, is the county executive's recommended operating budget along with a budget message to the county council (legislative branch). During the month of May, the county council reviews the budget and may decrease or delete any items in the budget, except the following: those required by the public general laws of the state of Maryland and any provision for debt service on obligations then outstanding or for estimated cash deficits. The county council has no power to change the form of the budget as submitted by the county executive, to alter the revenue estimates, or to increase any expenditure recommended by the county executive. The budget is adopted into law by the affirmative vote of the county council in May. In June, the college component of the county's adopted operating budget is presented to the board of trustees of the college, for its information. Table 11.3 presents the timeline for the annual operating and capital budget process used at CCBC.

## Expenditures by Strategic Direction

The key strategy in linking planning, budgeting, and resource allocation is the documentation of expenditures by strategic direction (see Table 11.4). Figure 11.3 demonstrates how expenditures are apportioned by use of a matrix to the eight LearningFIRST 1.0 strategic directions. Note that expenditures are primarily monitored by function and by category within each function. Note also that direct percentage allocations to students' learning (40.3%) and learning support (15.9%) total 56.2%. In LearningFIRST 1.0, integrating academic and student services creates a holistic environment that supports learning as the central focus of the college.

Another methodology for linking budget requests to strategic directions is the operational objectives form. Table 11.5 demonstrates how every budget request must be linked to a specific strategic direction in LearningFIRST 1.0. This process has been the driving force behind CCBC's effectiveness. Finally, Figure 11.4 illustrates how multiple institutional planning processes influence the annual operating budget, the capital budget, and the capital improvement program.

## Monitoring, Evaluating, and Renewing

The commitment to the culture of planning at CCBC is matched with an equally compelling commitment to a culture of evidence. A Vanguard Learning College must remain focused on implementing and integrating all programs and services that enhance the success and performance of its students. In the midst of increasing enrollments and declining state funding, colleges must maintain momentum and continue to focus on learning as their central institutional commitment.

Monitoring the implementation of the LearningFIRST 1.0 strategic plan is critical to maintaining the focus on vision. Guthrie, Garns, and Pierce (1988) warned that

**Table 11.3  Operating and Capital Budget Process**

| | Operating Budget (Annual) | Capital Budget (Biennial) |
|---|---|---|
| August | Budget parameters determined | |
| September | Revenue and expenditure requests formulated | Formulation of Capital Improvement Plan (CIP) |
| October | Chancellor's cabinet review, prioritization, and transition of working budget into administration's proposed operating budget. Presentation to the Board of Trustees. | |
| November | | |
| December | Presentation to and approval by Board of Trustees | Review CIP with County Office of Budget and Finance |
| January | Forward Board of Trustees operating budget to Baltimore County Office of Budget and Finance for review and revision | County Planning Board review and recommended CIP |
| February | | |
| March | | |
| April | County Executive's recommended operating budget | County Executive review and development of proposed CIP |
| May | | |
| June | County Council review and adoption of operating budget | County Council review and adoption |
| July | New fiscal year begins | New fiscal year begins |

## Table 11.4  Highlights of the Adopted Fiscal Year 2004 Budget

| Revenue | | FTE Data[1] | |
|---|---|---|---|
| County Appropriation[2] | $ 35,632,254 | Credit | 11,349 |
| Tuition and Fees | 45,529,226 | Non-credit | 6,390 |
| State Aid | 32,130,873 | Total | 17,739 |
| Other Revenue | 20,409,094 | | |
| **Total Revenue** | **$ 133,701,447** | **Cost per Student** | **$ 7,537** |

| LearningFirst Strategic Plan Expenditure Allocation | |
|---|---|
| Student Learning | $53,905,600 |
| Learning Support | 21,241,761 |
| Learning College | 21,586,800 |
| Infusing Technology | 12,725,080 |
| Management Excellence | 16,671,296 |
| Embracing Diversity | 2,348,822 |
| Building Community | 2,239,050 |
| Enrollment Management | 2,983,038 |
| **Total Expenditures** | **$133,701,447** |

| Expenditures by Category | | Expenditures by Function | |
|---|---|---|---|
| Salaries and Fringes | $ 92,387,186 | Instruction | $ 54,470,487 |
| Contracted Services | 10,388,058 | Public Service | 451,520 |
| Supplies & Materials | 3,314,256 | Academic Support | 11,841,624 |
| Communications | 1,582,160 | Student Services | 9,256,819 |
| Conferences & Meetings | 935,510 | Institutional Support | 24,799,928 |
| Mandatory Transfers | 21,379,063 | Operation & Maint. of Plant | 11,502,006 |
| Utilities | 2,552,622 | Mandatory Transfers | 21,379,063 |
| Fixed Charges | 576,318 | | |
| Furniture & Equipment | 586,274 | | |
| **Total Expenditures** | **$ 133,701,447** | **Total Expenditures** | **$ 133,701,447** |

[1] FTE = full-time equivalent students. Thirty credit hours equal one credit.
[2] Includes debt service of $2,534,040.

**Figure 11.3 LearningFIRST Strategic Plan Expenditure Allocation**

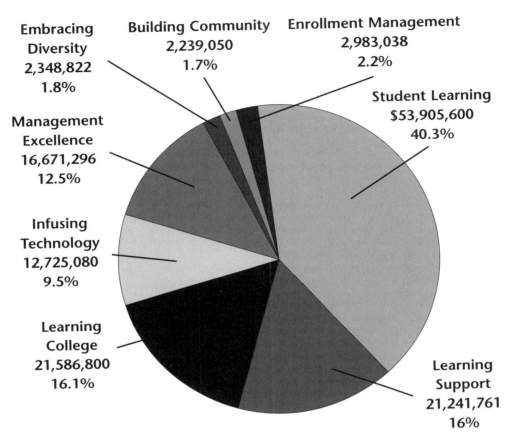

colleges must allocate resources in accord with agreed-on priorities based on the plan. This becomes a collaborative function of the chancellor's cabinet. The principal tools for monitoring, evaluating, and renewing the strategic plan are the quarterly review process and the broad-based distribution of mid-year and end-of-year accountability reports.

Each quarter, the chancellor meets with every member of the chancellor's cabinet to review progress on assigned areas of responsibility in the annual operational plan. The focused discussion centers on the operational plan accountability form (see Table 11.6) that is completed by each cabinet member and backed up with appropriate documentation.

The mid-year report is issued to internal and external constituencies. It serves as a catalyst for communications throughout the community and helps to keep everyone focused on the primary institutional commitment to students' learning. A comprehensive end-of-year report is prepared each August and is widely distributed throughout the institution.

## Table 11.5  The Community College of Baltimore County FY2004 Operational Objectives Form

**Fund #:** 6000

**Organization # / Name:** 61195-PA Collaborative Program

**Program #:** 10

**Cost Center Manager:** Carol D. Eustis

---

**Project:** Physician Assistant Program

**Objective:** To serve the educational needs for the licensing of physician assistants

**Description:** This program, in collaboration with Towson University, prepares students for licensure by engaging in a 57-credit certificate program offered by CCBC and a 33-credit master's in physician assistant studies.

---

**Strategic Direction:** Student learning, learning support, learning college, infusing technology.

**Strategic Plan Objectives:** To create a learning-centered environment that enables students to develop and achieve the professional skills they will need for practice.
To prepare students for licensure.
To provide students with state-of-the-art technology to further enhance their skills.
To better prepare students to move into the clinical setting.

**Funding (Base/Tier/Technology Fee):** Tier

**Technology Plan Link:**

**Timeline for Completion:** August 15, 2004

---

| Category/Description | Account # | $ Request |
|---|---|---|
| Instructional Equipment | 7030 | $75,000 |

**Justification**

The clinical simulation model, Sim-Man, is a state-of-the-art patient that can be programmed to provide medical scenarios covering a broad range illnesses and systemic malfunctions. The model serves to replicate situations that students may or may not see in clinical rotations. Therefore, it not only  serves as a "without harm" patient for students to perfect skills but also provides a vehicle to further expand their training prior to licensure and practice. Students are provided immediate feedback as to the appropriateness of their plan of care and the consequences of their critical thinking in dealing with symptoms, illness ,etc., as programmed and demonstrated by Sim-Man. This learning tool serves to enhance students' preparation and training. Sim-Man includes the full form patient able to accommodate the insertion of IVs, injections, detection of heart and breathing sounds, and coughing, to mention a few, and can also be programmed to respond verbally to the students. The associated computer and hardware provides for a real patient in the laboratory setting.

## Figure 11.4  Primary Planning and Operational Resources

Institutional (CCBC) Academic Plan

Strategic Plan LearningFIRST (Long-Term)

Campus Plans (3)
- Catonsville
- Dundalk
- Essex

Annual Operating Plans (Action Planning Worksheet)

Continuing Education and Economic Development Business Plan

Technology Plan

**Annual Operating Budget (MOE + Tier)**

**Capital Budget & CIP**

Strategic Enrollment Management Plan

Vanguard Plan

10-Year Facilities Master Plan

Annual Unanticipated College Priorities

Turnover Assessment

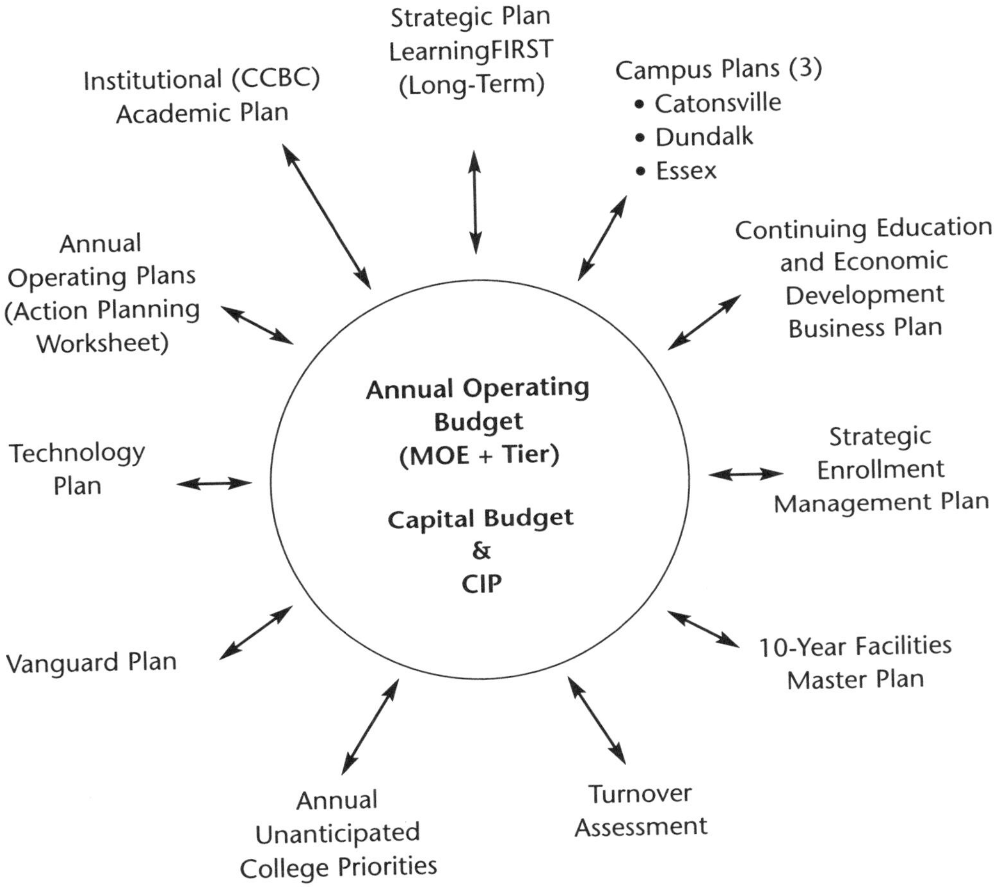

*Note.* This graphic represents the primary planning and operational resources affecting the development of the annual operating budget, the capital budget, and the capital improvement program.

## Leadership's Role in Linking Strategic Planning, Budgeting, and Resource Allocation

The literature suggests that organizational leaders cannot rely solely on strategic planning to create linkages between the many components of the organization. Bryson (1995), for example, argued that strategic planning is not a substitute for effective leadership; instead, strategic planning is simply a set of concepts, procedures, and tools designed to help leaders think and act strategically on behalf of their organizations and their stakeholders.

Leaders are called on to perform political, spiritual, and intellectual functions as well as managerial and group maintenance tasks. These range from providing vision and strategies for change to mobilizing a constituency to facilitating group decisions or

## Table 11.6   Operational Plan Accountability Form (OPAF)

CHANCELLOR'S CABINET
2002–2003 OPERATIONAL PLAN
OPERATIONAL PLAN ACCOUNTABILITY FORM

NAME: Henry Linck

TITLE: Vice Chancellor for Learning and Student Development

QUARTER:

I _____      II _____      III _____      IV ____X____

KRA: Student Learning

OBJECTIVE: 1.2.1 To conduct five high-impact learning outcomes assessment (LOA) projects.

STATUS:          COMPLETED          ____X____
                 ON SCHEDULE        _____
                 BEHIND SCHEDULE    _____

                                    _____

SIGNIFICANT ACCOMPLISHMENTS:

The CCBC *Guide for Learning Outcomes Assessment and Classroom Learning Assessment* (enclosed) has been distributed to all full-time faculty and will soon be available via the CCBC Web page. A number of other colleges have requested a copy of our Guide and continue to "borrow" the excellent work that we have done at CCBC to develop their own LOA policies and procedures. CCBC has been recognized as a national leader in the area of Learning Outcomes Assessment—most recently in an article entitled "Benchmarking Best Practices in the Learning College" by the Vanguard Learning College Project Evaluator, Kay McClenney.

All five high-impact LOA projects for FY03 have completed the first phase of their assessment. Baseline data have been collected for HLTH 101, PEFT 101, CINS 101, and SDEV 101. The ENGL 101 project included a pilot phase to test the writing prompts and scoring rubric that will be used to assess the data. More than 400 writing prompts have been collected. The prompts will be scored during summer 2003. The first round of data from the other four projects will also be analyzed during the summer, and faculty will begin developing curricular changes in fall 2003.

Another significant accomplishment is the approval of the Learning Outcomes Assessment Advisory Board's (LOAAB) Core Competencies Learning Outcomes Assessment Initiative by the Learning/Academic Affairs Council (see attached). LOAAB has done tremendous work this year to get the Assessment Initiative written and approved. CCBC now has an approved definition of assessment, an assessment mission statement, and four core competencies that will be addressed (and eventually assessed) in every CCBC course. The four core competencies are Communication, Critical and Analytical Thinking, Global Perspective and Social Responsibility, and Independent Learning and Personal Management.

ATTACH APPROPRIATE DOCUMENTATION:

creating coalitions. Unless the organization is very small, no single person or group can perform them all. Effective linking of strategic planning, budgeting, and resource allocation functions is a collective phenomenon, typically involving sponsors, champions, facilitators, teams, task forces, and others in various ways at different times.

Linking strategic planning, budgeting, and resource allocation at CCBC has occurred amidst the onslaught of bad financial news, stagnant or shrinking revenue, and growing public pessimism. The expectation is that colleges must do more with less. The following leadership strategies have enabled me to work collaboratively with the cabinet and all key constituent groups in managing through gloomy financial times (McPhail, 2003).

### Strategies for Leaders

Tie the numbers to vision. A college's vision and mission must drive college operations. Budgeting is no exception. Quite frankly, it may be the college function most critically linked to vision and mission, because no activity can take place without appropriate funding. At CCBC, every budget request item is evaluated in terms of whether or not it advances learning-centered priorities. How well it stands up to the litmus test of supporting students' learning determines its fate.

Build it from the bottom up. With the college's vision and mission emanating from the top and flowing down and out, a bottom-up approach to budget building is crucial. First, it makes people and departments accountable. More important, it enhances buy-in for the vision and mission throughout the organization. Everyone grows accustomed to thinking strategically and for the good of the college. A sense of unity and a commonality of purpose evolve. The resulting budget clearly demonstrates that the whole is greater than the sum of its parts.

Avoid a pie-in-the-sky approach. There is no room for wishful thinking in today's economy. Realistic expenditure and revenue projections should become second nature. Revenue projections, in particular, require a strong partnership among a college's finance, enrollment management and planning, and research arms. Budget managers need to rely on their joint expertise for scientific projections. But do not stop there. Adopt a holistic approach to budgeting. View projections in light of past performance of peer colleges and up-to-date environmental scanning. It is about more than the numbers.

Give finance a real seat at the table. Make the chief financial officer (CFO) a leader at the table in terms of college decisions, not just financial ones. See budgeting as more than pure fund appropriation. Funding is pervasive to every decision, every action. That is why it is important to appoint a member of the college's finance team to standing college committees, such as strategic enrollment management. Such front-line and executive-level financial guidance goes a long way toward ensuring sound financial decisions.

Be ready to shift gears. Virtually every speaker on the motivational circuit today promotes the concept of balance. This principle applies to budgeting as well. Balance control with flexibility. Stay on top of spending by working with the CFO and other college leaders throughout the year to identify and fund those unanticipated college priorities. Otherwise, the system will not be as fluid and responsive as it must be.

Make friends with technology. If vision is the vehicle that drives all college operations, then technology is the engine. To be at the forefront of the information revolution, colleges must integrate technology into all that they do, including budget management. At CCBC, the online information system, BANNER, is used to make up-to-date budget information immediately accessible to all budget managers. There is no need for managers to wait for monthly budget office reports when they can more easily monitor spending on a daily basis. It generates goodwill, gives them direct oversight, and leads to better management decisions.

Do not rush a good thing. Details require time. The budget planning and approval process must not be rushed. CCBC allows 4 solid months from the onset of budget planning to the final adoption by the board of trustees. Along the way, training workshops for all budget managers throughout the organization demonstrate how to write clear, detailed, line-item justifications. As a result, the answers are ready if either trustees or the county executive question specific items. The college can respond quickly and appropriately. This builds credibility and trust.

Be open year-round. Regular and honest communication with all stakeholders is important. It is not enough to work with budget managers during the planning phase, with trustees during the adoption phase, and so on. Assign a finance representative to each major area of the college organization. Make sure each manager has a trusted contact to call on for help with budget decisions or transactions. Invite representatives of the college's funding agencies to board of trustee meetings. Keep the lines of communication open and avoid surprises. When tough decisions need to be made the college will already have the board's support.

Raise the bar. Encourage excellence and seek third-party validation to acknowledge it. This will not only build internal confidence for a job well done, but will also enhance credibility with trustees and funding agents. As a college that seeks to attain premier, learning-centered status, CCBC is committed to the highest principles of government budgeting. Earning the Government Finance Officers Association (GFOA) Distinguished Budget Award affirmed this commitment.

Be willing to take a stand. When funding is dwindling and resources are stretched to the limit, not all programs can receive all they ask for. In the end, to try to meet every department's request will lead to poor quality, which is counter to the college's vision of excellence. Budget managers will have to make allocations based on priorities. CCBC recently made structural changes that, although difficult, will free about $1.5 million over the next two years to help fuel priorities and preserve core programs and services. Ultimately, this may be one of the best ways to safeguard the college's mission.

## Conclusion

CCBC has developed creative new links among strategic planning, budgeting, and resource allocation to meet the challenge of sustaining organizational transformation and becoming more learning-centered during a period of fiscal decline and retrenchment. The efforts for the past 6 years have proven counter to the conventional wisdom and evidence regarding integrating planning with budgeting and resource allocations.

In a pioneering study, Williams (1999) surveyed all 107 California community colleges to determine, among other things, the extent to which the planning, budgeting, and financial resource allocation processes were integrated. Williams concluded that such integration did not exist or was very weak. This is the general conclusion reached in the planning and budgeting literature.

CCBC continues to evolve its planning, budgeting, and resource allocation model and to search for best practices. The success of the LearningFIRST 1.0 journey has suggested much in the way of assembling the elements of strategic planning, budgeting, and resource allocation such that the newly introduced LearningFIRST 2.0 2003–2008 strategic plan is enhanced by these integrative processes.

## References

Below, P. J., Morrisey, G. L., & Acomb, B. L. (1987). *The executive guide to strategic planning.* San Francisco: Jossey-Bass.

Bryson, J. M. (1995). *Strategic planning for public and nonprofit organizations: A guide to strengthening and sustaining organizational achievement.* San Francisco: Jossey-Bass.

Guthrie, J. W., Garns, W. L., & Pierce, L. C. (1988). *School finance and educational policy: Enhancing educational efficiency, equality and choice.* Englewood Cliffs, NJ: Prentice-Hall.

Massey, W. F. (1996). *Resource allocation in higher education.* Ann Arbor: University of Michigan Press.

McPhail, I. P. (1999, September). Launching LearningFIRST at the Community College of Baltimore County. *Learning Abstracts, 2*(6).

McPhail, I. P. (2003, March 18). 10 steps to better budgeting in "blue" budget days. *Community College Times,* p. 2.

McPhail, I. P., & Heacock, R. C. (1999). Baltimore County: A college and community in transition. In R. C. Bowen & G. H. Muller (Eds.), *Gateway to democracy: Six urban community college systems* (pp. 75–83). San Francisco: Jossey-Bass.

McPhail, I. P., Heacock, R. C., & Linck, H. F. (2001, January). LearningFIRST: Creating and leading the learning college. *Community College Journal of Research and Practice, 25*(1), 17–28.

Meisinger, R. J. (1990). Introduction to special issue on the relationship between planning and budgeting. *Planning for Higher Education, 18*(2), 1–8.

Schmidtlein, F. A. (1990). Why linking budgets to plans has proven difficult in higher education. *Planning for Higher Education, 18*(2), 9–24.

Wildavsky, A. (1979). *The politics of the budgetary process* (3rd ed.). Boston: Little, Brown.

Williams, J. E. (1999). *Linking strategic planning, budgeting, and resource allocation in California community colleges.* Unpublished doctoral dissertation, University of LaVerne, CA.

# PART 5

# Surviving and Sustaining the Paradigm Shift

# CHAPTER 12

# When Do You Know You Have a Learning College?

RENATE KRAKAUER

Over the past few years, colleges have implemented many innovative methodologies intended to improve and expand learning. Solid evidence of change is still scarce, however. How do colleges know whether real changes have been achieved or whether the new methodologies are merely window dressing? How do educators know whether the changes are deeply embedded in the fabric of the college or whether they will fade away when a new administration with different priorities takes over? As the learning college movement gathers momentum, colleges may want to clarify their status as they prepare to move forward. In this chapter, I suggest practical ways in which colleges can assess their level of learning-centeredness in all areas—academia, administration, leadership, instructors, and students—to establish a baseline from which improvement and expansion of student learning can proceed.

## Improving and Expanding Learning Through Self-Assessment

With conflicting pressures to be simultaneously more responsive and more fiscally conservative, colleges must stay focused on their commitment to learning-centered principles as part of their long-term goals. A vision of what your college would look like as a learning college and a plan for how to get there must be embedded in the mainstream of the college's business and not be marginalized as an ad hoc collection of projects. A self-assessment will help guide you in this direction.

Societal and workplace trends are making the learning college model more attractive for community colleges. By recognizing the importance of work-related learning, the learning college can respond to the changing nature of work, including the expansion of part-time jobs, the emphasis on teams, the introduction of new technology into work processes, and employers' requirements for independent, self-directed employees (Foot & Stoffman, 1998). The knowledge age has become pervasive as a workplace phenomenon (Norris & Malloch, 1997), and the workforce needs to be learning constantly to keep up to date. The learning college prepares students for the lifelong learning necessary to succeed in this kind of environment.

Another trend is the increase in the number of older students; older students make more demands on the postsecondary education system. According to O'Banion (1997), the needs of this growing group of students, who have been in the workforce for a few years and want to upgrade their skills or change careers, are not being met effectively by the current system. In addition, with the increasing diversity of the student population, the benefits of a learning-centered education are becoming even more apparent.

In this chapter, I also describe how a self-assessment process can be designed to help a college (or a department within a college) determine how its level of learning-centeredness and how a college or department can use that information to improve and enhance learning. Because colleges, like students, differ from one another and vary in strengths and weaknesses, each college should create its own self-assessment tool using the suggestions provided.

## Where to Start

To avoid a piecemeal approach, it is important to start with a commitment to learning-centered education from the college leadership and a collegewide self-assessment that is coordinated and integrated into the strategic planning process. If enthusiastic staff members undertake isolated initiatives without centralized support or a respected champion, the initiatives will not be part of the mainstream of college activity. Individual efforts may be based on different criteria and may not be understood and accepted by the college community. Those same initiatives enacted within the framework of a centralized self-assessment will have a greater impact and will be more useful for college leaders in ongoing strategic planning for the improving and evolving environment.

After gaining senior-level commitment, develop a common understanding of and language for the underlying principles, theories, and models of learning-centered education within the college community. This is a significant learning project for staff and students that can be implemented through open forums, lunch-and-learn sessions, faculty debates, and other opportunities to gather the college's community members together for open discussion and dialogue. For students, the most opportune time for such discussion is probably the orientation session at the beginning of the school year. These sessions will help gauge the readiness of students, instructors, and other staff members to undertake self-assessment. After a decision has been made to conduct a self-assessment, whether throughout the college, in selected departments, or as a pilot study, a cross-functional, multidisciplinary, and multilevel committee should be created to steer the process. The role of the committee will be described at the end of this chapter.

In the next sections, I outline the categories of self-assessment that I have developed through my research and experience at my own college (Krakauer, 2001). The insights I gained as my institution began to use the self-assessment process in 2000 have helped me to formulate the questions presented in each category. All major aspects of college life are covered, including leadership and organization, delivery and design of curriculum, students and teachers, learning outcomes, specialists, and college culture.

## What To Consider in Self-Assessment

### *College Leadership*

The board of trustees and senior management of a college should act as champions of learning-centered education. They define the college's strategic priorities and can demonstrate that learning-centered education can be integrated at the highest level of college business. Senior managers, who have primary responsibility and accountability for the college's performance, need to show their commitment to students' learning and whatever it takes to improve it. Leadership also can be reflected in the performance of individual staff members and groups of employees who understand the concept of a learning-centered education and their role in facilitating learning.

Revisiting the mission and vision statements of the college is a good first step, even if the college has already started on the learning college journey. These statements should indicate clearly to the internal and external community that learning-centered education is an integral part of the college's regular activities. The mission and vision statements should be meaningful and should be reflected in action to avoid cynicism among staff and students.

Commitment to learning-centered education also needs to be demonstrated in budget allocation. Learning can be enhanced with appropriate financial support not only for excellent teaching and support staff but also for strategic information technology, a clean and pleasant physical environment, appropriate and up-to-date laboratory equipment, and the development of innovative curriculum and techniques for assessing students. Such support provides staff members and students with evidence that the leadership of the college puts its values into practice.

The following are some sample questions that can be asked in the college leadership category:

- Do the college mission and vision statements refer to student learning?
- Does the college leadership advocate for learning-centered education internally with staff members and students and externally with stakeholders and funders?
- Has management established financial priorities for those aspects of college life that have the greatest direct impact on learning?
- Does the college have long-term plans for items such as information systems, physical plant development, and academic equipment that support teaching and learning and are aligned with learning-centered education?

## *College Organization*

Some colleges, in their efforts to become learning colleges, are applying the management principles of total quality management (TQM) and learning organizations. (For examples of how these principles have been applied at Sinclair Community College, Ohio; Jackson Community College, Michigan; and Maricopa Community College, Arizona—see O'Banion, 1997). TQM ( also called continuous quality improvement) is helping colleges to develop more streamlined and efficient processes, eliminate duplication, involve employees in problem solving, and become more customer focused. These approaches can help colleges make substantial changes in their systems and structures and create open, participatory organizational cultures, which may bring about greater support for learning-centered education.

The concept of the learning organization is sometimes confused with that of the learning college. The fundamental differences relate to purpose and emphasis. The learning college places students and their learning first, both as an institutional value and as a central focus around which the whole institution is organized. The learning organization is focused on employees learning to make the organization more effective. Systems thinking, shared vision, and transformational and collaborative learning are some of the ways in which employees can participate more fully in organizational life to make their jobs more meaningful and to contribute to the long-term goals of the organization (Senge, 1990). These new behaviors are fostered in a learning organization by its flattened hierarchy, empowerment of employees to use their creativity and intelligence to make decisions, and involvement of employees in developing organizational goals (Krakauer, 2001).

Although TQM and the learning organization model do not address the central issues of learning-centered education, they are useful tools for improving the overall organization of a college, its administrative systems and procedures, and its student support services. The focus on employees' learning is particularly important for fully engaged participation in the learning college initiative. Financial rewards are not the only or necessarily preferred method of recognition, but they can be used to support improvement in employees' performance. Employees also need to be told regularly whether they are doing a good job, especially in the area of innovation and support for students' learning.

Sometimes colleges develop policies that contribute little to the institution except more bureaucracy. All policies should be thoroughly overhauled; how they affect learning should be examined. O'Banion (1997, p.12) referred to the bureaucracy inherent in colleges as the "efficiency-bound architecture of education." With focused policies and new, sophisticated information systems, more flexibility should be possible. One department that many colleges have been able to make more student-friendly is student services. Students should have convenient and timely access to registration services, financial aid, housing, and counseling.

Educators are sometimes uncomfortable with the word customer when applied to students. In the learning college, learning is a partnership between those who deliver and facilitate it and those who participate as learners—it is not merely an exchange of goods and services for money. Nevertheless, the customer service metaphor is useful to represent the service aspect of the partnership. The following are some questions to ask in reviewing the organization of a college:

- How many layers of decision making exist in the college? That is, does bureaucracy get in the way of engaging students in relevant, flexible learning?
- Do all employees understand their roles in facilitating learning in a learning college?
- Does the budget process allocate adequate support to learning-centered objectives for employees' development?
- Is the remuneration system tied to performance? Do performance appraisals include achievements based on learning-centered criteria?
- Are college policies regularly reviewed to determine whether they support student learning?
- Is there a rigid schedule or timetable for learning, or can students create their own timetable (with assistance) to meet their learning needs?
- Are diversity and student differences accommodated?
- Are learning resources, on site and by remote access, available 24 hours a day/7 days a week, with user-friendly technical support?
- Are student services organized around student needs?
- Are services and information readily accessible, accurate, and easy to understand?

### Learning Options

Learning options are about choice. In the learning college, students can choose from a wide variety of ways to receive the components of their programs. In this context, learning is understood as a process that refers to what happens when people engage in activities to meet certain needs and to achieve their goals or desired outcomes. Understanding the learning process helps educators to support individual students and to design learning options from which students can select those most suited to their learning style, life circumstances, or ability level.

One method of supporting the learning process is to provide self-directed learning options, whether through individual or group study. As more adults with more work and life experience are added to the growing diversity of the community college student population, they may prefer and may be more prepared to be self-directed. In addition, students who are very independent may want to select self-directed learning options. The availability of online study helps self-directed learners, whether they select this delivery method because they prefer it or because attendance at the college campus conflicts with home and work responsibilities.

Working together on academic projects also can be a preferred method of learning for students because it combines self-direction and collaboration—which is excellent preparation for the workforce. Problem-based learning (Barrows, 1986; Boud, 1985; Checkley, 1997; Woods, 1985) and situated cognition (Wilson, 1993) incorporate collaboration and self-direction; they stress the relationship of learning to real-world experience and fit well into the learning college. Providing these learning options for students gives them an opportunity to understand the relevance of what they are learning, to practice skills and knowledge as they learn, and to benefit from the mentorship of experienced professionals in the field as they learn to solve increasingly complex problems. To have a real choice of learning options, students must be offered a variety of methods for the delivery of content within the same program area and must not be penalized for selecting one option over another. For example, the content of a course offered online or through a work-study format should be valued at the same number of credits as it would be through the traditional classroom method.

The following are some questions that could be asked in the learning options category:

- Does the college offer a variety of programs, courses, and other units of learning through multiple delivery methods so that students have real options with which to create a learning plan to meet their individual needs?
- Does the college offer academic advising to help students make the right selections within this variety to meet their long-term academic, career, and personal goals?
- Does the college offer a variety of online and distance education learning options?
- Can students select and combine or replace traditional courses with independent study, collaborative learning, problem-based learning, situated cognition, or other nontraditional approaches and receive equivalent credit?
- Are students given academic credit for workplace learning?
- Can students vary the length of time it takes them to complete the requirements for credits?
- Can students select or structure learning options at their own level of difficulty depending on their abilities and learning or career goals?
- Can students select learning options across disciplines or departments to experience an integrated rather than specialized curriculum?

### *Learning Content*

When designing the curriculum and specific learning activities, instructors in a learning college rarely rely on the "sage-on-the-stage" or lecture method, although this may be a useful approach for providing a brief overview of the subject matter. Traditional methods are based on the behaviorist learning theory of "show and tell, repeat, and practice" and are useful in skills training, professional education, laboratory work, clinical education (i.e., the experiential education component for health-care professionals), and any work that requires repeated drill and practice to perfect techniques. Some technology-based learning is also behaviorist in nature, for example, that provided through computer-assisted or Web-based instruction. However, the process of transferring large and complex quantities of information in a lecture format combined with rote learning (i.e., behaviorist methodology) is not appropriate in the learning college because this method suppresses inquiry and dialogue (Krakauer, 2001).

Cognitivist and constructivist learning theories are much more useful bases on which to design learning activities in the learning college. Cognitivism recognizes that the learner is in control of learning as an internal process and not a process restricted by the environment. Cognitivists believe that learning is cumulative; as more information is accumulated, mentally manipulated, and stored, the learner's understanding and ability to make sense of future input of information is enhanced (Cross, 1999). Instructors in a learning college using this approach ensure that they design learning activities that involve students as active participants and that require "deep-level processing, thinking, and manipulating of content by the student … to increase the probability that effective learning will occur" (Boettcher & Conrad, 1999, p. 19). The instruments used to analyze a person's learning style are based on the cognitivist principle that recognizes the different ways in which people process information. Instructors can structure and adapt learning activities by analyzing students' learning styles so that their learning is enhanced.

Constructivist learning theory also supports the design of learning activities in the learning college. According to this theory, students do not acquire knowledge by a process of transmittal from an external source but create knowledge by extracting meaning from experience. Each student thus comes to the learning activity with different experiences, interests, emotions, and previous knowledge and will create her or his own construction of knowledge by interacting with the environment through internal cognitive processes. Social constructivists believe the process of creation of knowledge takes place through social interaction with others in discussion and group activities (Krakauer, 2001).

Problem-based learning and situated cognition are two examples of how the constructivist learning theory can be applied to curriculum design. Students take responsibility for what they need to know and how to learn it, including the sequence and pace of learning. Collaborative learning groups "in which people construct knowledge as they talk together and reach consensus" is another valuable application of constructivist theory to curriculum design (Bruffee, 1999, p. 84).

Technology-mediated learning provides opportunities for self-directed learning, collaborative learning, and real-life simulations (e.g., situated cognition). Technology-mediated learning contributes to O'Banion's (1997) conception of the learning college by enabling learning experiences to be offered anyway, anyplace, anytime. Students are released from the boundaries of space (location) and time (pace of learning). They can solve problems in simulations of real-life situations and can participate in collaborative learning that they might not have been able to do under normal circumstances.

In assessing your college in the learning content category, ask the following questions:

- Does the learning content (including curriculum and lesson plans) encourage critical thinking, higher levels of comprehension and evaluation, analytical skills, and the use of judgment?
- Is the curriculum designed to maximize students' inherent abilities and affinities?
- Is the curriculum regularly reviewed and updated to ensure that it meets the needs of the students, as well as employers and other stakeholders?
- Does the curriculum incorporate real-life work experience as a learning activity?
- Is the curriculum designed to incorporate simulated and problem-based learning modules and self-directed learning?
- Are students active participants in designing learning activities?
- Does the curriculum demonstrate sensitivity to the students' life experiences, prior knowledge, and diversity?

### *Students as Learners*

In the learning college, students are called learners to focus on their active participation as full partners in the learning process. It becomes the responsibility of the college to help students reach their full potential as learners not only while they are enrolled in its programs but also throughout their lives. The college should seek input and feedback from students on the ways learning is delivered, specific learning activities, assessment of outcomes, and all aspects of the learning experience. This does not mean that educators should abrogate their responsibility to control curriculum and standards but that they should be responsive and flexible and should attempt to accommodate students' needs and concerns as much as possible. In a learning college, individual differences are recognized and accommodated. It is therefore to be expected that some students will be less prepared to take responsibility for their own learning than others; these students will require more support.

According to humanist learning theory, each person is considered capable of learning to her or his unlimited potential and, by choosing to do so, takes full responsibility for himself or herself (Merriam & Caffarella, 1999). This theory may apply more to adult learners, but all learners have the potential to become more responsible for their own learning. As the diversity of the college population increases, more working adults are returning to school full time or part time to enhance their employability. These students are more vocal and assertive in their desire to control their own learning than younger students are. They also experience, like all students, differences in motivation;

barriers to participation in learning; and varying life experience, social contexts, and learning needs and styles. Educators must pay attention to all of these differences.

The following questions can help to determine the level of support that the college provides for students to become independent learners:

- Does the college help students take increasing responsibility for their own learning by providing assistance for them to identify learning needs, create learning plans, select learning options, and develop independent study skills?
- Are students' differences respected and accommodated? Are students treated with respect as adults?
- Are all students assisted in becoming more self-directed, self-evaluative, lifelong learners in their programs of study?
- Do students provide feedback on how their experience at the college has changed them?
- Do students give feedback on college programs, curriculum, policies, instructors, and administrative processes? Is appropriate and timely action taken on this feedback?
- Do students have a voice in the decision-making process related to programs and services through their elected representatives?

## Instructors as Learning Facilitators

An instructor's commitment and ability to make the transition to learning-centered practices from traditional instruction are crucial to the success of the learning college. Some instructors may think this new role reduces their importance in the teaching–learning relationship. In fact, in their new role, they are even more important, because it takes far greater skill and broad-based knowledge to be a coach and a mentor than it does to be a traditional instructor lecturing to students. In addition to the essential disciplinary expertise, the learning facilitator must have excellent interpersonal skills to relate to individual learners, design curricula to maximize learning, understand the learning process, and evaluate to what degree a student's learning outcomes have been achieved.

Carl Rogers may have been the originator of the term "learning facilitator." He based his theory of education on respect for the individual, the ineffectiveness of the lecture method, the need to share power between teachers and students, and freedom with responsibility for students (Merriam & Caffarella, 1999; O'Banion, 1997; Rogers, 1983). One of the most difficult things to change in creating a learning college is what happens in the classroom. The closed door behind which teachers do their work is almost as sacrosanct as the proverbial closed bedroom door. This tradition needs to be challenged for the benefit of instructors as well as students. A collaborative approach has been found not only to enhance students' learning but also to increase instructors' job satisfaction.

The college should address instructors' recruitment, qualifications, professional development, and ability to adopt learning-centered principles. Instructors are both self-directed learners and collaborators in curriculum design and implementation; they serve as a powerful role models for students. Assessment of instructors' effectiveness should include questions such as the following:

- Does the college have a systematic recruitment and selection process for hiring new instructors? How is the commitment to learning-centered education evaluated?
- Is there a comprehensive and accessible professional development program, with a focus on learning-centered education and with financial support for professional development.
- Are instructors provided with assistance in curriculum design to transform their programs to meet the learning needs of students more effectively and to contribute to their learning outcomes?
- Do instructors make themselves available to students for guidance, coaching, and mentoring? Do they help students to prepare learning contracts and provide remediation if necessary? Does the college see this component as central to rather than as an add-on to the existing workload?
- Is there an effective developmental performance appraisal process for instructors that includes self-assessment and feedback from peers, students, and supervisors? Does this process incorporate demonstrated commitment to and implementation of learning-centered principles?

### *Learning Outcomes*

The results or outcomes of students' learning can be assessed on an individual or an institutional basis. The focus should be on demonstrable change in a student's knowledge, competence, and behavior on an individual basis or on an improvement in aggregate student achievement or in another indicator of the organization's effectiveness in promoting learning on an institutional basis.

Assessing student learning in a learning-centered way has been a major challenge for instructors. With large classes and complaints of overload, many instructors do not feel ready to give up multiple-choice exams. Even those who do forego these exams find it difficult to develop appropriate alternative assessment tools. The literature includes numerous examples of learning-centered assessment, such as those proposed by Jonassen (1991): using goal-free evaluation methodologies to avoid bias and the constraints of previously established criteria; assessing authentic, real-world tasks performed at different levels of complexity; performing task and content analysis with a focus on alternative sequences and conceptions to fit alternative evaluation needs; and evaluating higher-order thinking by assessing originality of arguments and solutions to problems.

Students can be evaluated as they acquire knowledge on the basis of evaluation guidelines available to the students and the facilitator beforehand. In this way, both students and facilitators can know how the students are doing as they proceed in the learning program. Evaluation also can be performed on the impact of courses of action proposed by students in case studies based on real-world contexts (Jonassen, 1991). Because the learning college combines theoretical learning with simulation and real-life experience, appropriate assessment tools are needed for both types of learning.

The following are some questions to consider about students' learning outcomes:

- Is assessment related to learning objectives and competencies? Do assessment measurements go beyond numerical or letter scores?
- Are a variety of formative and summative tools used to assess learning?
- Are a variety of assessors used when appropriate (e.g., on work-related projects), including employers, peers, and other instructors?
- Are students given an opportunity to negotiate how they will be assessed?
- Is a portfolio approach available for students to document their learning outcomes, achievements, and assessments at various stages in the learning process?
- Are students who experience difficulty identified early on the basis of assessment results? Are they supplied with remediation and tutoring?
- Is Prior Learning Assessment and Recognition made available to applicants to the college to recognize knowledge and skills gained in other jurisdictions or through nontraditional learning?

On an institutional level, the college needs to examine its methods of evaluating how effectively it is achieving the goals it has established for collegewide learning outcomes. This evaluation can focus on questions such as the following:

- Is there a comprehensive institutional system in the college for reviewing effective performance (e.g., key performance indicators)? If so, does this system incorporate criteria for evaluating learning outcomes?
- Does the college collect data on learning outcomes related to recognized standards of competency for programs that have external accrediting bodies or where national standards are available?
- Is information collected on a regular and recurrent basis, and does it take into account learning outcomes; completion, retention, and employment rates; and the satisfaction of students, graduates, and employers? Is this information used as feedback for improvement measures to be developed and implemented?

### Access to Specialist Resources

The availability of specialists (e.g., counselors, librarians, information technologists, curriculum designers, and professional development staff) depends on the size and financial resources of the college. When there are few specialists, a greater burden falls on instructors so that they have less time to support students in becoming independent, self-directed learners. Specialists also serve as facilitators of learning at the college, because they come in direct contact with students and support and enhance students' learning in a substantial and timely manner. Investment in specialized support is worthwhile not only in supporting learning, but also in integrating departments other than the traditional teaching departments as members of the team working to becoming a learning college.

The college should examine the availability and appropriateness of its level of staffing in this area by considering the following: Does the college provide adequate levels of expertise to

- Assess students' needs and learning styles?
- Design innovative and appropriate assessment tools to evaluate learning outcomes?
- Counsel students who need clarification on goals, values, expectations, family problems, financial pressures, and the like?
- Design technology-mediated learning and other innovative learning models and assist instructors in adapting their subject matter to these formats?
- Create necessary databases and assist in their retrieval and analysis for institutional and individual research?
- Increase the capacity of the system for individualization of programs?

## College Culture

A learning college fosters a culture that supports learning by paying attention to morale issues among all employees, the employee–labor relations climate, and students' satisfaction with the learning experience and student life. Culture is, however, one of the most difficult things to measure and change. Employees and students often can sense intuitively the quality of the working and learning environment. It also may be reflected in the college's reputation among prospective students and in the community as a desirable employer.

An assessment of this category should include instructor–student relationships, the predominant communication style used at the college, the ways in which people generally interact with one another, and how involved all levels of staff feel in the learning college enterprise—from the caretaker to the president. The mark of a positive college culture is the level of enthusiasm among all its members and their willingness to participate in learning-centered projects and activities. Such enthusiasm is noticeable in the hallways, in the offices, and in the library, but most of all in the classrooms and laboratories, and it can be a source of great satisfaction to all those who dedicate themselves to its creation and support.

The following are some questions that can be used to assess culture:

- Does the college have a publicly enunciated statement of values that incorporates commitment to learning-centered principles? Has this statement been developed in a collaborative and participatory way within the college community?
- Are satisfaction surveys conducted regularly with employees, students, graduates and alumni, and employers? Is follow-up action taken when necessary and appropriate?
- Is there open communication, both up and down, through a variety of accessible mediums (e.g., town hall meetings, newsletters, informal forums, debates, and discussions) on issues important to the learning college?
- Are instructor–student relationships and staff–management relationships based on mutual trust and support?
- If a union exists, are there few grievances and a positive approach to collective bargaining such as interest-based negotiation?
- Is there frequent opportunity for and demonstrated evidence of teamwork and collaboration across departments and organizational levels?
- Does the college community take time to celebrate its successes, especially those related to learning-centered education?

## Developing an Action Plan

As mentioned earlier in this chapter, a cross-functional, multidisciplinary, and multilevel committee should be created to steer the process of college self-assessment as well as to guide the implementation of learning-centered education throughout the college. For example, the committee can decide which departments, programs, or service areas are most receptive to the learning-centered education process. By starting with areas of the college in which learning outcomes or level of service can be demonstrated readily, the self-assessment process can be a positive experience and a boost to morale rather than a threatening exercise.

When the committee decides on a set of questions that it considers most useful and appropriate for its college, it should coordinate the formation of teams to conduct interviews; hold focus groups; review documents, promotional materials, and policies; and decide which surveys should be used. Collecting data for baseline information will take a considerable length of time and will require college support for employees involved in its gathering and analysis. The analysis is critical for identifying key areas to target for action. The timeframe for setting priorities for action should be 3 to 5 years, with regular progress updates to the whole community. The committee can devise a rating or ranking system for items or criteria in the self-assessment. In *Criteria for a Learning College* (Krakauer, 2000), I provide a simple rating scale for each criterion identified in the self-assessment. Committees may choose to follow the grading scale in Table 12.1 or create their own, to indicate the overall degree of progress for the college.

## Table 12.1  A Simple Rating Scale for College Self-Assessment

0            = No evidence that this item has been implemented at the college.

✓            = This item is being discussed, is in the planning stages, or, if present,
              occurs only marginally in isolated examples.

✓✓          = This item has been partially implemented or is in evidence in some programs
              in a visible and substantial way.

✓✓✓        = This item has been fully implemented across the whole college.

---

The process of becoming a learning college is long and will be different for each college. The long-term action plan helps to keep everyone on track in the same way that a roadmap does. The destination is the overall goal, and the stops along the way are the specific, targeted steps taken to arrive at the destination. An action plan should be carefully integrated into a regular review cycle both on the macro level (e.g., follow-up from surveys and feedback) and on the micro level (e.g., the performance appraisal process, which identifies the objectives and measurable targets for individual employees for specific learning-centered education components of their jobs). When responsibility centers and individuals who will follow up are clearly identified, the learning college transformation will move along steadily toward its goal and will not falter or get derailed in the years to come.

## Conclusion

I have described ways in which leaders and colleges can design and implement their own self-assessment process to become a learning college. I cannot emphasize too strongly how important it is to have a commitment to learning-centered education as a mechanism for meaningful, transformative change. The self-assessment process is not intended to support a piecemeal approach or a marginal tweaking of the system. Even if assessment is conducted department by department, the goal is to bring the whole institution into the learning college framework.

Change management has become a popular concept in recent management literature. With the self-assessment process, community colleges can become experts at change management, using a practical tool designed specifically for their needs. The reward will be the realization of their goal of becoming learning colleges.

## References

Barrows, H. S. (1986). A taxonomy of problem-based learning methods. *Medical Education, 20,* 481–486.

Boettcher, J. V., & Conrad, R. (1999). *Faculty guide for moving teaching and learning to the Web.* Phoenix, AZ: League for Innovation in the Community College.

Boud, D. (Ed.). (1985). *Problem-based learning in education for the professions.* Kensington, Australia: Higher Education Research and Development Society of Australasia.

Bruffee, K. A. (1999). *Collaborative learning: Higher education, interdependence, and the authority of knowledge.* Baltimore: The Johns Hopkins University Press.

Checkley, K. (1997, Summer). Problem-based learning: The search for solutions to life's messy problems. *Curriculum Update,* pp. 1–4. Washington, DC: Association for Supervision and Curriculum Development.

Cross, K. P. (1999). *Learning is about making connections: The Cross papers number 3.* Phoenix, AZ: League for Innovation in the Community College.

Foot, D. K., & Stoffman, D. (1998). *Boom, bust & echo 2000: Profiting from the demographic shift in the new millennium (Rev. ed.).* Toronto, Ontario, Canada: Macfarlane, Walter & Ross.

Jonassen, D. H. (1991). Evaluating constructivistic learning. *Educational Technology, 31*(9), 28–33.

Krakauer, R. (2000). *Criteria for a learning college.* Toronto, Ontario, Canada: The Michener Institute for Applied Health Sciences.

Krakauer, R. (2001). *A learning college for health care: The applicability of learning-centred education to The Michener Institute for Applied Health Sciences.* Unpublished doctoral thesis, Department of Education, University of Toronto, Ontario, Canada.

Merriam, S. B., & Caffarella, R. S. (1999). *Learning in adulthood: A comprehensive guide (2nd ed.).* San Francisco: Jossey-Bass.

Norris, D. M., & Malloch, T. R. (1997). *Unleashing the power of perpetual learning.* Ann Arbor, MI: The Society for College and University Planning.

O'Banion, T. (1997). *A learning college for the 21st century.* Phoenix, AZ: AACC and ACE/Oryx Press.

Rogers, C. R. (1983). *Freedom to learn for the 80's.* Columbus, OH: Charles E. Merrill.

Senge, P. M. (1990). *The fifth discipline: The art & practice of the learning organization.* New York: Currency.

Wilson, A. L. (1993). The promise of situated cognition. In S. B. Merriam (Ed.), *An update on adult learning theory* (New Directions for Adult and Continuing Education Series No. 57, pp. 71–80). San Francisco: Jossey-Bass.

Woods, D. (1985). *Problem-based learning and problem-solving.* In D. Boud (Ed.), Problem-based learning in education for the professions. Kensington, Australia: Higher Education Research and Development Society of Australasia.

# CHAPTER 13

# Beyond the Rhetoric: The Learning College in Action

### CYNTHIA WILSON

I n January 2000, the League for Innovation in the Community College launched its 5-year Learning College Project. The goal was to assist community colleges in the United States and Canada to "become more learning-centered by creating a network of Vanguard Colleges strongly committed to the learning college concept, whose efforts would serve as a basis for model programs and best practices" (League for Innovation, 2000–2004). The League invited all community and technical colleges in the United States and Canada to apply for participation; 94 applied, and their applications were reviewed by an international panel of experts on learning, including leading thinkers in the learning-centered education reform movement. On the basis of their demonstrated progress toward becoming learning colleges, 12 were selected to become Vanguard Learning Colleges:

- Cascadia Community College, Washington
- Community College of Baltimore County, Maryland
- Community College of Denver, Colorado
- Humber College Institute of Technology and Advanced Learning, Ontario, Canada
- Kirkwood Community College, Iowa
- Lane Community College, Oregon
- Madison Area Technical College, Wisconsin
- Moraine Valley Community College, Illinois
- Palomar College, California
- Richland College, Texas
- Sinclair Community College, Ohio
- Valencia Community College, Florida

Project participants and staff soon discovered that the work required for this project was enormous, complicated, and demanding. Three years into the project, one participant acknowledged the intricacies involved in committing to an increased focus on learning: "We have not defined [the learning college] in 25 words or less. We have allowed it to be as complex as it is." To provide some parameters for this multifaceted project, the League defined five broad objectives for the project. The Vanguard colleges agreed to make progress toward becoming more learning-centered institutions in these areas: organizational culture, staff recruitment and development, learning outcomes, technology, and underprepared learners. As work on the project began, participants generally agreed that organizational culture encompasses the other four objectives. The colleges also found that the five areas are often so interrelated that distinction between them is difficult.

The complexity of this work also complicates the study and reporting of progress, so that an exhaustive discussion of the project would be required. Among the many themes emerging from the continuing work of the Vanguard colleges is a set of organizational traits that these colleges are developing, expanding, or enhancing as they focus more strongly on learning. Early in the project, participants' conversations focused on what has been called a "culture of evidence." As the project continued, participants spoke increasingly of a "culture of learning."

Other dominant organizational traits emerged as well, such as self-examination, commitment, and collaboration. These five traits (commitment, innovation, collaboration, self-examination, culture of learning, and culture of evidence), which are the focus of this chapter, are not exclusive. Instead, they provide a framework for discussing the progress Vanguard colleges are making on their efforts. These traits, as well as others not discussed in this chapter, have been identified through project activities, including seminars; focus groups; site visits; interviews; and Vanguard college project plans, reports, and updates. At the end of the project's third year, the project evaluator, Kay McClenney, and I, the project director, conducted site visits and focus groups at the Vanguard colleges. These site visits provided a rich source of data for this chapter and other writings about the project. The participants' statements, quoted throughout this chapter, come from notes taken during these site visits and focus groups.

## Demonstrated Commitment

Demonstrated commitment to an increased focus on learning was a prerequisite for participation in the learning college project. Applicants for selection as a Vanguard college were required to indicate their commitment to this work in a letter from the institution's president indicating that the college would be actively involved in the 5-year project and in the learning college movement. Colleges also were required to demonstrate their focus on learning by providing evidence of their commitment in documents and in deeds.

The commitment to becoming a college with a strong, conscious, and overt focus on learning manifests itself in several ways common among the Vanguard colleges. These include committed leaders—both formal and informal—and board members, as well as resources committed to enhancing and expanding students' learning. Many participants also spoke of the commitment to innovation.

### Commitment of Leaders

Project participants acknowledged the importance of presidential commitment to the learning college philosophy and the institution's journey. Vanguard college leaders demonstrate their commitment to a strong focus on learning in both symbolic and substantive ways. Some Vanguard college presidents and their executive teams, for example, have worked with new employees at orientation sessions to explain the learning college concept and what it means at their institutions. Some colleges have made the focus on learning and on evidence of that learning a central theme in their accreditation process. Lane Community College's (2004) Self-Study and Richland College's (2004a) Quality Enhancement Plan provide two examples. Vanguard college leaders also have ensured that learning is at the core of budgeting processes and decisions. Furthermore, while not downplaying the need for their own commitment, the leaders have emphasized the importance of conveying that commitment throughout the college.

Many Vanguard colleges reexamined their statements of the college values, vision, and mission and, when needed, revised those statements to reflect learning as a priority. College leaders stressed the importance of inclusion in creating and revising their institutional plans. At some Vanguard colleges, campuswide support for placing learning first was garnered by leaders who involved all college groups in planning, setting goals, and reallocating resources. Referring to various task forces, committees, and other collaborative structures, one team member pointed out the need for collegewide commitment to spending the time it takes to be inclusive.

### Commitment of Boards

To educate boards and help ensure their support, the project required that boards be represented on colleges' project teams. At several colleges, the involvement of the board in the project was central to gaining support and embedding the learning college movement in every aspect of college life and work. One college president pointed to the need for board involvement to help anchor the change so that the learning college movement would be not episodic but something enduring. Colleges helped ensure commitment of their boards by offering professional development opportunities for board members to learn about the learning college journey and to be involved, through local policy, in mapping the general route the college would take in becoming more learning centered.

At Madison Area Technical College (MATC), the board embedded the learning college principles in its policies, focusing decision making on how actions would increase opportunities and improve learning throughout the college. Board policies also ensure that the board will function as a learning cohort, for example, by participating in professional development and assessing the board's growth by using board meeting surveys, annual evaluations, and compilation of board activity throughout the year and other measures (MATC, 2004).

### Commitment of Resources

Several Vanguard colleges also reexamined their budgeting processes and revised budget priorities to support learning priorities better. The use of O'Banion's (1997) two fundamental questions in the decision-making processes became common: "Does this action improve and expand students' learning?" and the more revealing and more difficult question, "How do we know?" Lamenting the lack of resources was common early in the project, but as colleges progressed on their journeys—even during an economic recession that led to drastic cuts in funding—their perspectives changed. Becoming more focused on learning was perceived not as a matter of money, but as a matter of will.

By increasing their focus on learning, Vanguard colleges have found ways to reallocate resources. By asking the two aforementioned questions posed by O'Banion and answering them honestly, colleges have identified programs and practices that do not adequately support learning. They have eliminated or revised ineffective programs and restructured positions, facilities, policies, and procedures to focus more intently on learning.

Vanguard colleges also have committed resources to professional development that supports the learning-centered initiative. Valencia Community College's (VCC) Teaching and Learning Academy, for example, provides a variety of learning opportunities to provide development opportunities for instructors to support tenure candidates in achieving the outcomes of their individual learning plans. The curriculum is based on the VCC Learning-Centered Core Curriculum for instructors' development (VCC, 2004). At Richland College (2004b), the Thunderwater Organizational Learning Institute supports the college's learning organization goals by providing learning activities for all full-time employees as well as adjunct instructors. The institute's learning opportunities support the college's learning focus at institutional, departmental, and individual levels.

## Innovation

In committing to a conscious, purposeful focus on learning, these colleges also have committed to innovation. Project participants spoke openly and frequently about the need for an environment of trust and for the freedom to implement new ideas in a safe place that encourages thoughtful experimentation, celebrates successful attempts, and learning lessons from failure that help ensure success in the next effort. As one participant put it, "We have to be willing to play poker a little, to gamble, to take the risk." Commenting about the atmosphere on her campus, another participant said, "It's okay to make mistakes if we learn from them."

Several Vanguard colleges have funded programs to promote innovation directly on their campuses. Moraine Valley Community College's (2004b) Learning Challenge Grant program provides an example of such a program. This grant program, in place since 1996, "awards support, resources and funding to individual faculty members and/or teams for the purpose of developing creative and compelling approaches to the teaching and learning process." The Community College of Baltimore County's (CCBC) Council on Innovation and Student Learning is a dynamic, collegewide think tank involved in developing policies, processes, and infrastructure to support the institution's focus on learning (CCBC, 2004). At several Vanguard colleges, pilot programs have been implemented to promote innovation. A team member at one Vanguard college noted that piloting has taken the risk out; another compared experimentation with bureaucratic institutional structures that are "oldthink," confiding that "it's innovation, so we can skip steps."

## Collaboration

Each Vanguard college was required to develop a 10- to 15-member cross-college team to lead the learning college initiative at the institution. Some team members were mandated by the project, including the president, a board member, chief academic and learner services administrators, and formal or informal instructors and support staff leaders. Many colleges reported that these teams were a major factor in driving the work throughout the college. Cross-functional teams allowed various perspectives to be included in the organizational conversation and helped ensure that there were champions to support and encourage the work throughout the college.

This team approach created opportunities for colleagues who previously had little communication with each other to learn more about the needs, challenges, resources, and other issues faced by different areas. Team members learned to make use of this newfound camaraderie. One team member noted with some relief that the collaborative approach helped "allay the sense of overwhelming work and importance that comes with going it alone." Another spoke of sharing resources to help learning, explaining that "getting out of silos helped us focus on learning and helping each other."

One team described the "tectonic shifts" in students' learning and employee morale that have occurred, in part as a result of a "direct democracy planning process" the college used in putting the collective focus on students' learning. At another college, the president proudly described the team's development: "We have built a good team [and have] gotten focused on students and learning." He emphasized the cooperative spirit that had developed among team members as a result.

### Conversations About Learning

Several Vanguard colleges used collegewide "conversations about learning" (O'Banion & Milliron, 2001) to engage all members of the college in discussions about learning-related issues and challenges. At Sinclair Community College, "learning dialogues" have involved campuswide conversations on predetermined topics and have included detailed planning and guides for facilitators. Using an envisioning template; facilitator handbook; and process for collecting and disseminating the knowledge, ideas, and solutions gathered through the conversations for use in planning and practice, the learning dialogues have been a successful way to "spread the philosophy . . . engage more people . . . get ideas . . . [and] motivate action" (Sinclair Community College, 2002). Moraine Valley Community College's (2004a) Center for Teaching and Learning facilitates regular "conversations on learning," which cover various topics related to the learning-centered initiative.

### A Common Language of Learning

Vanguard colleges typically examined their language—terms and definitions about learning—in some cases continuing work that had started before participation in the project. Other colleges realized much later in the process that they needed a common language to speak about learning. A trend among the Vanguard colleges has been to adopt language that fits the college's culture, is consistent with a college's values, and is useful to internal as well as external constituents. The Vanguard colleges generally agreed that language is an important part of defining the college as learning centered and in ensuring that employees, learners, and others fully understand the institution's terminology. At several Vanguard colleges, after agreement was achieved, language was revised in print and digital publications, including catalogs, memos, handbooks, course syllabi, job applications, and performance review documents.

### Collaborative Learning

One of the six fundamental principles of the learning college defined by O'Banion (1997) is that a learning college provides opportunities for collaborative learning. The Vanguard colleges embraced the collaborative spirit. Perhaps the strongest evidence of success in collaborative learning comes from the several colleges that organized learning communities, particularly in developmental education or first-year experience programs. Lane Community College, for example, reported that learners who persisted through its Guided Studies Learning Community for Reading and Career and Life Planning had comparable or better success rates than did those who had not taken or were not required to take guided studies. The Community College of Denver reported similar success for learners in its First-Year Experience and other learning communities, as did Moraine Valley Community College in its College 101 freshman seminar.

Among the Vanguard colleges, collaborative learning is not limited to students. The learning exchange networks instructor development program, initially developed at Humber College Institute of Technology and Advanced Learning (2004a), has been used at several Vanguard colleges as a collaborative learning experience. Several Vanguard colleges have incorporated collaborative learning into other professional development activities through programs designed to share learning. The Community College of Denver's mini-grant program for professional development, for example, requires recipients to conduct workshops for their colleagues in which they share what grantees have learned through the grant-funded project. The conversations about learning, or learning dialogues, also provide a rich collaborative learning experience at several Vanguard colleges.

## Self-Examination

Part of the learning experience for some Vanguard colleges focused on becoming a place—culturally and organizationally—where honest, thorough, and thoughtful self-examination is possible. Some colleges realized early in the project that they had not been as thoroughly self-aware as they might have been; for others, this realization came later. For a few, this kind of candid self-examination was already a routine part of the college culture. For colleges that examined themselves closely, the findings were not always pleasant.

Some found barriers to learning across their campuses, and some found areas in which they were not adequately meeting learners' needs. Some colleges discovered inconsistency across disciplines and a need to assess all learning outcomes in credible ways. One team member described her college before beginning the journey: "We're amber: little fossils that are fixed in time." Through self-examination and honesty, this college has moved forward, becoming consciously competent as a result of its commitment and dedication to learning. One Vanguard college instructor noted that the journey had led to "more honesty and integrity in the work we do in the classroom. Is what I'm doing expanding student learning? How do I know? It forces honesty." A participant at one college defined the transformative process as follows: "Change is recognizing that you're not doing something as well as you could or should and then taking time to do something about it."

### Integrity

As colleges engaged in self-examination, they began to discover and acknowledge discrepancies between words and deeds. Finding and correcting these discrepancies became, for some, a fundamental part of the learning college journey. In one college, assessment had become so deeply embedded that one team member described "a constant review and questioning of processes, of what we're doing and how we're doing it." Another explained the importance of achieving "clarity with students and the community about what we are." Another advised, "Question everything. Question what you do and why you do it. Start dissecting what you're doing."

The president of one Vanguard college emphasized the importance of "focusing on what we're about, not focusing on the glitz." A team member from another Vanguard college echoed that concern, wanting "to make real, sustained change without being flashy." At another college, a team member explained, "This is the real deal. It's not something we've added on. It's who we are."

At MATC, involvement in the project and interaction with the other Vanguard colleges led to a focused self-examination process through which the team and others at the college were able to acknowledge areas that needed attention. The resulting discovery of gaps in service to underprepared learners led MATC to focus strongly on developmental education throughout the project. This concerted approach to finding solutions included bringing in developmental education experts for professional growth, visiting colleges with successful developmental education programs, and forming study groups to make recommendations for improvements in this area at the college. Work teams were charged with implementing the recommendations, and the work continues to be integrated throughout the college.

The board's support for this effort is strong, and the college has made developmental education a priority in its academic quality improvement program and annual planning. Even though budgets are lean, MATC has committed more than $1 million to the underprepared learner effort (C. Holmes, personal communication, May 20, 2004). The support has been valuable: Data indicate that learners who complied with placement test recommendations performed better than those who did not. Learners who also participated in the advising process and who followed the advice they were given "had a 17 percent higher probability of success than those who complied only with the placement test score" (J. Thrush, personal communication, May 20, 2004).

## Learning and Evidence

Learning and collecting evidence of that learning represent the core work of the learning college. In seeking answers to the ubiquitous "How do we know?" question, Vanguard college teams began emphasizing the importance of using data about learning (1) in planning, (2) in creating and assessing teaching and learning environments and experiences, (3) in supporting the learning process to ensure learner success, and (4) in every other aspect of the college's life. One participant admitted, "We are good at capturing data, but not so good at using it." A Vanguard college vice president explained that his college had been collecting data on learner outcomes "for quite a while," but the introduction of substantive conversations about learning "demands that folks look at the data, and talk about it, in ways they've not probably looked at it before." One team member explained a self-proclaimed "appeal to pride" tactic: "We know we're good. How do we prove it? We need data. We know we need to and can get better." Another participant explained that deciding to answer the "How do we know?" question involves learning to recognize "the importance of data in the change process, and not to be afraid of it."

Vanguard colleges examined their strengths and weaknesses and used evidence thoughtfully to improve courses, programs, and the entire institution. To gather the information they needed, Vanguard colleges used means such as the project's learning college inventory; campuswide conversations about learning; the thoughtful collection and examination of data; and the systematic examination and evaluation of existing policies, practices, and processes. In some cases, data collection processes themselves revealed needs for improvements and raised questions about the usefulness of data that had been collected traditionally. As campus community members began thinking about their work in terms of the focus on learning, they began to find additional data needs and to explore ways to get information that would give them an accurate picture of students' learning.

## Learning Outcomes

Learning outcomes are the most fundamental part of the learning college work. By clearly defining the learning and demonstrations of learning required for student success at the outset, all participants in the learning process—learners, instructors, resource providers, and others—are informed about and can be focused on offering appropriate support for learners. The learning outcomes work also has been generally regarded by Vanguard colleges as among the most difficult and challenging part of the journey. In some cases, colleges even seemed to avoid this work. One participant commented, for example, that it sometimes looked as though her college would do everything else first and then, when there was nothing else left, it would finally get to learning outcomes. Another team member noted that "learning outcomes can be threatening unless considered in a nurturing, collegial environment."

Despite the disheartening difficulty of this work, most of the Vanguard colleges made progress. Participants admit, however, that this progress has been slow. Some colleges have agreed on outcomes but have not reached agreement on the assessment of those outcomes. Some participants expressed concern about consistency and interrater reliability and began exploring ways to ensure consistency in the evaluation of students' learning. One college acknowledged that its progress had been slowed by instructors' concerns about measuring learning. A team member at that college clarified the concerns: "We all know that everything you get out of education is not measurable, so there's a great deal of resistance because it can't all be measured." Others talked about the role of "the unintended part" or "incidental learning" and wondered how or whether to measure that learning. They also questioned how to measure what one participant called "the transformative process of learning" and commented on how much they are "still learning about learning."

To make the learning outcomes work manageable, Vanguard colleges have found ways to focus on one or two aspects at a time. At Sinclair Community College (2004a), the Assessment of Student Learning Web site was developed for use by instructors, learners, and any other interested members of the college community. It contains a record of progress on the college's assessment initiative. The Community of Expertise Web site was created to support assessment and other work with a bank of successful practices contributed by practitioners (Sinclair Community College, 2004b). At Humber College (2004b), the Ontario "generic skills" provided one level of learning outcomes evaluation that gives insight into what and which students are learning. The college ensured that generic skills were embedded in courses and programs and tracked learners' attainment of the skills.

Kirkwood Community College instructors have been involved in an assessment project focused on evaluating the shared learning outcomes of transfer courses. In the process they have developed, instructors identify the level—1, 2, or 3—of assessment of a particular outcome that occurs in their course and then move toward the next level. CCBC's (2002) *Guide for Learning Outcomes Assessment and Classroom Learning Assessment* began at the course level with volunteers and continued with a focus on high-impact courses or those courses with high enrollment. All instructors, including full-time and part-time instructors, participate in this ongoing assessment project. CCBC has developed common course outlines as well as a common course template among its three campuses. At Cascadia Community College (2004), a set of four collegewide learning outcomes is at the heart of the college's focus on learning, and classroom assessment is linked to collegewide learning outcomes as well as course-specific outcomes.

### Nontraditional Documentation of Learning Outcomes

The sixth learning college principle is that "the learning college and its learning facilitators succeed only when improved and expanded learning can be documented" (O'Banion, 1997, p. 47). This documentation expands on traditional methods by providing a more specific, detailed record of what the learner knows and can do with that knowledge. To provide a thorough record of learning for students seeking employment or transfer, Palomar College, Cascadia Community College, and other Vanguard colleges developed electronic portfolios. At Cascadia Community College (2002), learners complete an electronic portfolio in which they "record and store a wide range of important materials and information, including career and educational goals, academic accomplishments, special projects, personal reflections and affirmations from others." Learners create their initial electronic portfolios in one of two introductory courses and continue adding "tangible products that demonstrate students' skills and showcase their accomplishments" throughout their college career.

Both college employees and learners create electronic portfolios; for employees, portfolios are used in the performance review process. At VCC (2004), the Teaching and Learning Academy supports tenure candidates' development of individualized learning plans and portfolios of learning evidence—paper, electronic, or hybrid—as part of induction to the college culture and preparation for tenure review. Colleges also have investigated other means of documentation. Kirkwood Community College's (2000) instructor-led Essential Skills Institute, for example, has explored certifying qualified vocational learners for three sets of workplace skills: communication, teamwork, and computation.

### Collective Responsibility for Learning Outcomes

One of O'Banion's (1997) six principles of the learning college includes having learners take primary responsibility for their own choices about learning. Vanguard colleges recognized that those community college learners who arrive unprepared for college-level work, who have had little or no success in other educational endeavors, and who have made an enormous effort simply to consider attending a community college are perhaps not in the best position to take immediate, primary responsibility for their own learning. Many Vanguard colleges embraced this principle by engaging learners as "full partners in their own learning" (O'Banion, 1997, p. 47).

CCBC, for example, has reported that 95% of learners who complete an individual education plan are retained, compared with 57% of those who do not complete such a plan. At VCC, early assistance is an important feature of the effort to ensure learners' success at the "front door." Learners may begin using Valencia's LifeMap during their transition to postsecondary education and continue through graduation and lifelong learning. LifeMap is "a student's guide to figuring out 'what to do when'" in completing career and educational goals; it links "all of the components of Valencia (faculty, staff, courses, technology, programs, and services) into a personal itinerary" to help learners succeed (VCC, 2003).

Sinclair Community College's (2004d) Process Learning Initiative program was designed to assist students in becoming lifelong learners. The program emphasizes students' learning and promotes information-processing skills, not only as tools for success at the college but also as tools for maintaining employment and "moving up the career ladder" (Sinclair Community College, 2004c). At Cascadia Community College, each employee is part of a learning outcomes team that corresponds with one of four collegewide learning outcomes. Each learning outcomes team serves as a shepherd for its learning outcome, meeting throughout the academic year to ensure that the outcome is represented institutionally in collegewide communication and in research, development, and assessment practices associated with the outcome. Each learning outcomes team also has an instructional role among instructors across the disciplines (Cascadia Community College, 2003).

Collective responsibility for learning outcomes extends beyond the college at some Vanguard colleges. The Community College of Denver (2004) has opened two "early colleges," which partner with area secondary schools to provide an option for "underserved students who have the potential to benefit from a rigorous academic curriculum offered within a supportive and nurturing environment." Learners enrolled in these early colleges have the opportunity to earn concurrently a high school diploma and an associate degree. Palomar College has established a "virtual matriculation" process with area high schools. This Web-based system has eased the entry process, which allows learners to use their high school Web environments for assessment, application, and registration.

## The Journey Continues

The Vanguard colleges first came together at the project's initial seminar in June 2000. The seminar was designed for the college teams to become acquainted with each other and to share their experiences. Through presentations, cross-college meetings, exhibits, and informal conversations, the Vanguard colleges showcased the progress they had already made on their journeys. This sharing of experiences allowed colleges to learn from each other's successes as they sought solutions to their own problems. The second seminar continued this process somewhat, but a realization emerged that despite the sharing of experiences, the Vanguard colleges were still grappling with the magnitude of the work of becoming a more learning-centered institution.

During the planning process for the third seminar, a significant shift in direction occurred. One courageous participant voiced what was apparently on the minds of several others when she commented that during the first two seminars, the Vanguard colleges had "strutted our stuff." Now, she continued, it was time to look more critically at the areas in which the colleges were not strongly focused on learning and to find the reasons for discrepancies between talk and action. She urged her colleagues to trust each other enough to "show the underbelly," the areas that still need work, that have problems, and that had not been featured at previous seminars. She and others acknowledged that they faced obstacles and challenges on their journeys and that with few or no models for overcoming them, they needed to create their own solutions and answers. They then designed the third seminar around a series of facilitated dialogues that addressed obstacles and challenges identified by the Vanguard colleges. The seminar planners spent 3 days in focused conversations about learning as they searched for and found ways to continue the journey despite the hazards along the path.

Becoming a more learning-centered institution requires resolute commitment to the idea that learning rightfully belongs at the center of college life—at the heart of every decision, action, policy, and practice. For more than 5 years, these 12 Vanguard Learning Colleges have been in the process of becoming more learning-centered institutions. The 5-year Learning College Project is nearing its formal completion, but the Vanguard colleges will continue the journey. They have not found all the answers they sought in preparing for that third seminar, nor have they solved all the problems. A more accurate statement might be that they have instead found more questions and encountered additional, unforeseen complications. With undaunted commitment, collaboration, and close self-examination, however, they have consciously and overtly directed their energy and resources toward learning. They are increasingly able to answer, with assurance and with evidence to justify their confidence, the question, "How do we know?"

## References

Cascadia Community College. (2002). *Cascadia's learning experience.* Retrieved May 9, 2004, from http://www.cascadia.ctc.edu/learningforthefuture/learningexperience.asp

Cascadia Community College. (2003). *The learning outcomes teams (LOTs).* Retrieved May 9, 2004, from http://www.cascadia.ctc.edu/vanguard/culture/LOTs.asp

Cascadia Community College. (2004). *Rubrics and learning outcomes.* Retrieved May 9, 2004, from
http://www.cascadia.ctc.edu/vanguard/OutcomeAssessment/rubrics.asp

The Community College of Baltimore County. (2002). *Guide for learning outcomes assessment and classroom learning assessment.* Retrieved May 9, 2004, from
http://www.ccbcmd.edu/media/cisl/loa_booklet.pdf

The Community College of Baltimore County. (2004). *CCBC CISL mission statement.* Retrieved May 9, 2004, from http://www.ccbcmd.edu/cisl/mission.html

Community College of Denver. (2004). *What is an early college?* Retrieved May 9, 2004, from http://ccd.rightchoice.org/EarlyCollege/index.html

Humber College Institute of Technology and Advanced Learning. (2004a). *Faculty & staff recruitment and development.* Retrieved May 9, 2004, from http://learning-college.humberc.on.ca/critical_problems3.htm

Humber College Institute of Technology and Advanced Learning. (2004b). *Generic skills.* Retrieved May 9, 2004, from http://genericskills.humberc.on.ca/#

Kirkwood Community College. (2000). *Features of Kirkwood Community College.* Retrieved May 9, 2004, from http://www.kirkwood.edu/vanguard/features.html

Lane Community College. (2004). *Lane self-study 2004.* Retrieved May 9, 2004, from http://www.lanecc.edu/selfstudy/index.htm

League for Innovation in the Community College. (2000–2004). *The Learning College Project.* Retrieved May 9, 2004, from
http://www.league.org/league/projects/lcp/index.htm

Madison Area Technical College. (2004). *District board policies: GP1 and GP2.* Retrieved May 9, 2004, from http://matcmadison.edu/matc/about/boardpoli-cies.shtm#Anchor-POLICY-23240

Moraine Valley Community College. (2004a). *Center for teaching and learning.* Retrieved May 9, 2004, from http://www.morainevalley.edu/CTL/events.htm

Moraine Valley Community College. (2004b). *Learning challenge grants.* Retrieved May 9, 2004, from
http://www.morainevalley.edu/Vanguard/outstanding/learning_grants.htm

O'Banion, T. (1997). *A learning college for the 21st century.* Phoenix, AZ: AACC and ACE/Oryx Press.

O'Banion, T., & Milliron, M. D. (2001). College conversations on learning. *Learning Abstracts, 4*(5). Available from http://www.league.org/publication/abstracts/learn-ing/lelabs0109.htm

Richland College. (2004a). *Richland College quality enhancement plan.* Retrieved May 9, 2004, from http://www.rlc.dcccd.edu/qep

Richland College. (2004b). *Thunderwater Organizational Learning Institute.* Retrieved May 9, 2004, from http://www.rlc.dcccd.edu/thunderwater/index.htm

Sinclair Community College. (2002). *How-to-do-it: Steps to deliver. Vanguard learning dialogs.* Retrieved May 9, 2004, from http://www.sinclair.edu/vlearning/pub/vanguard/learning_dialogues/ld_management_flow_chart_ncspod.pdf

Sinclair Community College. (2004a). *Assessment of student learning.* Retrieved May 9, 2004, from http://www.sinclair.edu/about/assessment/outcomes/index.cfm

Sinclair Community College. (2004b). *Best practices.* Retrieved May 9, 2004, from http://www.sinclair.edu/vlearning/pub/vanguard/what_community_expertise.htm

Sinclair Community College. (2004c). *Process learning.* Retrieved May 9, 2004, from http://www.sinclair.edu/about/plearning/index.cfm

Sinclair Community College. (2004d). *Process learning: The strategic plan.* Retrieved May 9, 2004, from http://www.sinclair.edu/about/plearning/plan/index.cfm

Valencia Community College. (2003). *LifeMap.* Retrieved May 9, 2004, from http://valenciacc.edu/lifemap

Valencia Community College. (2004). Valencia's Pre-tenure Faculty Development Program. Retrieved May 9, 2004, from http://faculty.valencia.cc.fl.us/development/Programs/TLA_academy/tla_description.htm

# Moving Beyond the Learning Paradigm Toward a Learning-Centered College Culture

CHRISTINE JOHNSON MCPHAIL

Throughout this book, the authors have described critical features of the learning-centered college movement that directly affect institutions and learners. This book has focused on what learning-centered community colleges do and why they do it. The goal of this book project was to expand the knowledge base about the transformative values of the learning-centered college to inspire individuals and colleges to continue with their efforts and to encourage others to launch learning-centered college initiatives.

Learning principles have provided a conceptual framework for the strategies discussed in the book, and the authors have demonstrated how adopting learning-centered principles in curricula, programs, and services is changing community colleges. The authors presented advice on how to initiate and sustain the learning college, an education reform that may fundamentally change the way community colleges function. It is clear, however, that although the learning college revolution offers a uniform sense of direction, community colleges will need to demonstrate the capacity and versatility to implement learning-centered activities that improve and enhance learning in ways unique to their environments.

## The Shift From Teaching to Learning

Throughout the chapters in this book, especially the later chapters, the authors have characterized the learning college as a higher education institution that embraces and creates change. Colleges embarking on the learning college journey will face a transitioning paradox: how to maintain the integrity of teaching connected to the old instructional paradigm without stifling the potential and benefits of the new learning paradigm. It is a struggle to change to the new and different and to explain why the change must occur. Commitment to the learning college means walking away from habits and practices that sometimes stagnate the integration of learning-centered concepts in programs and services. In essence, becoming a learning-centered college means changing the culture of the organization.

A major theme of this book has been the focus on how the institution must change. By making this focus apparent, the authors called attention to the true effect of the learning college. I invite you to go beyond the learning paradigm shift to examine the implications of the organizational culture for sustaining the momentum of the learning college movement. There are many examples of organizational culture that foster institutional reform (Lieberman & Miller, 1990). The culture of the community college is invisible and is often taken for granted. The deeper structure of life in the organization is reflected and transmitted through symbolic language and expressive action.

As described in the previous chapters, the expressive action of the learning-centered colleges is the shift from teaching to learning. This action demonstrates how community colleges, by adopting learning-centered principles, are engaged in activities that reshape beliefs and behaviors and influence learning outcomes over time. The learning paradigm shift may seem to have had only curricular implications because it significantly influenced instructor–learner relationships. It is clear, however, that when colleges become learning centered, the culture of the organization changes. The shift from teaching to learning brings about not only changes in curricula but also modifications in the delivery of programs and services and the allocation and reallocation of funds. The authors suggested significant ways in which these learning-centered activities have been accomplished. Thus, adhering to learning-centered principles ensures that change permeates the entire fabric of the college.

The learning-centered college concept extends beyond the relationship between instructor and learner. It includes programs, processes, procedures, and services. While learning-centered activities are taking place, something deeper and not so tangible is also under way. In the best learning colleges, changes in the infrastructure have taken place. When colleges become truly learning centered, problems are defined and addressed using learning-centered principles.

## Learning-Centered College Culture

To fully understand the significance of the learning college, it is important to understand the cultural context of the institution. The culture of the college consists of the invisible and the taken-for-granted activities, assumptions, and beliefs that give meaning to what people do and say. The programs, services, governance, and decision making are all reformed when learning moves to the forefront. The concept of organizational culture continues to play an important role in discussions about the learning college. Each feature of organizational culture can be seen as an important environmental condition that affects programs and services at the college. Edgar Schein (1993), one of the most prominent theorists of organizational culture, gave the following very general definition:

> A pattern of shared basic assumptions that the group learned as it solved its
> problems of external adaptation and internal integration, which has worked well

enough to be considered valid and, therefore, to be taught to new members as the correct way to perceive, think, and feel in relation to those problems. (p. 373)

How organizational culture relates to the discussion of the learning college beyond the paradigm shift may be explained best by Gareth Morgan (1997), who described culture as "an active living phenomenon through which people jointly create and re-create the worlds in which they live." Morgan suggested that elements of organizational culture may include the following:

- Stated and unstated values
- Overt and implicit expectations for member behavior
- Customs and rituals
- Stories and myths about the history of the group
- Shop talk—typical language used in and about the group
- Climate—the feelings evoked by the way members interact with each other, with outsiders, and with their environment, including the physical space they occupy
- Metaphors and symbols—which may be unconscious but can be found embodied in other cultural elements

Morgan proposed four essential strengths of the organizational culture approach:

- It focuses attention on the human side of organizational life and finds significance and learning in even its most mundane aspects (e.g., the setup in an empty meeting room).
- It makes clear the importance of creating appropriate systems of shared meaning to help people work together toward desired outcomes.
- It requires members—especially leaders—to acknowledge the effect of their behavior on the organization's culture. (Morgan proposed that people should ask themselves, "What impact am I having on the social construction of reality in my organization?" and "What can I do to have a different and more positive impact?")
- It encourages the view that the perceived relationship between an organization and its environment is also affected by the organization's basic assumptions.

Translating these concepts into expressive action to maintain the shift from teaching to learning requires colleges to act according to the principles of the learning college. The beliefs and ideas that the college holds about the learning college and the changes made to make the shift must be clearly articulated to all stakeholders within the organization. The manifestation of the required shifts has been described throughout this book.

For the past several years, I have studied the activities of the 12 Vanguard Leaning Colleges. In addition to attending the annual meetings, I examined a variety of documents released by the Vanguard colleges and the League for Innovation in the Community College. I have observed how learning-centeredness (1) influenced the role of most community college personnel, (2) modified delivery of programs and services, and (3) influenced decision making on topics such as realignment of funding. In addition, as I stated in my chapter on learning-centered governance in community colleges, the learning principles should be at the forefront of governance. In other words, the infusion of learning college principles changes the culture of the college.

## Core Beliefs

When readers remember the messages delivered here about building and maintaining the learning-centered college, I hope they will consider the suggestion that various aspects and functions of the colleges need to undergo certain changes. The culture of the college influences the implementation of the learning principles in the programs and services at the colleges. Figure 1 shows how learning is at the core of the institution and permeates the culture of a learning-centered college.

Transitioning from a teaching paradigm to a learning-centered paradigm means that community colleges must change the way they respond to the needs and interests of the learner. Beyond the paradigm shift, colleges must sustain the learning college momentum and develop the ability to engage all constituent groups within the college

## Figure 1   Toward a Learning-Centered College Culture

in the politics of changing the organizational culture. The various discussions in the chapters show how the transition from a teaching paradigm to a learning paradigm will be different for different colleges. In this epilogue, I have tried to clarify that the transition process is not a "one-size fits all" proposition. In a learning-centered college culture, community colleges are no longer expected to do business as usual. Colleges are expected, however, to place learning at the forefront of all policies, procedures, and practices to best serve the interests of the learners and the learning-centered principles. Moving beyond and sustaining the paradigm shift require a college culture that consistently conveys strong learning-centered messages to all constituent groups, including boards of trustees, legislators, and community groups.

In general, the intent of this entire book, including this epilogue, was to ensure that all constituent groups understand the institutional commitment to the principles of the learning college. This commitment should result in a true consensus and institution-wide support for the principles of the learning college. The shared values and belief systems surrounding the learning college principles could serve to build the capacity to sustain the learning college beyond the learning paradigm shift.

Figure 1 shows that learning is grounded in a clear and rational way throughout the various parts of the college. This learning is at the forefront of teaching, planning and budgeting, governance, program and service delivery, and assessment and evaluation. The organizational culture is always focused on learning to guide innovation, problem solving, and broad participation throughout the college. So what is an effective learning-centered college culture? I believe that it is one that promotes higher levels of learning outcomes for all students.

This book will help community college professionals to assess the congruence of the theory of transitioning from a learning college to the implementation of learning college principles at all levels of the learning experience. The authors also hope that this inquiry into the learning college experience beyond the learning paradigm shift will lend valuable insight into the contextual activities of the learning college movement and provide additional information that will help colleges achieve the capacity to sustain the momentum. Last, the authors hope that many more community colleges will awaken to see new and different possibilities for using the principles of the learning college to transform and create new and different learning options for community college students.

## References

Lieberman, A., & Miller, L. (1990). Restructuring schools. What matters and what works. *Phi Delta Kappan, 71*(19), 759–764.

Morgan, G. (1997). *Images of organization.* Thousand Oaks, CA: Sage.

Schein, E. (1993). *Organizational culture and leadership.* Fort Worth, TX: Harcourt College Publishers.

# APPENDIX

# Selected Bibliography of the Learning College

TERRY O'BANION AND KELLEY L. COSTNER

*Note.* This bibliography was last updated updated December 1, 2002. Please add to this bibliography by sending suggestions to Terry O'Banion at obanion@league.org.

American College Personnel Association. (1994). *The student learning imperative.* Washington, DC: Author.

American Council on Education. (1996, May). *Guiding principles for distance learning in a learning society.* Washington, DC: Author.

Angelo, T. A. (1995, November). Reassessing (and defining) assessment. *AAHE Bulletin, 7.*

Angelo, T. A., & Cross, K. P. (1993). *Classroom assessment techniques: A handbook for college teachers.* San Francisco: Jossey-Bass.

Argyris, C., & Schon, D. A. (1978). *Organizational learning: A theory of action perspective.* Reading, MA: Addison-Wesley.

Armajani, B., Heydinger, R., & Hutchinson, P. (1994, January). *A model for the reinvented higher education system: State policy and college learning.* Denver, CO: Education Commission of the States.

Association of American Colleges and Universities. (1995). *The direction of educational change: Putting learning at the center.* Washington, DC: Author.

Association of American Colleges and Universities. (2002). *Greater expectations: A new vision for learning as a nation goes to college.* Washington, DC: Author.

Association of Colleges of Applied Arts and Technology of Ontario (ACAATO). (1995). *Learning-centered education in Ontario's colleges.* Toronto: Author.

Astin, A.W. (1985). *Achieving educational excellence.* San Francisco: Jossey-Bass.

Astin, A.W. (1993). *What matters in college? Four critical years revisited.* San Francisco: Jossey-Bass.

Banta, T. W., & Associates (Eds.). (1993). *Making a difference: Outcomes of a decade of assessment in higher education.* San Francisco: Jossey-Bass.

Barr, R. (1993, October). *A new paradigm for community colleges: Focus on learning instead of teaching.* Sacramento, CA: Association of California Community College Administrators.

Barr, R. (1994, February). *A new paradigm for community colleges*. San Marcos, CA: Research and Planning Group of the California Community Colleges.

Barr, R. (1995, March). From teaching to learning: A new reality for community colleges. *Leadership Abstracts, 8*(3).

Barr, R. (1998, September/October). Obstacles to implementing the learning paradigm: What it takes to overcome them. *About Campus, 3*(4), 18–25.

Barr, R., & Tagg, J. (1995, November/December). From teaching to learning: A new paradigm for undergraduate education. *Change, 27*(6), 13–25.

Barr, R., & Tagg, J. (1998, December). Accreditation in the learning paradigm. In *Eight perspectives on how to focus the accreditation process on educational effectiveness*. Oakland, CA: Western Association of Schools and Colleges, Accrediting Commission for the Senior Colleges and Universities.

Board of Governors, California Community Colleges. (1995, September 14). *The new basic agenda: Policy directions for student success*. Sacramento, CA: Author.

Boggs, G. R. (1993, September). Community colleges and the new paradigm. In *Celebrations*. Austin, TX: National Institute for Staff and Organizational Development.

Boggs, G. R. (1993/1994), December/January). Reinventing community colleges. *Community College Journal,* 4–5.

Boggs, G. R. (1995, Fall). The new paradigm for community colleges: Who's leading the way? *The Catalyst, 25*(1), 27–28.

Boggs, G. R. (1995/1996, December/January). The learning paradigm. *Community College Journal, 66*(3), 24–27.

Boggs, G. R. (1998, January/February). Accepting responsibility for student learning. *On the Horizon, 6*(1), 1, 5–6.

Boggs, G. R. (1999, January). What the learning paradigm means for faculty. *AAHE Bulletin, 51*(5), 3–5.

Bradford, P. F. (2000). Illinois community college presidents' perceptions of leadership for creating or maintaining learning colleges (Doctoral dissertation, Northern Illinois University). *Dissertation Abstracts International, 61*(6), 2115.

Brown, J. S. (1997, January/February). On becoming a learning organization. *About Campus, 1*(6), 5–10.

Caine, R. N., & Caine, G. (1990, October). Understanding a brain-based approach to learning and teaching. *Educational Leadership, 48*(2), 66–69.

Chickering, A. W., & Gamson, Z. F. (1987, June). Seven principles of good practice in undergraduate education. *The Wingspread Journal, 9*(2), 1–4.

Cleveland, J., & Plastrick, P. (1995). Learning, learning organizations, and TQM. In A. M. Hoffman & D. J. Julius (Eds.), *Total quality management: Implications for higher education*. Maryville, MO: Prescott.

Committee for Economic Development. (1994). *Putting learning first: Governing and managing the schools for high achievement* [Executive Summary]. New York: Author.

Cross, K. P. (1986). A proposal to improve teaching. *AAHE Bulletin, 39*(1).

Cross, K. P. (1998, June). *Opening windows on learning* (The Cross Papers No. 2). Mission Viejo, CA: League for Innovation in the Community College and Educational Testing Service.

Cross, K. P. (1999, June). *Learning is about making connections* (The Cross Papers No. 3). Mission Viejo, CA: League for Innovation in the Community College and Educational Testing Service.

Cross, K. P. (2000, February). *Collaborative learning 101* (The Cross Papers No. 4). Mission Viejo, CA: League for Innovation in the Community College and Educational Testing Service.

Cross, K. P. (2001, February). *Motivation: Will that be on the test?* (The Cross Papers No. 5). Mission Viejo, CA: League for Innovation in the Community College and Educational Testing Service.

Cross, K. P. (2002). *The role of class discussion in the learning-centered classroom* (The Cross Papers No. 6). Phoenix, AZ: League for Innovation in the Community College and Educational Testing Service.

Cross, K. P., & Angelo, T. A. (1988). *Classroom assessment techniques: A handbook for faculty.* University of Michigan, National Center for Research to Improve Postsecondary Teaching and Learning.

Dibella, A. J., Gould, J. M., & Nevis, E. C. (1995, Winter). Understanding organizations as learning systems. *Sloan Management Review, 36*(2), 73–85.

Doherty, A., Riordan, T., & Roth, J. (Eds.). (2002). *Student learning: A central focus for institutions of higher education. A report and collection of institutional practices of the student learning initiative.* Milwaukee: Alverno College Institute.

Dolence, M. G., & Norris, D. M. (1995). *Transforming higher education.* Ann Arbor, MI: Society for College and University Planning.

Doucette, D. (1994, October/November). Transforming teaching and learning through technology. *Community College Journal, 65*(2), 18–24.

Education Commission of the States. (1996, April). What research says about improving undergraduate education. *AAHE Bulletin, 48*(8), 5–8.

Ehrmann, S. C. (1995, March/April). Asking the right questions: What does research tell us about technology and higher learning? *Change, 27*(2), 20–27.

Ely, E. E. (2000). Developmental education in the learning college (Doctoral dissertation, University of Texas at Austin, 2000). *Dissertation Abstracts International, 61*(8), 3035.

Ewell, P. (1997, December). Organizing for learning: A new imperative. *AAHE Bulletin, 50*(4), 3–6.

Flynn, W. J. (1999, September). Rethinking teaching and learning. *Community College Journal, 70*(4), 8–13.

Flynn, W. J. (2000). *The search for the learning-centered college* (New Expeditions Issues Paper No. 9: Charting the Second Century of Community Colleges). Washington, DC: American Association of Community Colleges.

Flynn, W. J. (2000, September). This old house: Revitalizing higher education's architecture. *Community College Journal, 71*(1), 36–39.

Gabelnick, F., MacGregor, J., Matthews, R. S., & Smith, B. L. (1990, Spring). *Learning communities: Creating connections among students, faculty, and disciplines* (New Directions for Teaching and Learning No. 41). San Francisco: Jossey-Bass.

Gardner, H. (1983). *Frames of mind: The theory for multiple intelligences.* New York: Basic Books.

Garvin, D. A. (1993, July/August). Building a learning organization. *Harvard Business Review, 71*(4), 78–91.

Gilbert, S. W. (1995, March/April). Teaching, learning, and technology: The need for campuswide planning and faculty support services. *Change, 27*(2), 46–52.

Guskin, A. E. (1994, July/August). Reducing student costs and enhancing student learning. *Change, 26*(4), 22–29.

Guskin, A. E. (1994, September/October). Restructuring the role of faculty. *Change, 26*(5), 16–25.

James, T. (1999). *Learning support and success: Determining the educational support needs for learners into the 21st century.* Retrieved November 2, 2002, from www.bccat.bc.ca/pubs/learner.pdf

Johnstone, B. (1993, April). *Learning productivity: A new imperative for American higher education* (Studies in Public Higher Education, No. 3). Albany: State University of New York.

Kim, D. H. (1993, Fall). The link between individual and organizational learning. *Sloan Management Review, 35*(1), 37–50.

Krakauer, R. (2000). *Criteria for a learning college.* Toronto: The Michener Institute.

Krakauer, R. (2000). A learning college for health care: The applicability of learning-centered education to the Michener Institute for Applied Health Sciences (Ontario) (Doctoral dissertation, University of Toronto, 2000). *Dissertation Abstracts International, 62*(4), 1308.

Marchese, T. (September/October, 1995). Getting smarter about teaching. *Change, 7*(5), 4.

McKeithan, G. D. (2002). Navigating through a learning organization: A case study of a community college (Doctoral dissertation, North Carolina State University at Raleigh, 2002). *Dissertation Abstracts International, 63*(4), 1237.

McPhail, C. J. (2000). *Transforming community college leadership preparation: A cohort leadership learning model.* Unpublished manuscript, Morgan State University, Community College Leadership Doctoral Program, Baltimore, MD. ERIC Document Reproduction Service No. ED449852).

McPhail, C. J. (2000, December 12). Reframing governance: At a true learning college, trustees have a lot to learn, too. *Community College Times,* pp. 3, 6.

McPhail, C. J. (2001, Winter). Building a distinctly urban program to prepare community college leaders. *Trustee Quarterly,* 28–29.

McPhail, C. J. (2002, August/September). Leadership prep: The cohort leadership learning model. *Community College Journal, 73*(1), 46–48.

McPhail, C. J. (2002, September). Leadership by culture management. *Leadership Abstracts, 15*(10).

McPhail, I. P. (1999, September). Launching LearningFIRST at the Community College of Baltimore County. *Learning Abstracts, 2*(6).

McPhail, I. P. (2000, March 20). Building a learning college. *Community College Week, 12*(16), pp. 4–6.

McPhail, I. P., & Heacock, R. C. (1999). Baltimore County: A college and community in transition. In R. C. Bowen & G. H. Muller (Eds.), *Gateway to democracy: Six urban community college systems* (pp. 75–83). San Francisco: Jossey-Bass.

McPhail, I. P., Heacock, R. C., & Linck, H. F. (2001, January). LearningFIRST: Creating and leading the learning college. *Community College Journal of Research and Practice, 25*(1), 17–28.

McPhail, I. P., & McPhail, C. J. (1999). Transforming classroom practice for African-American learners: Implications for the learning paradigm. In *Removing vestiges: Research-based strategies to promote inclusion* (No. 2, pp. 25–35). Washington, DC: American Association of Community Colleges.

Michigan Community College Association. (1998). *Becoming a learning college: The building blocks of change.* Lansing, MI: Author. (Available from Michigan State University, Office of the Provost for University Outreach, 216 Hannah Administration Building, East Lansing, MI, 48824-1046)

Milliron, M., & Miles, C. (1998). Technology, learning, and community (TLC): Perspectives from teaching excellence award recipients. Mission Viejo, CA: League for Innovation in the Community College.

Milliron, M., & Miles, C. (2000). *Taking a big picture look at technology, learning, and the community college.* Mission Viejo, CA: League for Innovation in the Community College.

Myran, G., Zeiss, A., & Howdyshell, L. (1995). *Community college leadership in the new century: Learning to improve learning.* Washington, DC: American Association of Community Colleges.

National Association of State Universities and Land-Grant Colleges. (1997). *Returning to our roots: The student experience.* Washington, DC: Author.

The National Commission on Excellence in Education. (1983, April). *A Nation at risk: The imperative for educational reform.* Washington, DC: U.S. Government Printing Office.

National Commission on Time and Learning. (1994, April). *Prisoners of time.* Washington, DC: U.S. Government Printing Office.

O'Banion, T. (1995, June/July). School is out: learning is in. *On the Horizon, 3*(5), 1–6.

O'Banion, T. (1995, Fall). Community colleges lead a learning revolution. *Educational Record, 76*(4), 23–27.

O'Banion, T. (1995/1996, December/January). A learning college for the 21st century. *Community College Journal, 66*(3), 18–23.

O'Banion, T. (1996, January/February). Gladly would he learn. *On the Horizon, 4*(1), 1, 3–5.

O'Banion, T. (1997). *Creating more learning-centered community colleges.* Mission Viejo, CA: League for Innovation in the Community College and PeopleSoft, Inc.

O'Banion, T. (1997). *A learning college for the 21st century.* Phoenix, AZ: AACC and ACE/Oryx Press.

O'Banion, T. (1997). The learning revolution: A guide for community college trustees [Special Issue]. *The Trustee Quarterly, 1,* 2–19.

O'Banion, T. (1997). Transforming the community college from a teaching to a learning institution. In D. Oblinger & S. Rush (Eds.), *The learning revolution: The challenge of information technology in the academy* (pp. 138–154). Bolton, MA: Anker Publishing.

O'Banion, T. (1997, February). Innovation and educational reform. *Academic Leadership, 4*(2), 3–11.

O'Banion, T. (1999). *Launching a learning-centered college.* Mission Viejo, CA: League for Innovation in the Community College and PeopleSoft, Inc.

O'Banion, T. (1999, March). The learning revolution in American higher education. *Broadcast, 45.*

O'Banion, T. (1999, June). The learning college. *Broadcast, 46.*

O'Banion, T. (2000, September). An inventory for learning-centered colleges. *Community College Journal, 71*(1), 14–23.

O'Banion, T., & Associates. (1997). *Teaching and learning in the community college.* Washington, DC: American Association of Community Colleges.

Oblinger, D., & Rush, S. (1997). *The learning revolution: The challenge of information technology in the academy.* Bolton, MA: Anker Publishing.

Ohio Technology in Education Steering Committee. (1996, March). *Technology in the learning communities of tomorrow: Beginning the transformation.* Columbus, OH: Ohio Board of Regents.

O'Neil, J. (1995, April). On schools as learning organizations: A conversation with Peter Senge. *Educational Leadership, 52*(7), 20–23.

Parnell, D. (1995). *Why do I have to learn this? Teaching the way people learn best.* Waco, TX: Center for Occupational Research and Development.

Perelman, L. J. (1992). *School's out: A radical new formula for the revitalization of America's educational system.* New York: Avon Books.

Robles, H. J. (1999). Building learning colleges: Preparing community college faculty and staff (Doctoral dissertation, The Fielding Institute, 1999). *Dissertation Abstracts International 61*(2), 471.

Ruehl, P. A. (2000). A comparison of full-time and part-time community college instructors' awareness and application of adult learning styles (Doctoral dissertation, University of Florida, 2000). *Dissertation Abstracts International, 61*(12), 4655.

Senge, P. M. (1990). *The fifth discipline: The art and practice of the learning organization.* New York: Doubleday.

Senge, P. M., Ross, R., Smith, B., Roberts, C., & Kleiner, A. (1994). *The fifth discipline fieldbook: Strategies for tools for building a learning organization.* New York: Doubleday.

Skolnik, M. (Speaker). (2000, May 11). In praise of polarities in postsecondary education. The R. W. B. Jackson Lecture. University of Toronto. Retrieved November 19, 2002, from http://fcis.oise.utoronto.ca/~mskolnik/Jackson_lecture.html

Teahen, R. (2000). *Strategies for creating a more learning-centered organization: A community college perspective* (Doctoral dissertation, Michigan State University, 2000). *Dissertation Abstracts International, 62*(3), 889.

Traverso, E. (1996, December). Learning: Buzz word or new insight? FACCCTS, *3*(2), 19.

Twigg, C. A., & Doucette, D. (1992, August). Improving productivity in higher education: A paradigm shift needed. *Leadership Abstracts, 5*(6).

Wilson, C. (1999). Faculty in the learning college: An examination of theorist and practitioner perceptions (Doctoral dissertation, The University of Texas at Austin, 1999). *Dissertation Abstracts International, 60*(12), 4295.

Wilson, C. (1999, Spring). Faculty of the future in learning colleges. *Michigan Community College Journal, 5*(1), 75–81.

Wilson, C. (2002, March). The community college as a learning-centered organization. In N. Thomas (Ed.), *Perspectives on the community college* (pp. 23–26). Phoenix, AZ: The League for Innovation in the Community College.

Wilson, C. (2002, February). The learning college journey. *Basic Education, 46*(6). Retrieved October 30, 2002, from http://www.c-b-e.org/be/iss0202/a4wilson.htm

Wilson, C. (2002, July). Leadership for learning. *Learning Abstracts, 5*(7).

Wilson, C., Miles, C., Baker, R., & Schoenberger, R. L. (2000). *Learning outcomes for the 21st century: Report of a community college study.* Phoenix, AZ: League for Innovation in the Community College.

Wingspread Group on Higher Education. (1993). *An American imperative: Higher expectations for higher education.* Racine, WI: The Johnson Foundation, Inc.

## Web Resources

**Leadership Abstracts.** Available from the League for Innovation in the Community College Web site: http://www.league.org/publication/abstracts/leaderab_main.htm. Leadership Abstracts address issues on the learning college. Review them by following the above link or by visiting http://www.league.org, click on Publications, then click on Leadership Abstracts.

**Learning Abstracts.** Available from the League for Innovation in the Community College Web site: http://www.league.org/publication/abstracts/learnab_main.htm. Learning Abstracts address issues on the learning college. Review them by following the above link or by visiting http://www.league.org, click on Publications, then on Learning Abstracts.

**Learning College Project.** Available from the League for Innovation in the Community College Web site: http://www.league.org/league/projects/lcp/index.htm. This 3-year project coordinated by the League for Innovation includes direct access to the 12 Vanguard Learning Colleges. Review the Learning College Project by following the above direct link or by visiting http://www.league.org , click on Projects, then click on Learning College Project.

**Learning Quarterly.** Available from http://www.ctt.bc.ca. Published by the Centre for Curriculum, Transfer & Technology, Douglas College, Victoria, British Columbia, Canada.

# About the Contributors

**Robert B. Barr** is executive director of Institutional Research and Planning at Foothill-De Anza Community College District in California's Silicon Valley. Previously, Barr was director of institutional research and planning at Palomar College in southern California. Since joining the California community colleges (CCCs) in 1987, he has served in many roles and contributed to many projects statewide, serving as an officer of the Research and Planning Group and conducting a statewide math outcomes research project. He has been a state evaluator for the Middle College High School projects and has served on nine accreditation evaluation teams.

Barr has made numerous presentations at conferences and colleges throughout the United States and Canada, explaining and promoting a shift from the instruction paradigm to the learning paradigm. After publishing several articles on the topic, *Change* magazine published "From Teaching to Learning: a New Paradigm for Undergraduate Education" (with co-author John Tagg) in 1995. *About Campus* published his follow-up article, "Obstacles to Implementing the Learning Paradigm: What It Takes to Overcome Them," in 1998. Since then, he has published a number of other related articles, including several with John Tagg and Frank Fear.

Barr is the 1996 recipient of the University of Michigan Norman C. Harris Award for distinguished contributions and leadership in the community colleges and the 1998 Practitioner Award from AACC's National Council for Research and Planning. He received his PhD from the University of Michigan.

**Mark Battersby** began working for change in postsecondary education, when, as a teaching assistant in philosophy at the University of British Columbia (UBC), he was responsible for the creation of an integrated political economy course. He has taught in the Philosophy Department at Capilano College since 1975 and at a number of other institutions, including Fraser Valley College, Douglas College, UBC, Simon Fraser University, and Stanford. His primary interest is ensuring that curriculum truly serves to intellectually empower students. At Capilano, he was involved in an extensive variety of educational initiatives. He introduced critical thinking courses to Capilano and was founder and president of the BC Association for Critical Thinking Instruction and Research, which promoted critical thinking instruction K–16. He is an internationally recognized expert in critical thinking instruction and has given numerous workshops on critical thinking and educational reform throughout BC and elsewhere in North America. He also served as president of the College Faculty Association and on the Education Council and College Board.

From 1996 to 1999, Battersby led the Learning Outcomes Initiative for the BC Centre for Curriculum Transfer and Technology, giving numerous workshops on learning outcomes throughout British Colombia and Alberta and on a number of occasions at the Learning Paradigm Conference in San Diego. He has written a number of articles and editorials related to learning in the Centre's journal, *The Learning Quarterly*. He has learned a great deal about how postsecondary education really works from the information supplied by his six children, the two youngest of which recently completed master's degrees.

**George R. Boggs** is president and chief executive officer of the American Association of Community Colleges (AACC) based in Washington, DC. AACC represents more than 1,100 associate degree-granting institutions and more than 11 million students. Boggs previously served as faculty member, division chair, and associate dean of instruction at Butte College in California, and for 15 years he served as the superintendent/president of Palomar College in California. He served as a member of the Committee on Undergraduate Science Education of the National Research Council and has served on several National Science Foundation panels and committees. He holds a bachelor's degree in chemistry from The Ohio State University, a master's degree in chemistry from the University of California at Santa Barbara, and a PhD in educational administration from The University of Texas at Austin.

**Evelyn Clements** is president of the National Council for Student Development, an affiliate council with the American Association of Community Colleges. She is vice president for student development at Middlesex Community College in Bedford and Lowell, MA. She holds an EdD.

**Kelley L. Costner** serves as the senior research associate for the Community College Leadership Doctoral Program/Institute for the Development of Multicultural Administrators and Faculty at Morgan State University in Baltimore, Maryland. Costner is a graduate of the Community College Leadership Program at Morgan State University. She received her MEd from Goucher College in Baltimore, Maryland, and her bachelor's from Morgan State University. She previously served as the research assistant for the Community College Leadership Doctoral Program at Morgan State University. She also served as the assistant director of academic services and support at Loyola College, an adjunct English faculty member at the Community College of Baltimore County, and the Coordinator of the Academic Learning Center at Baltimore City Community College. Her research interests include faculty attitudes and beliefs toward teaching African-American learners, African-American learners in community colleges, culturally responsive faculty development, and the recruitment and retention of African American administrators and faculty in community colleges.

**Tara Ebersole** has 23 years of teaching experience, primarily in biology. She is currently working on her doctorate in the education policy track of the public policy program at the University of Maryland, Baltimore County. She also serves as the

Community College of Baltimore County (CCBC) Learning Outcomes Associate, aiding faculty teams in designing and conducting their course-level outcomes assessment projects. She is also a member of the CCBC Learning Outcomes Assessment Advisory Board and co-chair of the Council on Innovation and Student Learning. She conducts the New Faculty Learning Community, a yearlong professional development program for newly hired full-time faculty.

**Frank A. Fear** is a professor of Community, Agriculture, Recreation, and Resource Studies at Michigan State University (MSU) in East Lansing. He studies, writes, engages in, and teaches about forms of extraordinary change in higher education that results from engagement with civic society. His articles have appeared recently in *The Journal of Leadership Studies, About Campus, Innovative Higher Education, Metropolitan Universities, The Journal of College and Character*, and *Encounter*. He is a frequent contributor to *The Journal of Higher Education, Outreach and Engagement*.

Fear was the chairperson of the design team and inaugural director of MSU's leading student-centered learning program for undergraduate students, The Liberty Hyde Bailey Scholars Program. The Bailey program was cited by The Templeton Foundation for its contribution to students' character development and honored by the MSU chapter of Phi Kappa Phi with its Excellence Award for Interdisciplinary Scholarship. Fear also serves as a scholar–writer in Food Systems and Rural Development for The W.K. Kellogg Foundation, is president and CEO of The Greater Lansing Food Bank, and is a Fellow at Clemson University's Institute for Economic and Community Development in Columbia (SC). He holds a PhD in sociology from Iowa State University.

**William J. Flynn** has 33 years' experience as a faculty member and administrator in community colleges in Maryland, New Jersey, Arizona, Ohio and California. In 2001, he retired after 12 years of service at Palomar College in San Marcos, California, where he was dean of the Division of Community Learning Resources. For the National Council for Continuing Education and Training (NCCET), he has served as state liaison, regional director on the NCCET board, national conference director, and publications editor. He is starting his eighth year as editor of *The Catalyst*, NCCET's journal. In 1998, NCCET gave Flynn its National Award for Exemplary Leadership, and in July 2001, he became the managing director.

Numerous publications include a white paper on teaching and learning for the AACC New Expeditions project and numerous articles in the *Community College Journal*. Flynn is a regular presenter and keynote speaker at regional and national conferences and an active facilitator of professional development days at community colleges, having done more than 60 presentations in the last 4 years. He produced the annual North American Conference on the Learning Paradigm, held in San Diego 1997–2001, and currently co-chairs the annual Learning Summit Conference for the League for Innovation.

**Alicia B. Harvey-Smith** is dean of learning and student development at The Community College of Baltimore County-Catonsville in Baltimore, Maryland. She has served on the board of the National Council for Student Development in a variety of posts including secretary, Region III coordinator, and newsletter editor. She is currently a learning college liaison. She holds a PhD.

**Ted James** is dean of student development at Douglas College, a large comprehensive urban community college in metropolitan Vancouver in British Columbia, Canada. He has served as a Canadian representative on the board of the National Council on Student Development and as coordinator of regional representatives. He has also served as a board member for the Canadian Association of College and Student Services.

**Renate Krakauer** is a consultant on educational and organizational change. She recently retired from her position as president and CEO of The Michener Institute for Applied Health Sciences, a postsecondary education institution dedicated to the current and continuing education of applied health sciences professionals. She has a BS in pharmacy from the University of Toronto, a master's degree in environmental Studies from York University, and a doctor in education from the Ontario Institute for Studies in Education, University of Toronto. In 2002, Charles Sturt University of New South Wales, Australia, conferred an honorary doctor of health studies degree on Krakauer for her commitment to health sciences education and the development of innovative education programs in partnership with the Australian university.

Krakauer's professional experience has included service in senior management capacities in community college, municipal administration, and provincial government. She has served on a number of professional and community boards, task forces, and associations. She has had a longstanding commitment to innovations in education, especially as related to learning-centered education, lifelong learning, workplace training, and professional education. She has made presentations across Canada, the United States and Australia.

**Henry F. Linck** is campus dean of the Collier County campus of Edison College in southwest Florida. From October 1998 to July 2004 he served as vice chancellor for learning and student development at The Community College of Baltimore County (CCBC) in Maryland. He was the lead system office administrator responsible for advancing CCBC as a learning-centered community college.

Prior to this appointment he served as vice president and dean of instruction at Howard Community College in Columbia, Maryland, where he was instrumental in implementing the shift from a teaching-centered to a learning-centered environment. Linck has more than 12 years of full-time teaching experience in addition to 25 years of management experience in higher education and private industry. He holds an EdD in higher education administration from the University of Maryland, a Certificate of Advanced Study in Liberal Arts from Johns Hopkins University, an MA in English from Morgan State University, and a BA in English from Gettysburg College.

**Christine Johnson McPhail** is graduate coordinator of the Community College Leadership Doctoral Program at Morgan State University in Baltimore, Maryland. Formerly she was president and chief instructional officer for Cypress College in California. She serves as a coach for the Achieving the Dream: Community Colleges Count Project. A longtime advocate of cultural awareness, McPhail is a strong advocate of programs for families and children. Active in professional associations, she is a member of the Council for the Study of Community Colleges, the American Association of Higher Education, the Association of Institutional Research, and the American Educational Research Association, where she serves as the affirmative action chair for Division J-Postsecondary Education.

She is co-author of *Transforming Classroom Practice for African American Learners: Implications for the Learning Paradigm,* which won the 2000 Research Award from the Maryland Association for Adult, Community and Continuing Education. Her book, *Walk the Rainbow: When You Get Tired of Waiting to Exhale,* has been adopted as supplementary reading material in ethnic and women's studies programs at several colleges and universities. Community and civic organizations are also using the book as a resource and curriculum guide for workforce preparation and training in response to the Welfare Reform Initiative.

McPhail is committed to making contributions to the communities where she works and lives. She wrote a community preservation grant, which resulted in the establishment of permanent housing for the African American Historical and Cultural Museum of Fresno County in California. While serving as dean of students at Kings River Community College in Reedley, California, she created a model Retention Assistance Program to attract and retain Black men in college; other California colleges later replicated this project. She was the recipient of an American Association of University Women's research award for conducting a study on the career aspirations of teen parents.

The State of California Assembly recognized McPhail for her leadership in California community colleges, and McPhail also received recognition from the cities of Fresno, Reedley and Cypress for outstanding contributions to higher education. She was recently inducted into the State Center Community College Educator's Hall of Fame and recognized as Outstanding Alum of the Year from Fresno City Community College (1990) and California State University, Fresno in 1998. The American Association of Women in Community Colleges named Johnson McPhail Woman of the Year in recognition of her leadership in community colleges. In 2001, Governor Paris N. Glendening awarded Johnson McPhail the Governor's Citation in recognition of her contributions to higher education in the State of Maryland. She received the Kathleen Kennedy Townsend Award for service to the community in 2001 and was inducted into Maryland Women for Responsive Government, Inc.

McPhail earned an AA degree from Fresno City College, BA and MA degrees from California State University, Fresno, and a PhD in education from The University of Southern California. Her postgraduate training includes The Kellogg Expanding Leadership Fellows Program, Executive Leadership Institute at Bryn Mawr College, Professional Administrators' Development Institute, and the Washington Leadership Experience sponsored by AACC.

**Irving Pressley McPhail** has been the chancellor of The Community College of Baltimore County (CCBC) since 1998. During his tenure, he has brought the college national recognition as one of only 12 Vanguard Learning Colleges in the United States and Canada, known for its commitment to student learning. Prior to joining CCBC, McPhail was a faculty member and program coordinator at Morgan State College. He spent 2 years as an assistant provost at the University of Maryland at College Park and 3 years at The Johns Hopkins University, first as an American Council on Education fellow in academic administration and later as a research scientist at the Center for Metropolitan Planning and Research. McPhail served one year as chief operating officer of the Baltimore City Public Schools and has held senior tenured faculty appointments at Morgan State University, Delaware State University, LeMoyne-Owen College, and Pace University.

McPhail has received many honors and awards including The Certificate of Honor from the Baltimore County Public Schools, the Hearts of Love Award from Aunt Hattie's Place, Inc., the Service Above Self Award from the Rotary Club of Woodlawn-Westview, the Pioneer Award from AACC's National Council on Black American Affairs, the Valued Hours Award from the Fullwood Foundation, Inc., and the Yes I Can: Role Models for Minority Youth Award from the St. Louis Sentinel newspapers. McPhail holds a bachelor's degree in sociology from Cornell University and a master's degree in reading from Harvard Graduate School of Education. He was a National Fellowships Fund Fellow at the University of Pennsylvania, where he earned his doctorate in reading and language arts.

**Mark David Milliron** is the president and CEO of the League for Innovation in the Community College (www.league.org), an international organization that has been catalyzing the community college movement for more than 35 years. With an innovative core of 19 CEOs from key community colleges and districts that make up the board of directors, close to 800 institutional members from 10 countries, 100 corporate partners, and a host of nonprofit, foundation, and governmental collaborators, the League hosts conferences and institutes, develops Web resources, conducts research, produces publications, provides services, and leads projects and initiatives.

Milliron is a distinguished graduate of the University of Texas at Austin, where he received his PhD. He has won numerous awards for his work exploring teaching excellence, student success strategies, leadership development, future trends, and the human side of technology change. He authors books, monographs, and articles; speaks at colleges, corporations, and conferences across the country and around the world; teaches in executive leadership and graduate programs; participates as a key resource for local, state, and national government programs; and serves as a member of several higher education and corporate boards.

**Rosalie V. Mince** is assistant to the vice chancellor for learning and student development at The Community College of Baltimore County (CCBC). She earned her BS in physical education from University of Maryland, College Park, and her MS in teacher education from the University of North Carolina at Greensboro. Mince's PhD is in human development from the University of Maryland, College Park. Since 1988, Mince has served CCBC as a faculty member, an associate dean, a division chairperson, a program coordinator, and a system senior-level administrator. Currently, Mince is responsible for coordinating course and program-level outcomes assessment. She is also the chair of the General Education Review Board and co-chair of the Learning Outcomes Assessment Advisory Board and the Vanguard Learning College Committee. Mince has given numerous presentations and consulted on general education and on learning outcomes assessment at the local, state, and national levels.

**Terry O'Banion** was president of the League for Innovation in the Community College for 23 years when he retired on December 31, 1999. Under his leadership the League became an international organization serving more than 650 colleges and was recognized by *Change* magazine in 1998 as "the most dynamic organization in the community college world."

In honor of his 41 years of service to education, three national awards have been established in his name. Following retirement he was named a senior league fellow and directs the international Learning College Project for the League for Innovation.

In a survey of 11,000 higher education leaders reported in *Change* magazine in 1998, O'Banion was named one of 11 "Idea Champions" who set the agenda for all of higher education—and the only community college leader on the list. He has consulted in more than 600 community colleges in the United States and Canada. He has written 12 books and 126 articles on the community college. *A Learning College for the 21st Century,* published in 1997, is in its third printing and was awarded the Philip E. Frandson Award for Literature in the Field of Continuing Higher Education.

O'Banion is one of the leading spokespersons in the country on the learning revolution. He has keynoted statewide conferences on the learning revolution in Illinois, Florida, Hawaii, Arkansas, Wyoming, Wisconsin, Michigan, Georgia, North Carolina, and in the provinces of Alberta and Ontario. He holds a BA in English and speech and an Med in guidance and counseling from University of Florida and a PhD in higher education administration from Florida State University.

**Mary Prentice** is an assistant professor in the Community College Leadership Doctoral Program at New Mexico State University. She serves as the program evaluator for the Community Colleges Broadening Horizons Through Service Learning project facilitated by AACC and is a research team member and college/community team coach for the Rural Community College Initiative. Before this, she was dean of social sciences at Illinois Valley Community College. She began her work in community colleges at Albuquerque TVI Community College as a psychology faculty member and service learning faculty coordinator. Her current interests include the integration of technology and instruction in community colleges, service learning and civic engagement, rural community colleges and economic development, and educational leadership preparation.

**David A. Shupe** has been an academic administrator since 1990, beginning at the University of Minnesota. He has served as vice president of academic affairs and student development at Inver Hills Community College in suburban St. Paul, Minnesota, and as system director for academic accountability for the Minnesota State Colleges and Universities system. Presently he is director of evaluation of student achievement for the *e*Lumen Collaborative in St. Paul. His 1999 article on the multiple constituencies in higher education described how the meaning of key terms depends on which constituency is using them. Shupe holds a PhD from Syracuse University.

**Shirlene Lofton Snowden** is currently serving as the program coordinator and research associate for the Institute for Development of Multicultural Administration and Faculty in Community Colleges at Morgan State University. Her professional background includes 12 years of progressive leadership and administrative experiences at the community college executive level, including positions as vice president for administration, dean for the Business and Information Systems Department, and chairperson for Business and Technology. She has more than 18 years of experience as a professor in higher education, teaching courses in accounting, business, auditing, and finance at the four-year and community colleges. She completed her doctoral studies in community college leadership at Morgan State University, Baltimore. Her studies include extensive research in the area of strategic planning resulting in her doctoral dissertation: *An Analysis of Strategic Planning in the Transformation of the 12 Vanguard Learning Colleges.*

**Cynthia Wilson** is vice president of learning and research at the League for Innovation in the Community College. She leads the League's Learning Initiative, serving as director of the Learning College Project and co-director of the 21st Century Learning Outcomes Project. She has authored or coauthored several publications, including the League's *Learning Outcomes for the 21st Century: Report of a Community College Study.* She has made numerous presentations on the learning college at national and international conferences and has served as a consultant for community colleges that are focused on becoming more learning-centered institutions. Wilson holds a BA and an MEd, both in history, from Southwest Texas State University and an EdD in educational administration with a concentration in community college leadership from The University of Texas at Austin. She spent 20 years as a faculty member before joining the League staff in August 1999.

# Index

## W